9021GROW

The Story of "Hollywood's Wizard of Weed"

9021GROW

The Story of "Hollywood's Wizard of Weed"

By
Craig X

2000 B.C.
Beverly Hills, CA

2000 B.C.

264 South La Cienega #468

Beverly Hills, CA 90211

Contact Information:
Director of Media Relations
Email: Webmaster@CraigX.com

2004096166 (PCN- LIBRARY OF CONGRESS CATALOG NUMBER)
BIO-026000 (BISAC)
ISBN—0-9747110-0-4 Hardback

Illustrations by Kevin Pearson & Gogue
Cover design: Kevin Byrd & Scott Rushforth

Please, visit our online community at CraigX.com

Acknowledgements

First, I want to say "thank you" to my editors, Thomas Brown, Stephanie Brennan, and Loxi Wyndle. Next, I want to give a special "thank you" to Robert Rudolf Ruchti III, Jason Roberts, Tara Taloma, my parents, Roland Manakaja, Robert Allen Roskind, Julia Roskind, my girls, Jessica Anne Rubin and Olivia Rose Rubin, and my son, Avi ben Israel (Christopher Avi Rubin), Ando, Brad Pitt, Ricky Martin, Drew Barrymore, Esai Morales, Lana Parrilla, David and Andrea Faustino, Tommy and Shelby Chong, Jack Herer, Eddie Lepp, Chris Bliss, Shiloh Massive I, Jill Ishkanian, Tony Frost, Eric Shevin, Alan Arkin, Jono Kohan, Jonathan Nadalman, Francois of the copy center at UCLA, Nicole Morgan, Armando Romero, David Lawrence, Neil Lipsky, Valerie Roberts, Bob Marley, the Havasupai, Jennifer Anniston, Jimmy Vines, Pearl Jam, Lisa Bay, Elan Sassoon, Catya Sassoon R.I.P., Luca Scalisi, David Sassoon, Pauly Shore, Peter Shore, Eden Sassoon, Michael Bay, Mitzi Shore, the whole freaking crazy Shore and Sassoon families, Eddie Griffin, Green Day, Eddie Greene, Mark Killian, Martha Stewart, Joel Cohen, Josh A., Robin Gronvall, Dice, Sammy, the seventh son of the seventh son, John Trudell, Leonard Peltier, Todd McCormick, Dennis Peron, Rod Stewart, James Katz, Randy Kast, Daniel Guss, Brown "Crash" Smith, Kristie Rivington, Walt Disney, President Reagan, the dancers and singers of the world, farmers, poets, animal lovers, kids, Tom Gilsenan, Hempfiles.com, Tito Ivan, Rod Serling, all the people who ever shopped at 2000 B.C., and all you members of the "420 Tribe" who are making the seed thrive.

Reader, I dedicate my book to you!

In the past two thousand years, it has taken billions of individual people—your ancestors (humans have two biological parents)—to create just one of you. All of this genetic variation in the world has led to a new generation of hemp activist, especially in the United States of America. This new breed envisions a radical new future in which hemp replaces petroleum as the source fuel for the world's economy.

This new breed of anti-prohibition advocate simply ignores marijuana laws. These conscientious objectors are practicing civil disobedience in such large numbers that marijuana laws, in their current state, are impossible to enforce in an effective manner. Law enforcement officials

know the war against this plant will never be won. The
government's drug warriors are justifying prohibition with
any small battle they win because their jobs and budgets
depend on it, but the fact remains, the war against
marijuana will never be won.

The numbers "420" are synonymous with this fresh approach
to legalization (what I call "overgrowing the government"),
so I have used the number to name a tribal society that I
see emerging: the "420 Tribe." The leaders of this tribal
society are identified as "420 Elders."

Think of the evolution that has occurred among different
cannabis strains that exist today. Now think of all that
had to occur precisely the way it did for you to be here
right now, reading *9021GROW*. There is a reason for
everything in this world, including the reason this book
came to you when it did. So, enjoy my work. It is
dedicated to you, the reader.

God bless you!

I would also like to thank my illustrators. Gogue is one of
the cartoonist illustrators for this book. He is from
Spain. You can find his work at http://goguetoons.com/.
Kevin Pearson of the United Kingdom did the other drawings
for *9021GROW*. You can find his work at
http://kevinpearson.com/. I met both of these artists over
the Internet and they live and work outside the United
States, which shows the power of the Web to bring people
and businesses together. Kevin Byrd, who designed the dust
jacket, is available at Rickey-Rat.com.

Thank you to the fonts **Courier New** and **Century Schoolbook.** The body
of the text is in Century Schoolbook and the credits and titles are in Courier New.

Table of Contents

Introduction

Foreword by Eric Drew Shevin, Esq.

Section I: A Hollywood Story with a "Save the World" Ending

Introduction

I know that books on most people's shelves are never read. If you were nice enough to buy my book and put it on your shelf without reading it, thank you for the money. I'll put it to good use in my effort to end the prohibition of hemp. However, I want you to get something for your investment. If you plan on reading the book, I hope you enjoy it and tell a friend. If you are on the fence about pot but purchased it anyway, thanks again. Here is what you are about to miss:

With my book, I give pot smokers a new vision of themselves as heroes who have saved the seed that will save the planet. In my opinion, the modern industrial world in which most earthlings live is coming to an end soon. However, pot smokers are going to be part of creating a society that will replace it.

I think our current problems are a result of our culture not connecting to the natural world and especially our unique relationship with plants. The modern industrialized world, demographically speaking, lives in cities. Entertainment and readily available resources in cities are alluring and have driven this demographic shift from rural America. The trouble is that city living is not connected to the garden. In the city, food comes from a truck and is sold in a market and not a plant. This perspective needs to change because it is dependent on foreign oil. Pot helps people reconnect to the natural world and the Creator, regardless of their location on earth and hemp is a resource that allows them to do that.

"420 Elders" is a group that I identify as being made up of people who recognize *cannabis* as wonderful and good, despite what world governments are saying. I call them elders because years from now everyone will use cannabis to survive and this generation, who saved the plant through prohibition, will be looked back on as Elders. *Cannabis* is a great plant that helps human beings live better lives. The plant bears a multitude of fruits, natural resources, for a contemporary, mechanized, industrial society, and modern farmers have discovered ways to make this plant bear fruit 12 months a year.

Hemp farmers should feel proud of the work they are doing. Growing any plant and bringing it to market is hard work. Farmers are not lazy people, and they are doing honest (I am making a distinction between legal and honest) work that will eventually save our industrialized culture from devastation. Right now, pot farmers and brokers are looked upon as thieves and criminals, but future generations will see them as heroes and pioneers.

In *9021Grow*, I tell of growing up in Beverly Hills. My stories include Native American prophecy from the Southwest and interesting Hollywood and celebrity buzz. I have written for *High Times* magazine and have received source checks from celebrity gossip magazines. I invite you to enjoy this collection of personal stories and humorous anecdotes. I think that after reading my story people will find it difficult to continue to persecute this beneficial plant.

Craig

Foreword

Craig is the true "Hollyweed Revolutionary," and he has never backed away from his life goal of ending the prohibition against marijuana and becoming the world's largest, legal *cannabis* businessman. When I first met Craig X Rubin, I was impressed that someone was willing to expose himself to losing his freedom in order to fight for the cause of legalizing marijuana. Craig's one-of-a-kind bong shop, 2000 B.C., never attempted to hide the true nature of his vision: namely, to sell merchandise aimed at promoting the growing and smoking of *cannabis*, in addition to marketing all the other wonderful hemp by-products of this "sacred herb."

During our first meeting, Craig told me that he was staging a pot legalization rally at the Federal Building and asked if I would speak. I agreed and prepared an informative speech to enlighten the throngs of followers as to their constitutional rights. As I arrived at the Federal Building, the first words I heard were those of Craig, fully amplified on a large wooden stage, asking those who would like to smoke some weed to raise their hands. Every hand in the crowd went up. Then, Craig asked who in the crowd didn't have any weed to smoke, and only a few hands were still raised. Craig then ordered those who *had* to share with those who *had not*. It was at this moment that the level of Craig's dedication resonated with me and I knew that I would support his cause with all of my heart and energy.

After the raid of Craig's bong shop, Craig was very concerned over the irrational politics that could criminalize the word "bong" regardless of the intended use of the device. When the narcs came to seize all of Craig's bongs, they treated Craig like a common drug dealer and the narc even commented to me that Craig was no different than a heroin dealer. This attempt to muscle out Craig and his store ultimately failed, and all of Craig's bongs were returned after the city prosecutor agreed to dismiss the case. I will never forget how dismayed the narc was when I called him to tell him that the case had been dismissed and that the court had ordered the return of all the bongs.

Craig was the one client who personified all that I truly wanted to be—only I was too scared to speak out prior to obtaining my law degree. And now, my efforts are better served helping warriors like Craig; and in doing so, I, too, become a warrior. I have had many battles concerning the injustices of the laws criminalizing marijuana, but I have noticed a trend towards compassion, starting with the medical marijuana laws spreading throughout the country and reflected in the attitudes about marijuana among prosecutors and judges. Craig's amazing powers of visualization may not be totally responsible for this trend, but in getting to know Craig and the strength of his convictions, I cannot say they have played no part.

We are all lucky that Craig and those like him are not afraid to speak out against the incredibly unfair drug laws in our country that seek to demonize the sacred herb. Fortunately, Craig has realized that in writing this book, he will reach a greater audience and, hopefully, more quickly realize his vision for the benefit of humanity. As Craig stated at the end of his television ad, "Can't we all just get a bong?"

Eric Shevin, Esq. Los Angeles, 2005.

Section I

A Hollywood Story with a "Save the World" Ending...

Chapter 1— Enemy of the State

"Long hair minimizes the need for barbers."
—Albert Einstein

By the time you read my story, I will be sitting in the White House as president of the United States; but if I'm not, I'll probably be in jail. Only God knows what the future holds. I am a modern-day Native American warrior, but who is my enemy? My enemy is the country that I love, the United States. I belong to a Native American tribe that did not exist at the time of Columbus' landing in the New World. We are an organic creation of this land. Where else in the world but this continent could we call our home? This is my home. I am a free American, but for how long? How long until an RFID chip is implanted under my skin?

The United States of America is my country, and this is my story. As a 420 Elder, I am risking my life to protect others in my tribe by providing guidance and counseling in the form of this book. How else am I am going to reach my people? What is my tribe? The 420 Tribe is made up of people who break the law. They are pot smokers. They relax or self-medicate by smoking what they call His "sacred" herb and keeping this seed alive, the seed that will save the modern world. The plant, *cannabis*, which is harvested 12 months a year, is what unites tribal members.

Personally, I use it because it makes me feel better, but there are a multitude of industrial uses besides making people feel better when they smoke it. I believe that *Cannabis*, earth's medicine, is going to save our modern world. That is the reason I am spending my life working towards ending the prohibition of marijuana in the United States. It is that important. I am not alone. I am simply near the tip of a spear point that will change our society soon. There are fellow warriors whom I am following, such as Jack Herer, Tommy Chong, John Trudell, Roland Manakaja, and millions more who are stepping forward to join them. This vast multitude of future elders and warriors is following right behind the spear tip, so this trend will not be stopped; in my story, I am the town crier, letting the broader society know what is coming.

1

What thanks do these activists, tribal members, currently receive? Scorn, ridicule, and insolence are the answers. At least, that has been my experience. Marijuana activists find it difficult to make a living without peeing in a cup, and worse, they can lose their children to state services for choosing to smoke this beneficial herb. Smokers have an expectation and conviction that their toking will be rewarded in bliss, regardless of prohibition; so they smoke, but the plant could be used for so much more than it is currently being used for.

Already, smokers make marijuana the number one cash crop in every state in our union. Instead of attacking the marijuana industry, why doesn't the government just legalize it and collect the tax money? Currently, in at least one state, brave souls risk incarceration for life if caught growing only one *cannabis* plant. While here in California anyone with a note from their doctor can purchase marijuana with credit card. My fellow warriors and I know that the leaves of the hemp tree were given to the world for the healing of the nations. It is written in the Bible. It is the prophetic Native American "Herb of Understanding" from Black Elk's vision.

I am a *rebel with a cause* against the prohibition of hemp in the American tradition of non-cooperation and civil disobedience. It all started when I was a kid. My best buddy, Christopher Grakal, stole some marijuana from Ringo Starr, the former Beatle. Christopher's father was the lawyer and manager for Ringo, and my bosom buddy, Chris, was being a sneaky 12-year-old. He had stolen two joints from Ringo's "fag bag" ("fag" is the British word for "cigarette"). The bag was a male purse or some early version of an organizer. I am proud to say that the first pot I smoked was from Ringo Starr, and so began my journey toward becoming a "Hollyweed Revolutionary." The sad part was that I didn't get high.

As a revolutionary, I didn't rebel against my country, which I love so much; I was more a rebel at home, where true politics start. I am willing to, but I don't want to die for, *the cause*. As a child, it was a dream to one day be president of the United States, not some revolutionary living in the woods growing pot on federal land—yet it did almost turn out that way and still might.

I trust that with God's influence, people are going to wake up to the reality of the benign nature of marijuana. It is obvious, judging by marijuana's popularity, that people recognize some valuable quality in the forbidden plant. Actually, banning marijuana has forced this plant to evolve more rapidly than if it had not been prohibited because now people play more with the plants genetics.

The economic forces of supply and demand work even in this illegal business. The fact that people love this plant so much and demand its cultivation has lured many producers into production to supply the market's demand. This fact has actually changed the plant's genetics. If you look at a plant's ability to reproduce, genetically speaking, *cannabis* is one of God's great success stories. The reason for its prohibition and success are the same: This little plant, when smoked, alters one's consciousness.

My personal battle began the first day I smoked marijuana. On that day, I made a pledge to myself to end the prohibition of this beneficial herb, and I will not surrender.

(My editors told me that I should leave God out of my book because it is not "cool," but like Bob Marley, God is a big part of my life. It is impossible for me not to include Him. I am a God-fearing, pro-hemp Republican!)

On the front lines of the Drug War, I am fighting my own battle against terrorism—the kind of terrorism you see on television when planes knock down buildings. I don't work for the government, but I try to inform my California friends about the real danger of international terrorist who want to kill Americans. However, there is the daily terrorism for everyone in my tribe who has said, "Just say *Know* to marijuana" that is more pressing and that is what I am fighting for.

"Holy Shit, where did this come from ?"

I am fighting:

> The daily terror of losing one's job because you smoke weed.

> The ever-present terror of losing the natural environment. Paper is made from trees rather than hemp. Gasoline comes from the Middle East instead being grown on the plains of Middle America. And the ground water becomes polluted as cotton, rather than hemp, is used for making clothes.

> The real terror of your life, liberty, and pursuit of happiness being denied every day in an American police state that takes children from parents who smoke marijuana for relaxation and enjoyment in their personal pursuit of happiness and the American dream.

Knowledge is the only cure for that type of terrorism. When the truth is known, it is possible for people to see and create different types of business models. New business development brings new workers in an organic fashion. People move to where life is good. Personnel will develop new communities using the resource, hemp.

Cannabis/hemp is such an incredible resource that it will allow communities to develop in remote areas and be truly off the grid, making hemp fuel, food, and fiber. These could be autonomous, self-sufficient entities, something that was tried in the early 70s; but without the diverse natural resource of hemp, these organizations were unable to become self-sustaining and eventually most failed.

Cannabis, or "hemp," is the paramount natural resource of fiber in an industrialized society. When I am president, America will manufacture a superior replacement for gasoline from this harvest, eventually replacing the majority of commodities currently relying on petroleum by-products; this will end our dependence on Middle East oil. Additionally, by using synthetic building compounds and hemp paper, it will be possible to save our indigenous forests. Hemp will be healthy competition to the supremacy of the lumber industry in producing fiber products. Hemp is an ideal source of cellulose—in fact, better than farmed monoculture forests intended for either paper pulp or building composites.

I became a dedicated hemp activist and then capitalist because of my family background. As a child, my father encouraged me by saying, "One day, you could grow up to become president of the United States." I believed my father. That dream has always made me look for ways to make our country a better place. When I leave this earth I want it to be better off for me having been here.

I always respected my parents by telling them the truth. One significant turning point in my life occurred when I was a young man. It was when my parents picked me up from Christopher Grakal's house the night after Chris stole Ringo Starr's weed. My parents asked me if I saw people smoking marijuana at the Grakals' house. The Grakal house was a constant party back in the

1970s. I met many a rock legend there. Chris' father is a famous business manager in the music industry besides being an entertainment contract lawyer.

I told them, "Yes, people were smoking there." I was acting naïve and didn't mention the type of smoke as if I didn't know the difference, but I knew what they were talking about.

They asked, "Do you know what marijuana is?"

"A plant of some kind I guess?"

I answered their question hesitantly because I knew what was coming next. I was thinking, "It is rolled into hand-rolled cigarettes with star-shaped designs or American flags on the paper." I was slipping; I was not smart enough to keep my mouth shut.

"Did you try any?"

There it was—the question that I knew was coming; and I knew that I couldn't lie to my parents. They had always told me that if I told the truth, I wouldn't get in trouble, but somehow I knew this was different. I went against my gut feeling and trusted my dad's previous words.

Suddenly, I could relate to my childhood idol, the United States' first president George Washington, when his father asked him, "Son, did you cut down the cherry tree?" According to the myth, which I thought was reality at the time, George says, "I cannot tell a lie!" And then admits to the crime.

Had they only asked me if I "smoked" any, I could have honestly answered "no," because I really didn't inhale. The marijuana had no effect on me. When Chris tried to get me to try the pot, my mind jogged back to the day that my father encouraged me to try my first cigarette at the age of six years old. At the time, I thought I was going to die. There was no way I was going to inhale that noxious smoke and I never became a cigarette smoker.

I pinched my lips together and exhaled before saying the truth. "Yeah, I tried it, but..."

I was instantly cut off before I could explain that I hadn't inhaled. An argument between my parents and me started. The next thing I knew, I was grounded by my father and I wasn't allowed to watch television for the rest of my natural life. The next punishment that was imposed upon me was 10,000 times worse. Today, it might not sound so horrific, but my dad took me to the barber and told them to give me a crew cut! (in the late '70s?)

I was the coolest kid in sixth grade, with beautiful long, curly blonde hair. I was a grade school rock star. As I watched my locks fall to the floor, I thought my dad had gone mad as he ordered the barbers to butcher my hair. I made several pledges to myself. One was that I was not going to remove my baseball cap for at least sixth months. Another was that I'd never do that to my kids. And the most important pledge that I made to myself sitting in that barber chair watching my hair fall on the floor was that I would end the prohibition of marijuana. I didn't know what it would take, but I made a commitment that I have stuck with until today.

The next time I was with Chris, I tried marijuana for real. If I was going to be punished, I at least wanted to actually experience what I was being punished for. I found out that my father's reasoning for the drastic haircut stemmed from the fact that Chris and his brother, Dean, both wore their hair long and both were smoking pot as teenagers. Therefore, he came to the brilliant conclusion that people who have long hair obviously are more susceptible to smoking weed than people who have short-trimmed, conservative Republican cuts. My father thought that the way to avoid the "wrong crowd" (potheads, to be specific) was to butcher my hairstyle. Obviously, it was rather traumatic because I still remember the event quite vividly.

For a short time, I lost sight of the vow I had made as a youngster. It wasn't until I got my driver's license and could actually go and buy pot that I started to smoke on a more regular basis.

Summer vacations were spent at Supai Village in the Grand Canyon. It was opened to the public for camping as a way to create income for the tribe in the late 1960s. "Uncle Pete," our family's paid guide (he was not a real uncle), led trips down the canyon to Havasupai. He was born in 1889 and was the son of Grand Canyon miners. Pete was in great shape for an older man and knew the Havasupai's canyon like the back of his hand. He shared stories of his youth with me, and I imagined myself being in the canyon back at that time.

My mom and aunt, who had introduced me to the Supai, had met Uncle Pete in 1971 on their first trip together. The following year, they took me. After the third trip with Uncle Pete's group, my mom and aunt decided not to pay for guides anymore and started organizing trips for themselves. From the time I was six years old in 1972 until I graduated from high school in 1984, my mom and aunt took my cousins, some of my mom and aunt's girlfriends and their kids, and my brother and me to the canyon for a week every summer. The husbands were left at home. It was the women's chance to hang out with the kids and smoke pot without their husbands giving them grief.

It was there that I smoked some pot one afternoon when I was alone. I was eighteen years old and occasionally smoked with my mom, but every once in a while she would act disapprovingly. So, I was glad that I was alone and I wasn't feeling great. My mom didn't approve of me getting high when I was in high school, but she didn't live with us, so there was not a lot for her to say. That afternoon when the family was off on a hike, I was in camp with a fever, but still wanted to get high. While I was under the weather and high on marijuana, I had a vision that reminded me of my childhood pledge. It was vivid and real.

At a young age, it became clear to me that having a goal in one's life gave one's life meaning. It gave me a reason to go to college. I was going to be a lawyer and convince a major tobacco firm to hire me as a lobbyist in Washington, D.C., to end marijuana prohibition for their corporate profit.

8

As a Beverly Hills teenager that is how I saw my goal being accomplished. My aspirations were, and still are, to bring pot to the world. By the reading my story you are helping me in that goal. By the end of this book the reader will know why I am Hollywood's Wizard of Weed. More importantly, they'll understand how marijuana relates to ancient prophecy and why at this time in history a new tribe has come into being. I am an American writing only of the American experience, but this new tribe is global.

Chapter 2— Conspiracy Theory

"Nothing is illegal if 100 well-placed businessmen decide to do it."
—Andrew Young

I know that most people reading my story have no idea who I am. *High Times* magazine marked me with the moniker "Hollywood's Wizard of Weed." Still, that didn't make me famous enough to have the booker for Jay Leno call. David Letterman doesn't know my name and Larry King hasn't called, asking for a personal interview with "Craig X." If *High Times* were more popular, I'd be famous, but now I am only a rock star in the pot world.

Former U.S. Attorney General John Ashcroft is not a pot enthusiast. In fact, he was attending a local press conference in Pennsylvania, announcing the charges against the owners of wholesale pipe companies, when he stated, "This billion dollar industry will no longer be tolerated." Tommy Chong (of the Cheech and Chong movies) was only one of the many people across the country indicted for "selling drug paraphernalia across state lines," but his factory was the only one raided that day on national television.

There was an entire task force for Tommy Chong, complete with a news helicopter and SWAT team. Their years of experience in law enforcement dictated this level of force. Police officers never know what type of resistance to expect, so they always go in with overwhelming force as if they were the military. Was it possible that a millionaire film and television star and part-time bong maker would come out guns a-blazing? Would he run and shoot down a police helicopter? What was the threat that led to tax dollars being wasted in this manner?

According to Ashcroft at the press conference, the indicted were to face a possible fine of up to $250,000 and three years in jail. Since these arrests were creating such a stir in the "industry," my first response was to call the writer I knew from *Star* magazine, a celebrity tabloid, and ask her if she knew anyone interested in *my*

11

pot story. For two years, I had been trying to sell her on the idea that my life was a good story. I thought the timing would be perfect and it was a perfect time for me to get out of the glass blowing business.

More than 130,000 new Americans were drawn into the American injustice system in the year 2003. Tommy Chong was one of those people. The "correctional population," 3.2 percent of the adult population in the United States, reached a new high in 2003—6.9 million American people. At a time when crime nationwide has been stable for years, more and more Americans are being locked up. At a time when many states and local communities are faced with budget deficits, the government is locking away millions of potentially productive citizens for marijuana or possession of marijuana paraphernalia.

Of those people discharged from prison in 2003 for serving their due time, almost 40 percent were returned to prison, mostly for technical violations, like failing a drug urine test. A large percentage of parolees absconded and can't be located by the government. Nearly 10 percent of people getting out of our injustice system (I say that partially joking because the U.S. justice system is more fair than most countries in the world, but it is much more fair to the affluent) would rather take their chances on the lamb or leave the country altogether.

Bush's home state of Texas leads the nation with 534,260 people on probation or parole, followed by California, with 485,039. Remember that the majority of prison growth is a result of the Drug War, and 80 percent of all arrests are marijuana-related.

My question is, "What the heck is America thinking?"

I am sure that everyone thinks his or her life would make an interesting story. A piece of history starring me is not nearly as interesting as most people think, at least not for 100 years. My reason for writing this story is that I think my life's story sheds light on a part of current history, the history prohibition in American, to be specific the prohibition on marijuana.

Growing up in Beverly Hills I came to know many celebrities from pop culture. I had become friends with Tommy Chong through the "pot industry," so when Tommy's factory was raided, I became very nervous. After all, Tommy and I were in the same general business. I closed 2000 B.C., my hemp store, when my wife and I separated. I wanted to spend more time with my children. I started blowing glass pipes at home. By working at home, it was possible to make money and care for my kids.

Within an hour of Tommy's arrest, people started calling me and asking, "What does it mean for the industry?"

I didn't know. I thought that my little home shop might be next. It was the first day that I had hired a sales person to help me with sales. She was a fellow comedian whom I had met performing at the Comedy Store, but she quit after the first day because she was afraid of being arrested. My business was finally starting to go well, even with the sales girl quitting that day. I thought of getting out of the business and I called my friend in the gossip industry. I had to think about my future, my children, and what I was going to do. I started keeping a journal that night.

It was obvious why they were going after Tommy Chong, he was famous. It was all over the press and shook up the industry for two days. The first thing I wrote in my journal was, "How did I personally know Tommy Chong?"

I first met Tommy on a *High Times* photo shoot at his house. I was invited along by the photographer to help hold the backdrop and reflectors. Also, I was bringing the pot for the photo shoot. You can't do a High Times photo shoot without pot and the photographer wasn't bringing it out from New York, so he called me. Tommy and I hit it off right away, as I told a few jokes and made him laugh. He was such a cool guy, and nothing like the character he plays in the movies. As we pulled up he was in his garage wearing a denim work apron and turning household objects into bongs. This was before he opened the bong factory, so bong-making was just a hobby of his. Who doesn't love craft projects? Tommy Chong is the Martha Stewart of the pot industry.

After the photos were taken, and we sat around joking, Tommy asked me to go on his roof and give him some advice on a pot plant that he was growing. It was the most pathetic-looking plant that I had ever seen, and my advice to him was, "Don't lose your pot dealer's number."

It was fun being at his house. He was one of my childhood idols, and I asked about Cheech. Tommy ragged on about Cheech in a joking way for being a "sell-out" to corporate America for his cheesy television show. However, there is a rumor that those two will come back together on screen. I always loved Cheech and Chong movies. However, Tommy's portrayal of a stoner has always been a little bit of a "sell-out performance," even though I am a huge fan of his.

Tommy's depiction of a stoner is over-the-top and far-fetched in almost every performance. His caricature of a stoner is "way out there," but in real life, he is a philosophical health nut in his mid-60s with a sharp mind and the body of a 40-year-old that looks great. I am 25 years younger than he is and I'm sure he could still kick my ass!

On television Ashcroft was bragging about his victory in "Operation Pipe Dreams," the D.E.A.'s operation that nailed Tommy Chong and the others, when he made some asinine comments. I think the nation's top justice official has seen one too many episodes of "The Sopranos." This entire performance was for the cameras, including the "made for television" bust of Tommy's factory.

After the arrests of pipe and bong manufacturers and distributors across the country, John Ashcroft had these choice words at the press conference: "Putting a bong in the hands of a pothead is the same as selling a silencer to a hit man." Did he write that "made for television" line himself? Was that straight out of the Ministry of Propaganda that created Bush's line, "We going smoke 'em out"?

14

Tommy wasn't one of the biggest pipe manufacturers. He was targeted because of his fame in both Hollywood and the pot world, not because of his success in the pipe distribution industry. In fact, he wasn't deeply involved with the company. It was his son who started and ran it.

What was Ashcroft's success? When he should have been smoking out the terrorists, Ashcroft was busy putting away a father. Was Tommy Chong a threat to our society? John Ashcroft put away a man who loves his family, loves America, and simply thinks differently than the attorney general. Tommy Chong thinks for himself by thinking that marijuana is good. Will Mr. Chong campaign for the Republicans in the future? I don't think so, unless I am running.

Tommy Chong pled guilty and was sentenced on September 11, 2003, in Pennsylvania. He was just released after nine months in jail in July, 2004.

When I called Tommy on the phone, shortly after the bust and subsequent plea agreement, I asked him, "So, what is the deal? I heard from some upset people in the industry that the feds forced you to sign something saying your stuff was for marijuana and now they are going to use that statement to prosecute others."

"I am not sure what they are going to do to prosecute others, but that is right," he said. "I signed something saying it was for marijuana use, but I wasn't forced to. It was something I wanted to do."

He was preaching and I was listening. "John Ashcroft is a cocksucker and right-wing religious zealot. He's out of control and there's no fighting him right now. They are such assholes I couldn't fight them because they told me if I did they'd go after my family. It is like dealing with the mafia. I just want to get out of the government's way and get on with my life."

"Why did you admit it was for marijuana?" I asked. My thinking was that they would have to prove it was for marijuana *smoking*, which is not an easy task.

"Well," he explained, "they were not going to let me go." Ashcroft was out for his blood.

Tommy continued, "Marijuana is a misdemeanor in every state (actually, you can still get life in prison for growing only one plant in Oklahoma), so when there is a friendlier administration in office, I am going to petition the court to have my conviction overturned. I just didn't want to fight these guys. I don't think they're going to send me to jail, but I'll get house arrest."

It was disheartening to hear someone I looked up to not willing to fight. He continued, "Ashcroft doesn't care about civil rights." Tommy's breathing was noticeable. "He doesn't care about the Constitution or freedom."

Continuing to speak of Ashcroft, Tommy said, "Ashcroft has said, 'I only answer to Jesus Christ.' What makes him any better than the Taliban who say the same thing? People who take their orders directly from God scare me."

Tommy said this before knowing he'd be sent to real jail. At the time, he thought he would get house arrest like the other 54 people arrested in "Operation Pipe Dreams." Tommy didn't have any idea at the time that he would be sent to a real prison. Everyone else arrested that day was given house arrest. He really didn't do anything wrong in my mind or his. It is Ashcroft who is over the top, in our opinion. From what I understand, Tommy thought by pleading guilty that he'd be serving his time under house arrest and doing community service. He's been in jail longer than O.J., I think. It is not as if he is a threat to society. He didn't kill anyone! Okay, maybe a few brain cells, but only the weak ones.

I joke, but a war is being waged. The former Los Angeles Chief of Police, Daryl Gates, believed potheads should be "taken out and shot," and that was *before* King George W. and his attorney general began calling potheads "terrorists."

I agree with Bush and Ashcroft that terrorists are using the black market and illegal drug sales to fund their activities. Pot is even being smuggled into America by organized crime. So why give them an increased profit by continuing an unjust prohibition?

The government's Drug War has been a dismal failure if their goal is to end drug use. We are wasting money. Eighty percent of all drug arrests are pot-related, and millions of Americans are smoking a product that is unregulated. In addition to that, pot smokers are not going to stop smoking pot. Pot potency has increased because of more sophisticated growing techniques that growers are developing. Black market marijuana producers have advanced techniques for production and have genetically altered the species to affect the potency and production rate.

The government bureaus that are carrying out the war are just short of becoming criminal organizations themselves, deriving large percentages of their budgets from seized assets. The Constitution is in tatters. Sadly, the government funds anti-drug organizations without much oversight or questioning of these organizations' budgets. Ashcroft said the pot industry was supporting terrorism, but the sad fact is, I feel as if my own government is terrorizing me by continuing the Drug War.

How do I fight our government when I am impoverished by comparison to their colossal budgets? A book is a great medium for expression. My only weapon is my story and my personal computer. Let's hope the ink is mightier than the sword because if it isn't, I'll probably be hauled off to jail like Tommy Chong, movie star, fellow warrior, and my friend who was arrested along with 54 other business people in the pipe industry. Remember, free speech is only free if you can afford the airtime.

With my book, I have the chance to tell my story in place of the lie that the government is spreading. My tale is a rock-and-roll story with a "save the world" ending. I am the rock star and hemp is going to save the modern industrial world from ending up polluted and past the point of livability. I don't think humans have the power to destroy the world. However, we do have the capacity to destroy our ability to survive on the planet, and we are testing that limit now by continuing to ban hemp.

Chapter 3— L.A. Story

"Half the people in Hollywood are dying to be discovered and the other half are afraid they will be."
—Lionel Barrymore

After one failed year at the University of Colorado at Boulder, I returned to Los Angeles. During the summer that followed, Norm, my dad, was in Europe with my family. I was supposed to have gone to Europe as well, but my cousin went in my place because I had to go to work now that I wasn't going to college. I had an apartment in Beverly Hills with my best friend from childhood, Christopher Grakal. I just wasn't able to take a vacation and still pay my rent without asking my dad for help, so I decided to stay and work at my new job in Santa Monica, selling leases and listings for a real estate office.

I was getting tired of eating buttered noodles night after night, so I stopped at my Granny Annie's penthouse in Beverly Hills. She had always said that it was okay for me to stop by any time, but for some reason, I felt shy about going over there when her card games were going on (which was all of the time). I had quit smoking pot when I started my new job. I was turning over a new leaf everywhere in my life. It was the summer of 1985 and I was 19 years old. At that point in my life, it was my dream to be a real estate mogul. At 19 years old, your goals change often and I had momentarily lost sight of my pot vision. At that time, money was my goal, but all of that was about to change.

When I arrived at Granny's, she made me a grilled cheese sandwich and some french-fried potatoes. My cousin Denyse (whom I call Denny) happened to be playing cards with all of the old ladies that night.

My cousin was taking a break from the game. Denny whispered loudly from Granny's covered penthouse patio, "Craig, Craig, I think you want to come out here."

Denny and I had been very close (I am close with my whole family), but Denny and I were particularly close. She was the first person in the family I ever smoked pot with. She is eight or nine years older than me and used to baby-sit me when I was little. When I saw her out on the porch, my eyes opened wider.

"What the heck are you doing?" I whispered. I could clearly see that she was rolling a joint of some pungent Northern California "outdoor dank." (Check "dank" in the glossary in the back of this book as well as other stoner vocabulary.) As opposed to marijuana grown indoors, this was 1985, and market pressures had not yet driven the growers into the closet.

"You want to have a smoke with me?" my cousin asked.

"No!" I said, shaking my head. "I am not going to smoke at Granny's. Are you crazy?" Then I said loudly, "Does she know you are doing this here?"

"Shush!" Denny said, "I don't want to create a scene." That was cool with me, so I sat as she finished rolling. "If you are not going to smoke, then just keep me company."

She finished rolling the joint, and suddenly Granny appeared like a ghost from the kitchen. I went a little pale. After Denny sealed the cigarette paper with her tongue, the joint was moist. She lit the lighter and ran the cigarette back and forth in the flame. (By not stopping in one place, the moisture dries and yet the cigarette doesn't light.) Denny then lit the joint right in front of Granny. I was shocked. Granny didn't seem surprised at all. I stared at Denny in bewilderment as she looked at me and tried to pass me the joint.

I said politely, "No thank you," shaking my head and raising one eyebrow at her.

I was about to say, "No way, Jose." I was not going to smoke in front of my grandmother. But then Denny passed the joint to Granny, and Granny didn't just hit that thing; she *inhaled* it. As my tiny Granny in her robe and slippers huffed back, drawing marijuana smoke into her lungs, the cherry ember on the end of the joint blazed crimson red. After she sucked back what looked like a huge toke, she paused a moment, winked, and double-clutched the joint. It was insane seeing my tiny Granny take such a big hit. My only inclination was to throw her a high five as if she were Kirk Gibson who had just hit the game-winning home run in the bottom of the ninth inning of the World Series against the A's.

She slapped my hand hard, and I said, "You rule, Granny!"

Granny then Jedi-mind-tricked me and handed me the joint. "Go on! Hit it," she said in her elderly, scratchy voice that enlightens a listener that she's been smoking since the age of twelve. "It's okay."

It was an offer that I could not refuse. I was getting peer pressure to smoke weed from my grandmother and I collapsed under it. How could I pass up an opportunity to get high with Granny? It was just cool seeing my Granny puff with me. I wasn't going to "just say no" to the matriarch of my family.

My dad had taught me a memory trick when I was younger. Simply by saying to myself, "I am going to remember this for the rest of my life," it creates a catalogued memory that can be accessed at any time. When I gave Granny that high five, I said to myself right then, "I am going to remember this moment for the rest of my life."

I took a toke, and the three of us got high on that warm summer evening. We were all standing in a circle the way my friends and I puff. The patio looked east, with a view of the tall buildings downtown. Some nights—well, about half the nights in Los Angeles—the buildings were not visible even though they were only eight miles away, but on that night, it looked as if you could see into the office windows it was so clear and warm. The Santa Ana winds were blowing in from the east rather than the cool ocean breeze from the west.

21

At that moment, I knew the reason that I didn't go to Europe. Before that, I had been anxious and upset that they went without me, even though it was my choice, but by the time that doobie was a roach, the whole world seemed clear.

Right before we stepped back inside, my Granny said, "Do me just one *little* favor." Her request, in my mind, was a moment late. I had already smoked with her. I was going to tell someone I puffed with my Granny. I paused and listened. "Just don't tell your father," was all she said.

"Don't worry, Granny, I ended up with a crew cut last time I made that mistake," I said. "Believe me, he'll never hear about this." I am not sure if she believed me, but the thought that my grandmother was afraid of my dad knowing she smoked pot made me laugh.

It wasn't that my dad hated pot. He hated the fact that his son had tried smoking it and liked it. I don't know what he would have said to his mother if he knew she was smoking that "devil weed." My dad once told me, "As far as I am concerned, every toke of marijuana is like sticking the heroin needle in your arm." I always thought that it was a matter of politics for him. I am sure he had no idea his mother smoked until her 80th birthday. My dad was considering becoming a future congressman and he was not going to jeopardize a future political career by smoking himself or endorsing his son's smoking. My dad still won't admit that his mom smoked the "chronic."

Several years passed and I was attending UCLA to get my B.A. in history. I started a Free Speech Club and began running free speech rallies weekly. Now, I was never one known for keeping secrets well, and besides, I had dreams of becoming a stand-up comedian. On Granny Annie's 80th birthday, everyone was asked to write a story—an "Annie-Dote," a humorous story about my Granny. I told the story of "smoking pot with Granny" for the first time. She was embarrassed, but didn't deny it. She just loved me for who I was, and we were good friends. But she did say later, "I told you not to tell your father."

The Gulf War broke out during my time at UCLA. My small free speech group on campus grew, and I became well known around the university. The mother of another student liked my speaking and thought I would make a good politician one day. I told her, "I am going to be the president one day—or at least the governor of California."

She told me that if I was serious, I was welcome to stay at her home in Mexico to learn Spanish (as it was the fastest growing language in the U.S.). I took her up on her offer. While I was in Mexico, my Free Speech friend rented my place in Santa Monica and kept the Free Speech Movement alive.

I moved to Merida, the capital city of the state of Yucatan. The Yucatan Peninsula is the thumb part of the country that sticks into the Gulf of Mexico. It was home to the Mayan Empire prior to its conquest by Spanish conquistadors. One night in Merida, I dreamt that my grandmother died, and I was heartbroken because I never spent enough time with her, learning about my family history.

It may sound like a simple bad dream, but it was much more than that to me. I believed my dream would become a reality unless I did something to change it. It was less than six months later that I returned to the United States. I was determined to learn from the experience of my dream and decided to spend more time with my Granny, and since I was a history major, learn the oral history of my own family. Not only did I share with her the dream I had in Mexico, I moved into her penthouse to live with her in Beverly Hills.

Yes, Granny Annie and I became roommates and she let me grow pot in the penthouse.

Chapter 4— Mr. Saturday Night

"You have to live for the moment and not care what people think."
—Drew Barrymore

It seems that everyone I know somehow becomes famous. I recall smoking pot with Ricky Martin behind my store and saying a prayer for his career, telling him how people I know just seemed to become famous. He was on "General Hospital," the soap opera at the time, so he was already somewhat well-known. However, even my childhood next-door neighbor, Jonathan Antin, a hairdresser, has an American Express commercial and a reality show on Bravo called "Blow Out." My best friend just finished a few years on "NYPD Blue," and another close friend of our family, Danny Comden, had a show on ABC for a season. Danny was the best thing on the show, and he's still in the Hollywood mix. David Schwimmer, one of my high school friends and classmates, just finished up a stint on NBC's "Friends." I suppose one could say about my life, "location, location, location."

The Weasel derived his name from the verb, *To Weiz; definition: to take without giving back, to sponge off others, to generally take advantage and act opportunistically.* This is Pauly Shore's characterization of his own life. I met Pauly when he was a kid. My dad's twin, my Uncle Nick, was Pauly's Little League coach. I had seen Pauly at the Comedy Store West, after Little League. The Comedy Store West was a comedy club that his mother owned, and underage people could go to it because they served food along with alcohol. My 14th, 15th, and 16th birthdays were held at the Comedy Store West (as opposed to the Comedy Store on Sunset that has an age limit of 21 years old). Pauly's older brother, Peter, would sneak my high school best friend, Luca, and me in to see shows when we were students at Beverly High, and not old enough to be there. I have always been a fan of comedy.

Pauly was a year or two behind us at Beverly Hills High, but we saw each other all of the time in school. Peter and Pauly had grown up "Hollywood," around a lot of celebrities in the entertainment business. Pauly's act reflected that reality. Recently, he self-produced a film originally called, *You'll Never Weiz in This Town Again,* but being released as *Pauly Shore is Dead.* It is about the end of his career and the rise of Carrot Top. I heard it was self-deprecatingly funny and loaded with celebrities.

I ran into Pauly in the local mountains, skiing, after he graduated from Beverly High in the mid-1980s. He invited me over the next day to listen to one of his cassette tapes, with a recording of himself performing comedy. It was pretty good. The big thing he was working on at the time was a tag line, a final joke that made reference to something said earlier. The tag was that his mom's boyfriends were just grown-up versions of him—lazy stoners sitting around his mom's pool scamming money from her. The truth hurts (listen to Howard Stern), but it usually makes for the best comedy.

When I told Pauly that I had always wanted to try comedy, he helped me get a spot: three minutes on amateur night. I was the first one on stage and there were only 12 people in the audience. It was great—an adrenaline rush that I'll never forget. Like the first time I had sex, only about two minutes longer.

While I was at UCLA, I started working at the Comedy Store. Since I was attending school full-time during the days, I had been eager to find a nighttime job. I was responsible for answering the phones and I had access to the greatest shows on earth.

Pauly Shore's career began to take off when he landed a job on MTV as a Video Jockey—a VJ (it sounds as if it could be sexually transmitted, but it can't). I noticed from the phones that people were suddenly excited to see him and he got more and more gigs in the Main Room, the largest of all the stages at the Comedy Store.

Pauly had to fight like all of the other comedians for good spots before he was on television but, after the MTV job, he was in the big room all of the time and no one complained about favoritism. Mitzi Shore helped Pauly by giving him advice on the business, and when he was ready, she helped him some more. He had paid his dues and earned it. It is just a reality in Hollywood that when your mom is a major player in town, you have a little more help than the Average Joe.

Pauly was popular on MTV. He then parlayed that success into a multi-million dollar, three-picture deal, and then his film career was over just as quickly as it started. No one was interested in a balding middle-aged "dude," and yet he was typecast as the "Super Dude." It is similar to the career of Andrew "Dice" Clay, or as his paychecks (which I watched accumulate in a folder of comedian's checks) said, "Andrew Silverstein."

The phone job was a piece of cake for me except when I smoked too much pot before work. On those nights, it was difficult to stay awake until 10 p.m. when I'd shut off the phones and head downstairs to watch the show for a few hours. Most of the time, the phone didn't ring that often. I only did the job to be closer to "The Store," where the comedy action was. I thought of it as "Comedy College." Comedians are circus performers moving from town to town learning their craft and changing the act. It was working there that trained me for the job I am now taking on as the self-appointed spokesperson for the marijuana industry.

It was also at the Comedy Store that I met Eddie Griffin, the skinny broke-ass, foul-mouthed, chain-smoking comedian who would go on to become a movie star, or at least a star in *Under Cover Brother*. The night I met Eddie, the club was packed with people trying to get in. There was a big line on Sunset in front of the club for the second show. The phones wouldn't stop ringing. Argus Hamilton, Eddie Murphy, Charlie Fleischer, Andrew "Dice" Clay, Sam Kinison, Arsenio Hall, and other famous acts were all on the bill.

Eddie was an interesting person. His birth name is Edward R. Smith and he is older than he claims to be. I suppose it is typical in Hollywood to change your name and age. My friend Carlos Mencia was Ned Holeness before Mitzi Shore made up his new name. Sometimes, a new name makes you a new person. Eddie was typical Hollywood—secretive about everything, as if he were on the run from the law. He claimed to be only 20 years old, but he was probably more like 26 since he had been in the military and was an experienced comedian.

It is not as if five or six years is a big deal, but it *is* a big deal in Hollywood because producers are investing in your career and how many years or films you might have left in you. Actors are a lot like sports stars, only with longer careers if they are lucky.

Eddie Griffin came up to where I was working on the phones to get an application to work at the Comedy Store. I was really busy, but he was patient and waited to speak with me after filling it out. When I wasn't answering the phones, we would get into more conversation.

We saw the world from two polar opposite places. I was a Reagan Republican and Eddie was a conspiracy theorist who thought the CIA created AIDS to depopulate the continent of Africa so that the *white man* could steal the resources. "Just wait until I am famous," he would state as we hung out together. "Then I am going to let people know the truth about how things are run around here." Then he would joke, "If I don't get shot."

We both loved comedy and had similar goals of using our fame to accomplish social change. Eddie had gotten off a bus from Kansas with enough money to survive for a few weeks, but barely that. However, he was determined that he was going to make it, no matter what. It was the kind of story you hear about in the movies. You could see he had the "Eye of the Tiger" and wasn't taking "no" for an answer when it came to him making it big. Eventually, he did make a movie about the experience called *Foolish*.

That night of Eddie's entrance, I explained my philosophy of the comedy business to him. "It is show business and there is not a show without the business. It is the business that pays for everything. The comedians who are famous bring people in. As more people come to the club, more drinks are going to be sold, and that means more profit to pay the talent. But, the most important thing in business is making money, and in the comedy business, it is no different. The money comes into the club by selling drinks.

That is the business of a comedy club—selling drinks. That is why there is a drink minimum. They don't *sell* jokes; people *steal* them all night long, and there is nothing you can do about it. The club sells drinks."

Eddie looked disheartened at that last comment. "Don't think your jokes aren't walking right out the door and ending up on some sit-com because they will." I wiped the corners of my mouth and continued. "Talent is a commodity to be bought and sold in the pictures. That is why you have to be famous, and in this society, it doesn't really matter if it's Joey Buttafuoco fame or Rob Lowe fame. They—the producers of shows and movies—want a name to give them free publicity and to invest in talent that is going to continue to pay off, making their property, the film, more valuable. Producers look for people who are committed to the industry or who already have established a name in the biz ... or unstable crazy bitches like Shannon D. of '90210' who'll constantly be in the press." Eddie laughed at my last comment.

I was on a roll, and Eddie was giving me his full attention, soaking up everything I had to say. Or maybe he was just looking for a place to hang out before going to spend the night at Denny's, the 24-hour restaurant where he had been staying most nights until dawn.

"Let's say that you make two or three low-budget films but are committed to the business," I continued. "One day, you are in a hit and suddenly the producers' 'low-budget' property—a film with you in it— is more valuable because you are more famous."

I was telling him what I had learned from the phones. "What I know is that fame sells tickets. So do something to make Eddie Griffin, the comic, famous. If you have any talent, use it to create some fame for yourself. Get in a movie or something that makes you credible and don't do shitty movies or your fans won't trust you. Fame creates marketability, period—end of sentence. If you have fame *and* talent, then, *maybe* you can become a star."

29

I didn't want to get too cynical, but that is part of my nature. There was a glint in Eddie's eye that led me to believe he'd become famous.

I continued, "The fact is that mass media is so compelling to watch and listen to; celebrities are just a by-product of the medium." I began to sound like a UCLA student for a moment until Eddie suddenly looked skeptically at me.

I got real again and told Eddie how great the Comedy Store was and that he should get a job as a doorman just to be close to the store and wait for the opportunity to show off his talent. Eddie filled out an application and was hired as a doorman. Sam Kinison had been a doorman once, so it wasn't a dead-end job. Eddie quickly capitalized on the proximity to the stage and stole as much stage time as he could. I say "stole" because once Eddie got on stage, it was difficult to get him off—and still is.

Mitzi, Pauly Shore's mom and owner of the club, ran the club like a general watching closely over her troops. She was aware of every little detail. She worked for her comics to get Comedy Store talent in the news and on television shows. Mitzi Shore was smart enough to recognize raw talent and had an ability to develop it. She was better than many casting directors in town at seeing people's talent and star quality. She recognized that Eddie Griffin had raw talent. She immediately gave him the doorman job and he was promoted to "non-paid regular," a status that guarantees 20 minutes of stage time a week. Then, one night, Mitzi needed an act in the Main Room and Eddie answered the call. He was working the door and when the phone rang, he was there.

"I'll send someone right over," he said. Then he showed up and performed and did well. He was a "paid regular" the next week.

I knew Eddie was going to be a star the minute I saw him perform. He was honest, and the truth is always the funniest thing. Some of his material wasn't that original or new, but his social and political comedy was hysterical. He told a childhood story about seeing Alex Haley's *Roots* on television. He talked about what it would have been like if white people had been the slaves in colonial America. His stuff was cutting-edge and truthful. I imagined us doing movies together, like Richard Pryor and Gene Wilder. It had always been my intention to meet other talented, like-minded people by working at the Comedy Store, so I was glad to get to know him.

Eddie and I became good friends. He even used my mom's place as his own for a television interview. With his first paycheck, he rented a basement room in a garage in West Hollywood near the Comedy Store. This place would not have been appropriate for television. His room had a hideous yellow shag carpet laid over a cement floor. The carpet was left over from the '70s. It didn't have a pad underneath and didn't look as if it had been vacuumed since it was installed. It was a two-room single, and Eddie slept on the floor of his room with only sheets as covers. And I'll never forget the disgusting yellow pillow that didn't have a pillowcase for his head.

The place was worse than I can possibly describe, and I imagine jail has better accommodations, but Eddie had faith in his future. His gay roommate/landlord of the dungeon named Noah lingered around "the cave" entrance and lived in a leopard bathrobe, wallowing around the garage in a black Speedo bathing suit painting trash and making it (in his words) "into treasure." He would then sell this recycled furniture to who knows what schmuck at some design store or something.

Seeing how broke Eddie was helped me to realize what a nice home my father provided for me growing up. Eddie lived in a dungeon. There is no mystery as to why he had a foul mouth and bad breath. He didn't go to sleep at night because who would want to? Or who could possibly sleep there? He was basically homeless, but he paid for a safe place to crash out in the morning. In the safety of the daylight, he would just pass out for a few hours until it was time to perform again.

Now that foul-mouthed *motha* is a millionaire. That is the type of possibility that still exists in California, and especially Los

Angeles. Our state's governor is a former broke immigrant turned actor.

We are called the "Golden State" because of our gold mining history and rapid growth that caused the state's population to swell in 1849. People came in search of the fame that came with striking it rich in the goldfields. People still move to California in search of wealth in the entertainment industry and now in the medical marijuana fields. A person can make the City of Angels his or her home, come as a broke "no one," and become famous and rich. The golden dream still exists here if you are willing to go after it and blessed enough to be one of the lucky few to strike it rich. Americans and citizens of the world still come to the Golden State seeking that illusive fame and fortune.

Chapter 5— It's a Mad Mad Mad Mad World

"This is a war and we are soldiers. Death can come for us at any time, in any place. Now, consider the alternative. What if I am right? What if the prophecy is true? What if tomorrow the war could be over? Isn't that worth fighting for? Isn't it worth dying for?"
—Morpheus 'Matrix Reloaded'

I went to San Francisco Easter weekend while at UCLA and I learned first-hand how the abuse of power and the gutting of the Constitution for our own safety was manifesting and morphing our nation into a troubled and divided society.

My cousin, who was going to school in Northern California, was visiting her family in L.A. for the weekend, and my girlfriend, Michele, who normally worked Sundays, was off. It was perfect. We rented a car and took a road trip up to San Francisco, where we crashed at my cousin's pad for the two nights.

I consider myself a fighter because I am engaged in an epic struggle for freedom to smoke, grow, and sell marijuana. Marijuana has the ability to show the user what life is really for and create warriors out of couch potatoes. My battle has been dangerous, but by the grace of God and the focusing of my will, I have managed to stay alive and out of the enemy's prison camps— jail.

In my opinion, life is to be lived fully, appreciated, and participated in, and part of life is children, the perpetuation of life. Every plant has a seed. These are the basic rudiments of life, and our technologic society doesn't support the genuine significance of being human. Our society doesn't support a healthy existence, and this is evidenced by the war it has been having on this harmless little *cannabis* plant.

A warrior is someone who recognizes that all human beings eventually die; that life is not forever and survival is not guaranteed. There is only one alternative to life—death. The

33

pollution created by the modern industrial world affects our sensibilities so that we forget what it is to truly live. People all around the world no longer think clearly. Humans have allowed their minds and bodies (the earth—our bodies are made up of the metals, minerals, and liquids of the earth) to be polluted, manipulated, and controlled for pocket change.

The Saturday before Easter was fairly romantic for Michele and me. We ate cheese and bread in Golden Gate Park while drinking wine straight from the bottle. We fed the ducks with some of our sourdough loaf and rode paddleboats around a lake I visited often as a young child when I lived in Northern California.

That night, Michele and I went to a Devo (short for de-evolution) concert. In the club, we got separated. Michele was a "rocker," or more into rock music than I was, so she stayed near the front of the stage while I wandered to the back of the club where it was a little easier on the ears. Don't get me wrong. I like music, but Michele was an adult groupie. One of her heroes was the girl who wrote, *I'm with the Band*, Pamela De Barres. Pamela was not speaking of the group named "The Band." She was speaking of a lot of groups. Pamela was a hot chick who slept around with different bands as a professional groupie. The fact that this was Michele's idol was a huge red flag on the relationship.

When I exited the club, I noticed the streets were blocked off to traffic. At both ends of the block, there were white construction horses with orange stripes on them and blinking lights atop the crossbar. It was there that I was to confront the face of fascism and the repercussions of the Drug War coming home to "us." It was there that I realized my life was on the line. For the first time in my life, I became a true warrior.

Historically, in this country there are two distinct groups: "us" and "them." A great deal of domestic history is based upon the conflict between these two groups. In the United States, I am part of the "us" and the "we" group because I am a rich, white, educated male. Guys like me are the ones who have traditionally made the laws. "We" don't make laws to put ourselves in jail.

That night, I learned what it was like to be "them" the way Eddie Griffin feels all of the time (or at least did when I first met him). I was kidnapped, assaulted, humiliated, and tortured by a police officer. The fact is, that is the American way—do something wrong until it is exposed and then make amends or "fix" the problem. Hardly anyone believed me, except Eddie, when I told them that the police beat me up. That is until the Rodney King video came out. *Then* suddenly I was credible. That is the strange thing about modern America. Nothing is true until it appears on television.

I can't expose the truth about Iraq prison abuse because I've never been there and don't know what is going on halfway around the world. From my perspective, what happened to the prisoners there was not all that bad when compared to what was done to Iraqis under Hussein. However, I didn't appreciate the treatment by the police, and I am sure the Iraqis feel the same way. My goal is to explain what happened to me in Northern California. I am an educated American from the Republican Party. As a result of my run-in with the SFPD—not an occupying force unless you happen to belong to a culture that smokes a certain prohibited herb—I became a warrior in America's Drug War.

Back to the action...I had just exited the club alone. As I walked onto that street in San Francisco, I was paying close attention because I was in a foreign city. I had the keys to the car, the apartment, and all of the money. My girlfriend needed me and might panic if she didn't see me right away. The streets were blocked off from both sides, and I noticed there was a short wall directly across the street. My plan was to stand on the wall to get a better view over the crowd and look for her. I made my way across the street to the wall and stood on it, but the height advantage didn't help much.

My eyes strained as I searched for one girl amongst the sweating masses pouring out of the club and into the street just after midnight. I didn't see her for what seemed like a long while. I imagined her getting invited backstage to go hang out with the band/or something. She had a way like that. Finally, I saw her

35

exiting the club and searching for me. In the sea of people, it was pointless to yell at her because she would have never heard me.

I jumped off the wall and walked toward her. When I was halfway across the street, I was stopped by a police officer. He asked where I was going and I explained that my girlfriend and I had gotten separated and that I saw her and was going to meet her.

He asked to see my driver's license and I shot back, "Have I done anything wrong?"

"No," he said. "I just want to see your I.D."

"I don't know what I've done wrong that would make you want to see my identification."

That was the first thing I did wrong—talk back to a cop. When I reached into my back pocket to get my wallet, I was punched in the chest with such force that I fell to my knees after having the wind knocked out of me.

As I was falling to the ground to catch my breath, the officer (who weighed more than 150 pounds more than me) jumped on me, yelling at the top of his lungs so that everyone, including fellow officers, could hear, "What are you reaching for?"

He then put one of his hands on the back of my neck and ground my face into the dirty spit-and-gum-infested street. Before I knew what was happening, I was put in handcuffs, slammed up against a police car door, and the officer was digging through all the pockets of my jeans. He took out my wallet and threw me in the back of a paddy wagon, holding onto my identification, credit cards, and cash.

My first thought was that he was going to rob me, and then suddenly I remembered Michele and thought of her safety. Michele was in a city alone with no place to stay, no car, and no money. My third thought was of the half-smoked joint in my back pocket. Things seemed to be moving in slow motion, and even now—years later—I can recall my thoughts in detail.

I had my hands restrained behind my back and was sitting on a bench in the back of the paddy wagon. However, I was thin enough to maneuver my hands to my back pocket. I felt the half-joint and grabbed it. I let it drop near my feet and I tried to kick it, but I felt something more solid with my foot. It was an object bigger than a roach.

I had only brought one joint for the weekend because Michele didn't smoke. I had smoked the first half at Golden Gate Park that afternoon. I was hoping to toke the rest after the concert but was glad not to get a "possession of marijuana" ticket for it. The vast majority of domestic drug arrests are marijuana arrests, and most of those are for simple possession. After the officer had gone through my pockets and missed the roach, I felt relieved that I wouldn't get a ticket, but what had I done to piss this guy off?

Now that the joint was out of my pants, Michele was my only thought. I was thinking about how to contact her to let her know where I was. I had lost eye contact with her. I tried praying, using mental telepathy, and thinking. I thought, whom could I call in Los Angeles to reach her? Whom would she be likely to call? This was in the days when college students didn't have cellular telephones because they were still too expensive. I hated the thought of being driven off to some location with no way of reaching her. I felt powerless. It was a horrible feeling and I was suddenly distressed.

I could see her through the one tiny window in the paddy wagon. I was on a bench, facing the back of the vehicle. The window was about six inches by six inches. I say "window," but it was not glass; it was wire cage material, in the steel wall at my back that separated me from the driver. I was able to turn my body, look through the little window, and then out the windshield in the front of the wagon. Michele was now urgently searching for me as the crowd was getting thinner and thinner and I was nowhere to be found. I told the guy driving the car the situation.

He told me in a rude manner, "Prisoner, shut up!" I thought it was weird that he called me "prisoner," but I would later learn of its significance.

Moments later, the first officer, the one who struck me, came back. He pulled me out of the wagon and stood me up. I was grateful because Michele saw me and began to come over.

The officer said, "I saw you drop something in the wagon."

There was *no way* he had seen me drop anything. "How could you?" I wondered aloud with disbelief, knowing he was lying. There were no windows other than the tiny one in the front of the wagon. I was slick when I took that roach out of my pocket.

"I saw you drop a needle," he said.

I had to laugh because I am deathly afraid of needles and still have my mother come with me to the doctor when I know needles are going to be involved. Besides, how could he have seen anything when he was outside a vehicle that had no windows? I was looking out the windshield, the only visible window, and I didn't see him. And how could he see if I had dropped anything in the van?

What I did not know is that the cop had planted a needle in the van. I knew I had kicked something, but I had no idea it was a needle. I just knew it wasn't part of a joint. He had placed it on the floor of the van to connect me with some incriminating evidence. He needed a reason to bring me into the station besides jaywalking.

The cop was searching the floor of the van. "Where did it go?" he shouted at me (but he was speaking to himself).

Then he asked me, "What did you do with it?"

I stared at him dumbly, not knowing what he was talking about.

38

"Oh, here it is," he said. "Why did you kick it?" You could see him thinking, "Why did you kick my needle?"

"I didn't do anything," I replied. "I am afraid of needles and, besides, you searched my pockets before you put me in the van. You know I didn't have anything on me."

At the time, I still had no idea what I had kicked. At first, I thought he had found my roach, but that wasn't what he was looking for. Then I realized that he was setting me up with a needle charge, but it was laughable because I am so afraid of needles.

"Oh, my God," I thought, "This is how it's done on television." I had never experienced a crooked cop before.

"I was trying to look out the window for my girlfriend," I explained, as she was now walking toward us. "I might have kicked your needle then. I am sorry." I continued, "But I promise you one thing—that is not my needle."

I explained to the officer that I didn't use needles. "You are welcome to check my arms for track marks."

I had learned what "track marks" were from all the television cop shows I've watched over the years. "I am scared to death of needles, so you won't find a mark on my body."

Half of what I know about crime was learned from television or the movies. Whenever someone says to me, "the media doesn't influence people," I ask them, "Then why would corporations spend millions for a 30-second spot during the Super Bowl if television didn't influence people?

At this point, the officer and I were standing between the paddy wagon and a patrol car when my girlfriend finally made her way over to us.

The officer said to her, "Speakenzee English?" when Michele first walked up to us.

It was a racist comment because Michele was not light-skinned. ("Speakenzee" is some sort of broken German. Michele was a Native Mexican-American; her family was fifth-generation Californian). She ignored the snide comment by the officer and proceeded to advocate for my release—and she was actually doing a good job.

She told the officer, "He is a straight 'A' student at UCLA, a wimpy guy from Beverly Hills. You can see by his license—he weighs about 115 pounds dripping wet. He is not a threat!"

With Michele insulting me and working for my release, I was taken out of handcuffs. I gave her the car keys and my cousin's apartment key and began to put my stuff back into my pockets except the wallet the officer was holding. The officer said that he was going to give me a jaywalking ticket. It seemed unfair to me since the street was blocked off and everyone was jaywalking, but Michele was urging me to keep my mouth shut, which I did.

The officer wrote the ticket and then had me sign it. Police officers wear a visible nametag or badge, but this officer wasn't wearing anything to identify him, as the law requires. His black jacket was zipped all the way to the top and it was impossible to see any numbered badge or name tag to identify him. He was a tall, intimidating man, well over six feet four. It pissed me off that I had no idea what this jackass's name was so I could report him. The guy finally gave me back my identification and wallet, but he did not give me a copy of the jaywalking ticket, which would have identified him.

I knew from my experience as a juvenile driver not to mess with the courts or the police. When they say, "pay a fine" or "show up," they mean it, and if you don't, the courts have the authority to issue a warrant for your arrest.

I inquired of the officer, "Am I going to get a copy of the ticket?"

He said harshly, "Yeah, you'll get a copy...in the mail."

I mentioned to Michele that he was supposed to give me a copy of the ticket because I had signed it, promising to appear in court or pay the fine. If he did not send it in until the last minute, I would end up with a warrant for my arrest.

Michele encouraged me not to argue for a copy of the ticket and to be satisfied with receiving it in the mail. She was from a tough neighborhood in Oxnard and had been messed with by the police before, so she realized that any time you walk away from an encounter with the police, you should consider yourself lucky.

"Well, can I at least get your name?" I asked of the officer. That was the last straw. In the officer's opinion, I should have listened to Michele's sage advice and kept my mouth shut. After that, he put me in cuffs and I was arrested and held in jail for the night.

Several officers that night called me a "long-haired white nigger" in an effort to humiliate me, but I felt more embarrassed for them. They had to call me a name like children in order to justify their mistreatment of me.

Everything done in jail is meant to dehumanize and humiliate you. It starts with calling you "prisoner." Why don't they use your real name? In my opinion, it would make it more difficult to control people. In penitentiaries, they use numbers similar to those the Nazis used on Jews. Only in U.S. prisons the number is on your photo and clothes rather than tattooed on your skin, as it was in Germany.

Prison guards or jailers in the United States don't use people's names. That would make it more difficult mentally to control them. The police identify persons in state custody as by either a number or a generic term for "inmate." This is a form of objectification that helps guards detach themselves from the idea— at least mentally—that ill treatment of "prisoners" is okay. If the controlling authority figure used the person's name that would be

41

an acknowledgement of the inmate's humanity, and that would make maltreatment of those individuals much harder—mentally, not physically. For this reason, law enforcement agents (who used to be called "peace officers") are taught this dehumanizing technique.

The morning came, and Michele picked me up from the police station at 7 a.m. I got into the car and drove back, having difficulty believing that the last night had been real. The arresting officer, Richard Balyac (name changed), had physically beat me and verbally threatened my life the night before, and now I was a free man.

As we drove back to my cousin's apartment, I was filled with rage and was plotting how to get Balyac back. At the apartment, we made love, and for a moment all of our "couple" issues disappeared. When we returned to Los Angeles, I was still reeling from the experience, which had left me a wreck and unable to deal with school for a week.

My plan was to go to law school when I first applied to UCLA. I was a history major, which is basically a pre-law major. I was going to become a lobbyist in Washington, D.C., for Phillip Morris Corporation or RJ Reynolds and work towards ending the prohibition on hemp. Giant tobacco companies would stand to gain an incredible market share of this emerging new product, marijuana, and they already had the distribution system in place to profit from prohibition ending. I have never understood why big tobacco and alcohol interests have funded the Drug War along with the government. Do they not want the competition?

When I was arrested and beaten in San Francisco, I decided not to wait until after law school to begin my goal of ending the prohibition on hemp. I wasn't sure I'd live that long in our current society where cops beat people up. I didn't want to wait to do my life's work now that I was a combatant in the phony War on Drugs. The truth was, it was a war on Americans. There are no drugs to surrender or sign a peace treaty with.

As I began my adult crusade to end prohibition, "There is no time like *now* to get started," I thought.

My experience with the SFPD caused my interest in politics to rise like never before. A reporter from the *UCLA Daily Bruin*, our school paper, interviewed me about my encounter with the SFPD. It was going to be my opportunity to tell my fellow students what a crock of shit the Drug War was.

I told the *Daily Bruin* reporter everything, including a "fun fact" that the guy who sold drugs to me in high school was the anti-drug "This is your brain on drugs" actor in that famous commercial paid for by the Partnership for a Drug-Free America (I scored pot while in high school from the actor, Sasha Mitchell, who would later go on to star in the famous "eggs in a frying pan" anti-drug commercial and appear as Cody in "Step by Step"—any questions?).

Two days later, the reporter called me up and said it was the official policy of the *Daily Bruin*, the third largest paper in L.A., not to write about white kids getting beaten up by the police. Police abuse, he told me, was only placed in the *Daily Bruin* when black or Latino kids were beat up. The excuse he used was that, "when white kids are beaten by the police, they usually deserve it." They did write a story about my free speech rally and accused me of being in jail for two weeks on drug charges. Our college newspaper writers weren't the best writers in the world, and they never called to check the facts of my story. I think they even misspelled my name in the article.

Back to my job, I worked the Comedy Store job because I also wanted to get time on stage. I knew having public speaking ability would be critical if I wanted to be a politician. I got on stage on "pot luck" or amateur nights, which were held every Sunday and Monday night. A good amount of my material was political and pot-related humor. I eventually used some of my San Francisco story as material for my comedy. The joke was that the racial make-up of the cops was so diverse that I had been beaten by a "rainbow coalition of cops," all calling me "a long-haired white nigger." My goal was to get people to think on their own, to form a

43

personal opinion about the society they lived in. My style of comedy was to tell stories about my life rather than individual jokes.

Summer vacation came and went quickly, and when I returned for UCLA's fall semester, I was inspired for my first rally of the new school year. The idea of continuing to have free speech rallies inspired me. Suddenly, the school was stalling. There was an incident with the police because of marijuana smoking on campus at my rally and the school paper's negative article. For all my years at school, it was never necessary to have a group before checking out a microphone. But, from the first rally of the year, the school was now saying, "You can't have another rally without forming a group." I explained that I needed the microphone just one day to attract enough people to my new Free Speech Club.

The administration was putting an obstacle in my way, but in the end, it worked in my favor because it forced me to give the Free Speech Movement (I chose the name after seeing the film "Berkeley in the 60s") some organization. It was one more example in my life of "everything happens for a reason." The school trying to stop me actually created more support for the club. I simply checked out a

44

microphone, and then started talking about pot legalization at the UCLA's Meyerhoff Free Speech Park. Amazingly, people gathered to hear me speak. When I invited the crowd to come up and overcome "the majority of people's number one fear," public speaking, they responded, and that was the birth of the club.

I first recognized how marijuana tore down social barriers when the Free Speech Club I created quickly became the most diverse club on campus. The majority, but not all, of people involved with Free Speech shared the common bond of smoking weed. Well, at least the ones I connected with on a personal level. It was then also that I realized that pot smokers were not a small minority. We were just a huge, unorganized group. Approximately 60 million American smokers can't be wrong.

When I first arrived at UCLA, the scene was very segregated and there was no institutionalized way to break through some of the boundaries. For example, each ethnic group had a club on campus. There was the African American Student Association, the Black Student Association, La Raza ("The Race," whose members are indigenous to Mexico), the Movemiento Estudiantes de los Chicanos de Atzlan (MECHA), and the Latin American Student Association (LASA). Groups had also formed based on sexual preference and/or orientation. It was as if everybody needed a freaking support group, and people from these various groups rarely interacted outside their particular community.

In no time, our Free Speech Club became the most diverse group on campus. We welcomed all to come and debate. There were people from the Liberal Arts end of school (the North Campus), scientists from the South Campus, and people from all different races, who were of various sexual orientations and of every shape and size gathering at the park. We had two things in common—our love for free speech and fondness or tolerance of weed.

The Free Speech Park became a free zone for weed smoking. There were always so many of us puffing all day long that the campus police chose to ignore the area. Funny, "crimes" were never committed there. At one rally, we actually declared the park a free country and read a "Declaration of Independence" and proposed a constitution that was adopted wholeheartedly by those present.

An incredible number of marijuana smokers came forward and had something to say, and not always about pot or pro-pot, either. The club's only political view was to non-violently promote the freedom of speech of all points of view. According to the Constitution of Meyerhoff Free Speech Park/Nation, "If police officers enter the country, citizens' only permissible form of self-defense is to point at them. The purpose of pointing your finger is to make the officers feel *so uncomfortable that they'll just want to leave.*"

Other students who didn't smoke but who appreciated this crazy activity, humor, and lively debate occurring on campus began to join in discussions on different topics. After awhile, we didn't talk about marijuana every day, but it was common knowledge that you could smoke on campus without being hassled at the Meyerhoff Free Speech Park in the center of UCLA's campus; it became a gathering place to hook up with friends.

Several members of the group were interested in botany, specifically *cannabis* genetics. A private sub-group from Free Speech was informally formed of UCLA's best pot growers. Smart people who loved to garden; the weed we were growing was insane. It came from newly bred strains, which crossed strong *sativa* and quick-blooming *indica* strains. As we developed our own strains, we gave them strange names to identify them.

As the demand and price continued to increase, fewer dealers wanted to go through the summer "drought." More and more pot began to be grown indoors around this period in the early 1990s. In the 1980s, dealers would hold onto their bad weed half a year until the "drought," when their crap would command top dollar because the supply was so low. This was before indoor pot became popular and the summer "droughts" ended. In an effort to get over the "pot drought" some of UCLA's top minds created famous strains of pot. This was in an effort to figure out how best to grow indoors. Techniques, such as, genetic selection and cloning, practiced in the university laboratory were applied to home-grown indoor gardens.

One of the worst droughts was occurring during finals week at UCLA. It was a hot June day. I had my skateboard on campus and I was flying around from final to final. I hadn't smoked all day and was heading into my last final exam for the quarter. My roommate and Free Speech partner came skateboarding by on Bruin Walk moments before my last exam. I asked if he had any weed on him and he said, "Yes." When the two of us went into a stairwell to smoke, he pulled out the tiniest roach I'd ever seen and handed me a lighter with an adjustable flame. The flame was set high, and as I went to light the small cigarette, I burned off half of my mustache. I had to sit through a three-hour final with half a mustache and the smell of burnt hair.

Chapter 6— True Lies

"She got her looks from her father... He's a plastic surgeon."
—Groucho Marx

Shortly after my graduation from UCLA, a young woman named Nicole entered my life. I met Nicole at the hair salon in Century City where my dad was getting his hair cut. She was getting her hair done as well. When the stylist was finished, Nicole approached me as if she liked me. She asked for my number and I gave it to her.

Nicole was not as good-looking as the women I usually dated, but I liked her forwardness. Unfortunately, I felt insecure dating women who were not exceedingly good-looking. She was not ugly, but not your typical Beverly Hills babe. She was strong, with thick thighs. Her skin wasn't flawless like the women I had grown up with who paid whatever it took to look beautiful on the outside but who were willing to scrimp on inner beauty.

Nicole seemed extremely confident, and when she called me on the phone, she told me that one of the reasons that she wanted to meet me was because I was wearing a hat with a pot leaf. I liked her forthrightness. She told me how she was really into pot. I told her how I was going to be the man to legalize it. She seemed interested and impressed by this, which was a turn-on.

Nicole and I hung out for a few months. I hadn't been sexually active for several years at this time in my life. Luca and David, my two best friends, called me "The Monk," because getting laid was the last thing on my mind. After getting a girlfriend pregnant and then getting crabs, I was smart enough to realize that I didn't have the best judgment when it came to choosing women and having protected sex. Okay, sex wasn't exactly the last thing on my mind, but I didn't want sex to cloud my judgment when it came to choosing a wife because having family and children was a priority for me.

I wasn't out like Luca and David, dressing fancy and wearing black clothes, trying to get laid every weekend. In my heart, I was hoping to meet someone to settle down with and raise a family. I didn't want to end up divorced like my parents or the vast majority of parents in Beverly Hills. I just wanted to be friends with a girl. Hopefully, getting to know her better *before* we had sex would keep things from getting confusing. Then, maybe, if this girl and I had similar values, we'd get married.

Nicole was all about smoking weed and hanging out. We went to hockey games together, she enjoyed the martial arts, we rock climbed together, and both of us were into camping and the outdoors in general. My feelings were growing stronger for Nicole. I expressed my feelings towards her and she made it seem as if she felt similarly about me. I remember the night I invited her to come with me to my birthday dinner at a nice restaurant.

My dad is generous with his money and takes me and several of my friends out annually for my "b-day." Norm, my father, likes living well (and thank God, in America, it is possible for the son of parking lot attendants to become a wealthy man, living in the nicest area of Beverly Hills).

What Nicole said when I invited her was, "I can't meet your father." It was the first time I had ever seen her react as if she were scared. She turned ghostly white and there was a look of panic in her eyes.

"Why can't you meet my father? What are you so scared of?" I asked directly.

Her reply was strange, but true. "I don't have enough character to meet your father."

I thought she meant to say that she didn't have enough *class* because she burped and swore like a sailor sometimes (I pretended not to mind because she was so cool in other ways), but she didn't have much class. Her choice of words was interesting, but I ignored it. I liked her and I was ignoring a lot of things because I was lonely, looking for love. I wanted to find someone to love and start a family with.

Nicole was an interesting bird. She asked me deep questions about my philosophy on life and I asked her about her past, but I didn't believe much of what she told me because she had a habit of contradicting herself. She claimed to be a UCLA graduate, but she didn't display many signs of a good education. I'm a good listener, and I had been noticing how little details like the names of cities and people, the years events occurred in her past, and the order in which things in her stories happened often changed. When I confronted her or tried to question her, she'd become extremely defensive.

"What do you think of me?" Nicole bluntly asked one day.

"I think you are a pig," I joked.

She was shocked, but I had no idea at that time why my comment petrified her. I tried to rescue myself from the harsh comment that obviously upset her. "I mean, at times you have absolutely no class whatsoever. You burp aloud constantly, you swear like a sailor, and you don't always tell the truth." I was not sure if I was doing a good job.

I raised my eyebrows, looked right at her, and smiled. She was not looking happy. I tried to recover again, a little more gracefully this time. "At other times, you are beautiful and I really enjoy being friends with you—you love marijuana as much as I do. You know, we like the same things."

She then relaxed a little. I didn't mean to hurt her feelings; I was falling for her and imagining a potential future with her.

"Aren't you worried about going to jail for selling weed?" she asked. It was a reasonable question to ask a person you are considering spending your life with.

"Yeah, I'm worried, but I have a vision that one day I will get busted and it will help accomplish my long-term goal of legalizing marijuana, so I am not afraid. What is the worst that can happen to me? I get killed? I am not afraid to die for what I believe in." I said this quite cocky and sure of myself. This is one thing that I believed in wholeheartedly. "This is what I am here on earth for—to legalize weed."

"What do you think jail would be like?" Nicole always picked my brain. She was a trained interviewer and I always told her the truth.

"I would probably die if I were incarcerated. It seems a pretty harsh penalty for someone who is growing, smoking, or selling flowers, huh?" I wondered where she stood on the issue. "What do think should happen to pot dealers?"

She didn't answer my question. Instead, she asked, "Why do you think you would die in jail?"

"Look at me Nicole. I weigh 120 pounds and have long blond hair. I am *hot* in jail. You don't think somebody would try to make me their 'bitch,' my first day in? You know that I wouldn't go for that bullshit. They'd have to kill me." I was not bragging. I was simply stating the facts as I saw them. I continued, "Jail is not a good place to be. The fact is, one in three male inmates is forced into non-consensual sex. How do you think that the prisons are dealing with that issue? They are not, so for me, going to jail—real jail, not 'Club Fed' (the imagined cushy prison where Ken Lay will be spending his time if he is ever convicted)—would be a death sentence. Now, do you see what I mean?" I asked.

Nicole looked at me. She was armed to answer every question I was going to throw at her with another question. Talking to her helped me, too, because I was able to analyze and articulate my thoughts and beliefs. She was one of the few people interested in what happened to me when the San Francisco police beat me up four years earlier, an event that I was still processing—trying to come to terms with the whole incident. I was still angry at the system instead of the person who disgraced the uniform.

I continued sharing my views with Nicole. "Friendly people who buy, sell, or grow pot go to *real* jail. It doesn't matter whether they ever acted in a violent manner or not. People like corporate executives who steal billions, ruining thousands of lives as they steal people's retirements, rarely go to jail, and when they do, it is more like a country club, with television, good food, and tennis and golf facilities. Would President Nixon have ever gone to a real jail for covering up the Watergate break-in had he been convicted? I don't think so. Several kids from my high school who were known as real assholes, thieves, bullies, and punks became police officers. When one of my former pot dealers was arrested, the cops reported finding $2,000 in cash when, in actuality, there was $8,000 in cash. The arresting officers pocketed the difference, and who was going to be the wiser? The lawyers and judges believe the police over drug dealers, and what is the pot dealer going to say? 'Hey, I was a more successful dealer than that! I had more cash. The police stole it.' It is not as if he is ever going to get his money back. It is sometimes difficult to have respect for the uniform when I've witnessed and experienced that kind of corruption first-hand." I was rambling.

Nicole continued our talk in my Granny's old Ford Maverick as we drove through Beverly Hills towards my new apartment. "Do you think your family would help you?" Nicole was very good at getting to the heart of the matter.

"Are you kidding?" I asked. "I think my dad has political aspirations. Maybe he'll be a congressman one day when he retires. My dad is such a straight arrow. Our poor housekeeper— my dad takes out taxes from her check and files with the IRS. My parents have been audited twice and got money back both times. I am pretty sure that my dad, like Daryl Gates, would rather have a son in jail for weed than have on his permanent record that he helped a *druggie* son."

I said to Nicole, "My brother says that our dad lives in Egypt and his house is right next to *denial*." It was a poor attempt at a joke, but I am my father's son and he is the *king* of bad jokes.

Chapter 7— Scar Face

"About all I can say about the U.S. Senate is that it opens with a prayer and closes with an investigation."
—Will Rogers

As my relationship with Nicole Morgan progressed, she began asking me about cocaine. I told her that I had tried it, but that my philosophy as a leader in the hemp community was, "I won't panic as long as it is organic," and cocaine was not organic, so it was outside of my illegal pharmacopoeia, which included peyote, mushrooms, and grass, all of the cool organic medicines that are prescribed.

Besides, I told her, "Everyone I know who does coke is an asshole. They never shut up about how much they love you and how great it is to be with you and blah, blah, blah. Beside, they never let me get a word in edgewise."

Cocaine was anything but organic, and I was turned off by the fact that she kept asking me about it. It made me wonder what kind of problem she was hiding. I admitted to trying coke, but found that it was no good for me. Still, she kept asking me about it. Even though she knew how I felt.

I knew selling marijuana, whether I called it "medicine" or not, was illegal, and that doing something illegal had consequences. "I am not afraid to die," I said. I had never been more serious. "Nicole, I am more afraid of not living life than I am of dying." This sort of shocked her, but I continued to express my faith. "God will use me in this life as He sees fit. I am not worried." I had her full attention.

I am not so naïve as to believe that the punishment for the amount of marijuana I was selling would carry the death penalty, but I am also not so delusional as to think that I could actually survive in jail. I am that prissy kid from Beverly Hills who likes to protest and smoke weed in public to show how benign it is. I get manicures for God's sake! Yet, after having gone to jail in San

Francisco (where I felt I faced my death), I accepted the fact that, one day, I would die.

"What do you mean?" She was interested in my story, my thoughts, and everything I had to say. It was nice to have someone paying such close attention to me. We had never had a conversation this serious before. I was thinking that, if she were really interested in me, she wanted to know my spiritual side.

I went on, "I mean, I am going to die some day, right?" She nodded in agreement. "When the cops in San Francisco beat me up, they also psychologically terrorized me. They said they could kill me and get away with it, and I believed them."

To this day, I have trouble seeing police cars. Adverse physical reaction is how I would describe it. My heart drops in my chest, my mouth goes dry, and I have difficulty swallowing. Sometimes, I'd just prefer to stay home than to see cop cars and police everywhere. I still drive out of my way to avoid seeing them.

I continued telling her about how I was beaten by the police, and I was beginning to fell anxious, antsy, and unnerved. It was hard to tell the story without feeling like I wanted to stand up and try to physically shake the feeling from my body.

I then told her something I had never shared with anyone before. "I used to lie when I was a kid. I would lie all of the time and people would believe me. I realized that some people who tell the truth are ignored even though they are speaking the truth. The fact that people believe me is a gift. It is a gift that I have to use wisely or I'll lose it. Once you catch someone in a lie they are no longer credible, so why lie? The gift of credibility is something everyone can have by simply telling the truth. A gift—if you treat it that way."

She was looking at me, waiting for the punch line as if I were telling her the obvious. "There is no secret; if people catch you lying, they don't trust you in the future. It is that simple. My truth is that if I am not living out my dream of ending pot

56

prohibition, then I already am dead. If I can't freely light a joint because it just makes me feel better in my city, then I don't want to live. I'm the Patrick Henry of pot. Give me liberty or give me death." There was a short pause in our conversation.

With a joking laugh, I ended the pause. "So, meanwhile, I spend my time taking care of my grandmother. Ha-ha."

She wasn't saying a word. "I am learning about my family, my past, and as much as I can about the medicine," I continued. As I did, my own conviction was strengthened and my vision made clearer.

"How is going to jail going to serve your purpose?" she asked next. She could sure ask the zingers. Some of her questions felt like being hit on that special place on the elbow that sends electricity down one's arm.

"Well, it's not my goal to go to jail, but if God put that in my future, I guess I would just accept it. I just know what my purpose is, and since my incident with the police in San Francisco, I am not sitting around waiting to start living out my reason for being here." Then I shared with her vision in the Grand Canyon, my dream in Mexico and why I was living with my grandmother.

My thesis to our conversation concluded with, "I refuse to live in fear. When I once asked my grandmother if she were worried about smoking pot, legally speaking, her answer was, 'The law doesn't make something right or wrong. God does. Everything the Nazis did to the Jews was legal according to the Nazi's law, but it wasn't right.' Just because something is legal doesn't make it right." I paused momentarily, thinking, and then piped in with, "However, my grandmother runs an illegal card business." Then we both laughed.

I continued, "I am too good a person to be put in jail. I care for my grandmother. I visit with other old people who just want some company. I help my younger cousins with homework and do good things in the community. I don't even litter! If the government puts me in jail, they will collapse. Not immediately, of course, as a

57

result of my incarceration. I don't have that big of an ego, but my death might inspire my father or someone else who might be a more credible character in mainstream society. I have conviction and a good education, but am smart enough to realize that there are more credible people than myself to spread the word that we are losing our best, most peaceful citizens to jail as a result of the Drug War. What will our society look like when all of the non-violent people are locked up and violent citizens run amok? A lot like today?"

Finally, I took a breath, but couldn't stop. "Our nicest, most thoughtful citizens, non-violent growers, smokers, and sellers of a *flower* are being removed from our society, yet we are not dealing with violent criminals. Look at the type of society that is left behind. We are a violent society, but is that what we want?"

Nicole's constant asking about cocaine was beginning to get on my nerves and I was thinking of ending the relationship with her. My grandmother didn't particularly care for her either.

My grandmother and I rarely discussed dreams or visions, but I knew she was someone who thought that dreams were significant. It was the week before I was going to move out of Granny's apartment that she told me about a dream she felt I should know. Nicole was hanging out at Granny's apartment with me when Granny asked if she could speak with me alone.

In replying to my grandmother's request, I said that it was okay for Nicole to join our conversation, but my grandmother insisted that we speak alone. So, I complied. She wanted my weed out of her house. I was keeping it there even though I was spending half my time in Bel-Air near UCLA at David's house since his father had recently passed away. My thinking was that granny's place was the safest for my medicine since she was there so much. She didn't mind, and it kept me going to her house regularly, at least three times a day to smoke, and that is when she asked me to take her here or there on our daily errands.

58

Granny told me that she dreamed that the police were going to get me and it was because of *that girl*—and she didn't mean Marlow Thomas. I believe visions, mental movies, daydreams, or sleeping dreams are ways the Creator uses your subconscious to communicate with your conscious mind. My grandmother warned me to be careful of Nicole.

I took her word of caution lightly. I was blinded by the fact that I was lonely and I had recently had a daydream in Supai that I was going to be a father soon. I saw myself being married there, in front of the Havasu Falls, and Supai spoken when I died. Supai is the single most isolated village in the continental United States.

And I digress...Havasupai are the people of the Grand Canyon, and their village, Supai, is the most isolated village in the United States. It is the only place in America where mail is still delivered by mule train. My mother first took me there when I was only six years old. I imagined getting married in front of Havasu Falls when I was a child. My wedding that was covered in *High Times* (Valentine's issue, 1996) took place in front of Havasu Falls in September, 1995.

I had a vision one day as I was exiting the sweat lodge next to Havasu Creek. I saw the full moon rising over a purple canyon wall to the east, as traditional Natives' doors always open to the east to welcome the morning sun. On this evening, the full moon had just crept over the canyon wall as I lay there, continuing to sweat even though we were now outside the lodge. My body was recovering from the heat and I couldn't move, but my head was full of daydreams and visions.

It was my vision in Supai as a teenager that led me back to my life's work of ending prohibition. I had another mental picture there as an adult that would also be significant in my life. Outside the sweat lodge, leaning against the mud structure, partially immobile, I closed my eyes. As my body slowly adjusted to the ambient temperature, I could hear the river and feel the moon. I wasn't trying to visualize anything special, but there was a mental movie of me holding a baby.

In my mind's eye, my parents were nearby and that is what made me think it was my child. Then an even clearer picture of me holding a baby came into my mind. I think there is a reason the mind's eye sees clearly something in the forefront of the consciousness. It was that image that allowed me to picture myself as a father, at least psychologically.

In my mind, I saw a blue football jersey on a baby with the number 22, and I kept thinking of the full moon in front of me. I had a blue football jersey with the number 22 when I was a boy. I interpreted the vision to mean that I would have a son 22 months later. Instead, 22 months later I had a daughter by a young girl that I met at a hemp rally at the Federal Building. The younger girl making hemp purses was named Genevieve.

Everything in the world has been dreamed into existence, including the language you are reading and the clothes you are wearing. I try not to be too attached to the images that come to me hundreds of times a day. Daydreams are like children blowing bubbles in the summer sun. Thoughts lasting momentarily and then bursting into oblivion, but some bubbles are more impressive than others. Every once in a while, my thoughts are accompanied by a visual image that make a deep impression in my consciousness, that is impossible to forget. The thought becomes as real to me as historical event. I pay attention to what my thoughts are, and occasionally a memory of a vision comes into sight. Why at that moment? What is the significance of a memory of a something that only occurred in your mind?

If you believe as I do that everything happens for a reason, then of course, there was some reason that a particular memory arose at that moment or that I am who I am and you are who you are.

My memories are from films I've seen as much as my from the life I've lived. I constantly compare things to and make reference to films. It is second nature being from Hollywood, movie capital of the world; everyone around here references *the business* in everyday conversation. I was raised on movies and cable television. I can describe my life and book in terms of a movie pitch: a *Ferris Buehler* meets *Dazed and Confused* hero story with a "save the world" ending starring a pro-pot Republican who's into Jesus and the Bible. Oh yeah, *that's* going play big in Middle America, the red states.

Okay, now back to my grandmother's warning about Ms. Morgan. Nicole and I left Granny's house and I shared with Nicole what Granny told me. Nicole looked pale as I was speaking to her. I don't think that she believed in dreams or visions, but Granny and I felt strongly about them. I shared with her Granny's dream and told her that my grandmother didn't trust her. Nicole didn't take it well. I assured her that Granny was just an old lady looking out for her grandson. I should have trusted my grandmother's instincts and not said anything to Nicole, but I was blinded by my emotions.

When I was asked by Granny to get my own apartment, I was a little bummed, but at least now I knew why. It was because she didn't trust Nicole. Maybe my grandmother thought Nicole was on cocaine. Who knows?

It only took one afternoon for my brother and I to find a small place on North Oakhurst that became our "Smokehurst pad." The place was perfect for our needs—hanging out, puffing bowls, and playing Madden Football. The culmination of thousands of years of culture summed up in front of a television with Cap'n Crunch, chronic, and an electronic gaming device. My ancestors followed their visions to the free shores of the United States so I could smoke pot, play video games, and loaf in style.

Nicole was a frequent visitor at our apartment and spent the night a few times, but we never kissed or made love, although I got the impression that she wanted to because she was constantly showing me her naked or half-dressed body. My brother and I didn't have beds. I had been sleeping on the guest bed at my grandmother's, but I didn't mind sleeping on the floor. My brother and I both laid down sleeping mats at night and camped out on our apartment floor in our one-room apartment.

Granny wanted me close and was happy that I found a place
nearby and so quickly. She felt secure in her place, and I was only
a few blocks away. I was still her main source of transportation
and loving company. No one else had time to listen to her stories,
and as her life was coming to an end, she wanted to reflect back on
her experiences. She was taking personal inventory of her life by
sharing with me her ups and downs and the world's history that
she had witnessed.

Annie was put into the hospital a couple of months after I moved
out. She had been in her penthouse for 20 years, and that place
was everything to her. "Where do they want me to live? What
about my games?" she asked.

"I know it's an important meeting
sir, but we've been working on
the computer all night"

Granny was dying in the hospital, and what worried her most was
who was going to run her card games. When she found out that
she didn't have a place to go back to, she began to fall apart and
lose her will to recover.

My father and his siblings had decided not to pay the rent for my grandmother's apartment. She was in the hospital and had been there for almost two weeks. She wasn't doing well, obviously, and was probably going to die soon. The doctor had found a tumor in her stomach. The doctors told my elder relatives not to tell her and they didn't, but she knew. You don't live into your eighties and not learn something about life, your body, your family, and what you need to survive. My grandmother needed her social life and her penthouse. She had been there for nearly 20 years and was hoping to die there. She had told me so.

Granny Annie could still talk and had her sense of humor. All she wanted to do was get home. She didn't want to die in the hospital. My dad didn't think it was important for me to be with my grandmother. He implicitly understood that she was not going to live much longer but didn't realize that she was my best friend besides being my greatest link to my family's story.

My grandmother was interesting. Annie had been born before cars were popular or planes were seen in the sky, and she died when people were making reservations over the Internet. She tried skateboarding at the age of 80 years old because I was into it. Before Granny died, she had time for me and was interested in whatever I was doing at the moment. Her family stories are now my children's stories.

From my dream in which Granny had died, I learned that I had to spend quality time with her before she left my life forever. From that time forward, I acted on my vision and made my life better by getting to know her as a result.

January rolled around and Granny's health wasn't improving. This one night, I had been up late, praying, banging on a drum, and burning sage until two o'clock in the morning. At 5 a.m., there was a knock at my apartment door. It was Nicole. I was groggy, having just gone to bed, and she had a bandage on her finger.

She said, "My dad dropped me off at the Cedars Sinai last night and I walked from there."

I don't recall why she claimed to be wearing the bandage, but it had something to do with an injury in the middle of the night, an emergency. I was in no shape for critical thinking. I wanted to go back to sleep. She asked if she could come in, and I let her. After she was in and I had fallen back asleep, she woke me up and asked me to give her a ride home. I asked her if she could just rest with me for a few more hours, but she said that she really just wanted to sleep in her own bed because she had been up all night.

I said, "Let's go then."

She insisted that I take a shower to help wake me up. I told her that it wasn't necessary, but gave in to her whining. I got my tired and sleepy butt into the bathroom for a clean-up. When I was in the shower, she stole $5,000 worth of pot. I didn't see her do it or realize it was missing for a few hours, but I knew it was Nicole.

I called pot "medicine" even before Proposition 215 passed because the Havasupai Indians taught me that hemp was a medicine from the Native point of view. I was selling weed to friends and family to support myself and to care for my grandmother. "Weed seller" was my official job title and I was proud of that fact.

I wanted to pay Granny's February rent to shame (a method of influence used by Native Americans) my elders into letting her come home. They would have still had to pay for a nurse to care for her until she died, but I would have paid the rent. I knew she was going to die. Everyone close to her knew she was going to die. Everyone dies. The question is, do we die the way we want? The way we have dreamed of dying?

It was shortly after Nicole stole my pot that I realized she was a police officer. Everything hit me all at once—my grandmother's dream, the fact that she wouldn't go to my birthday because she didn't have enough "character," how she would show me her naked body but didn't want to hold my hand in a loving way, and was incredibly great at martial arts.

When I said she was a "pig," in our conversation, the look on her face said it all. Her asking me about cocaine several times, even after I told her my feelings about anything not organic, and the fact that she had stolen my weed—it all enlightened me to the fact that *she was a cop.*

Chapter 8— Return of the Jedi

"The Beatles were *so* high; they let Ringo sing a couple of tunes."
—Bill Hicks

Upon first realizing that Nicole Morgan was a police officer, I panicked. What was I going to do? For sure, my family would not help me. I turned to a trusted high school friend, Jonny. The professional Jonathan thought my story was unbelievable. The high school friend Jonny tried to believe me. He only found credibility in my story because he had known me for so long, but it took a lot of faith on his part to swallow it.

"Should I hold a press conference and call out the undercover cop before she arrests me?" I wondered aloud.

I was lost, confused, and didn't know where to turn. I was scared and wanted some answers. My grandmother was about to die and I was going to jail. The last time Jonny and I were together, it was singing outside of my grandmother's window on Fairfax at the place where she died. It was not a pretty scene, with me babbling at his house. If I were watching this unfold on screen, I'd be biting my nails, but this wasn't Hollywood make-believe. This was real life, my life.

"That's your call," Jonathan said calmly, as he was not involved other than caring about me as a friend going through a crisis. His professional job was working as a therapist. "If they don't arrest you, it will make you look crazy, though." He paused a moment. "In the end, that could work in your favor." Jonathan was trying to be funny because he is a shrink, but at the time, it was difficult to see humor in anything.

After realizing Nicole Morgan was a cop and not getting any solid advice from my friend other than his support and understanding, I was still left not knowing what to do. How could he understand? Was I simply being unreasonably paranoid?

Jonathan had never been through something like this; what kind of context could I ask him to put this situation into for me? I was hoping that he would have some answers.

He said, "I'll support you no matter what happens."

I was looking for direction, and instead I got a Hallmark response. I wanted to be grateful, but I wasn't. To me, his answer sounded empty.

My life seemed like a movie. Suddenly, I had the vision of my family completely rejecting me as a felon, my life's work being ruined for the same reason and I didn't want to die in jail. It was time for a scene at the bottom of the Grand Canyon. I hid the rent money in the apartment because rent wasn't due yet. I had enough, the $225 to pay my half of the rent, with some left over to get to Supai and back. I loaded up the Ford Maverick and split for Arizona. Maybe I would have a vision there that would save me from this mess that I had created for myself. That was the thought I had as I pulled out of Los Angeles and headed to Arizona.

Roland Manakaja, my friend, was the family's patriarch and Havasupai tribal leader. Roland wasn't expecting me; still, I was always welcome at his and his wife's home. I had been in the Grand Canyon only a few weeks before, selling some weed and hanging out with his family, so they had no idea I'd be back so soon.

When I arrived in Supai, I told Roland what had happened and how I realized Nicole was a police officer. He clearly didn't believe me, but saw that I was distressed. (Every pot dealer and hemp activist believes the government is out to get him or her. Ninety-nine percent of the time, it isn't true, although the fear is real. But my paranoia was deserved and I knew it deep in my heart.)

I didn't want to go to jail and die, but I was equipped for whatever fate lay ahead for me.

Roland said, "We'll take a sweat lodge and together we will pray for an answer."

It was the first thing that made me feel better. That first night in Supai, I went into the sweat lodge and took some positive action by praying and asking the Great Spirit for direction.

After the sweat, we returned to Roland's house. Roland's family went to bed, leaving me alone with my thoughts. I was guided toward a book in the Manakaja's personal library. It was the cover that drew my attention. Why do adults always judge books by their covers and tell children not to? The book was about a man named Edgar Cayce.

I read the whole book that evening. Edgar Cayce (1877-1945) is known as an American Prophet. In his time, Mr. Cayce was famous for healing people. He was not a doctor, but he had a psychic ability to heal people. He dealt with complex questions about the universe and uncomplicated questions like, "How do I get rid of a wart?" He was known to give "readings" to people to help them answer life's deeper questions as well. Many books have been written about him in the years since his death.

The book had been left by a tourist. The Grand Canyon was visited by thousands of tourists each year, and they left many books, foods, and musical tapes with the Indians. One specific section of the book really stood out in my mind. It was a descriptive story of an earthquake in Los Angeles. The next day, as I helped Roland chop wood for the family, I couldn't get the story out of my head.

Cayce wrote of our modern world. He wrote about Hollywood (which was famous even in his day), and described it as being revived and modernized. He wrote that the men looked like pirates, and I found it to be a little more than coincidental that I had just made that same comparison a week before—that the "in" style of bandanas, goatees, tattoos, wallet chains, gold loops, and diamond stud earrings made guys look like modern-day pirates making their living off the black market. "Ahoy mates, all hands on deck!"

The next day in Supai and the following days in California, I kept imagining an earthquake in Los Angeles. In my vision, my lack of fear saved me. The earth was shaking and fell away all around me, but because I knew who I was and wasn't afraid, the ground I was standing on was stable. I kept thinking about the book when I returned to L.A. and that I was on stable ground and that Nicole Morgan was on shaky ground in the Creator's eyes. She was helping with the prohibition of this incredibly useful plant.

There was going to be an earthquake soon, and I knew in my heart that my premonition would somehow save me, so I acted on that intuition. I returned to Los Angeles with renewed confidence that God would guide my life in a way that I'd be a father and not a convict. I knew that only God could send me to jail and that the police had nothing to do with it, so I wasn't afraid of them. I was grateful for what I believed was God's faith, and I continued on the straight and narrow path that I was on.

I returned to Los Angeles and didn't worry the slightest about Nicole. I began to prepare for the coming earthquake. I started by going to the market and collecting 2.5-gallon plastic bottles of water until I had 50 gallons. My little apartment was lined with the liquid. Nicole then called me and I confronted her on the fact that she stole my "medicine." We both knew I was speaking about my pot, but I used the word "medicine" to make a point and incase our conversation was being taped for prosecution purposes. I was not angry. I explained calmly to her what it meant to me. She denied stealing it, of course, but I knew.

I then asked if I could borrow money from her, since she claimed to be so rich. I explained that I needed the money to care for my dying grandmother. I offered to give her my Social Security number and whatever other information she would require to check my credit. I would have paid her back even though she was a police officer. I acted like a perfect gentleman. I would not go to jail kicking and screaming profanity without my shirt on as if I were on the television show "Cops." If I were going to jail for pot, I would go down intentionally, with the class of Rosa Parks in her stand for civil rights. I knew exactly what I was doing, and had no problem facing the consequences in defense of liberty.

I did, however, want Nicole to stay convinced that I didn't know she was a cop, but that I no longer wanted to be her friend. She had lied to me, stolen from me, and cheated me out of the opportunity to help my grandmother have a peaceful death in her own home. The only emotion I showed towards her was compassion. She was about to see an earthquake and the death of my Granny Annie, whom she had met and spent time with. I knew that she was going to feel badly when my grandmother was dead.

I did meet with her once after returning from Supai. We met to discuss the possibility of her helping me with money. We were in a laundromat on Santa Monica and Beverly Glen that is now a Coffee Bean. My head and stomach hurt from fasting. I kept putting my head down on my fist and thinking, "She isn't going to help me. Why am I here?" I had been praying and fasting for three days, hoping that she would loan me the money, but the meeting wasn't productive and I left feeling sick that my Granny was going to die in a hospital.

I told Nicole, "I have to go get ready for the earthquake, and it is going to be huge. If you are not going to help me, my grandmother will be dead within the month and she won't die at home. I have stuff to do."

And with that, I left and went home. Thank God, I wasn't arrested right there on the spot.

When I next spoke with Nicole on the telephone, I acted convinced that she must have a cocaine problem. If she wasn't a cop and I was wrong, the only way to make sense of her behavior was that she had a coke or crack addiction. I called Ron Siegel, the famous UCLA pharmacologist who studied animal intoxication (he happened to be a family friend) to ask if he could see her. He had helped my childhood friend overcome his addiction to cocaine, and if she was not a cop, I figured he could truly help her. If she was a cop, at least I was doing the right thing. If I went to court it would

71

look good for me that I wanted to help her. Also, it would highlight an alternative to prosecution. She denied having a problem, but I brought up the fact to her that she had been constantly asking me about coke. Why would she do that if she didn't have a problem?

Then I told her, "Nicole, I can no longer be your friend since you lie, cheat, and steal, and refuse to get help for your cocaine problem. With a resume like that," I joked, "you should find getting a job with the government, no problem." I was sending a subtle message that I knew she was a cop and that I wasn't afraid of her. This is when students believed that the CIA brought cocaine into the poor communities to raise money for black-ops and off the shelf projects. Also at the time, President Clinton was admitting to our government doing human testing on institutionalized people.

The next day, at the market, I ran into a girl I knew from high school.

"Hey, what are you doing here?" Ronny Reed asked.

"I am buying water. I think there is going to be a big earthquake," I said. When I saw her ten minutes later in line, checking out, I had 12.5 gallons of water in my cart (five 2.5-gallon plastic jugs) and nothing else.

"I guess you do think there is going to be an earthquake, huh?" she asked upon seeing my basket full of water.

"There will be," I said with confidence.

The earthquake rocked Southern California on January 17, 1994, and my grandmother died on February 10, less than one month later. It was beyond upsetting to me how Nicole prevented me from doing a better job of caring for her; but, I did what I could to make her last days on earth comfortable, and I held her hand as she passed away. I was starting to wonder if God were looking out for me or if it was all a coincidence. When things like that occur, it has to make you wonder. Does stuff like that happen to everyone? Or is just me?

I don't know if my logic is often correct, but my intuition is good and I trust my hunches. I feel as if I have inherited this gift from the Creator through my Jewish heritage. For a few thousand years, the Jews have been staying a step ahead of death and evil. I can read the times by the signs. I can imagine future events and actions in my mind's eye that I am not witnessing in person, but feel confident that my imagination is close to reality because I have worked to develop this skill intentionally and practice using it.

There are so few Jews in the world, and yet you hear about Jewish people every day on the news. The Jews who are alive today are here because, in spite of all of the trials and tribulations our ancestors have suffered, they are insightful enough to survive and reproduce. That is the goal of all living things, including the hemp plant. The irony is that marijuana has become much more successful at reproducing and passing along its genes during prohibition than it was before its intentional eradication. Is it possible that prohibition might have been this plant's reproductive strategy and that humans are just pawns in this plant's little game?

Nicole called January 24, one week after the quake, to ask how I knew it was coming. I told her that I had a vision in Supai, but we did not see each other much after that. I was busy thinking about Granny's funeral plans and what I would say to eulogize her.

At Granny's funeral, I delivered a memorable speech that caused my father not to speak with me for several hours. Several members of the huge audience shared with me, "That was the best funeral I have ever attended." For me, it was quite a compliment, considering that the audience was large and for the most part, they were not young. Let's say this was not the first "funeral for a friend" that they have attended, and for some, there was a possibility that it might be their last. At Granny's service, I spoke the truth, but I told true stories of Granny's pot smoking, and my dad was furious.

After the funeral, I moved out of my "Smokehurst pad" and into the back of a building I was leasing that was going to become 2000 B.C., my store on Melrose. I slept in a hammock that I had from living in Mexico. I didn't forward any of my numbers, and the last time I saw Officer Nicole Morgan was on December 5, 1994.

I shared many intimate details about my life with Police Officer Nicole Morgan. Now, the intimate details of my life are part of some government record, as if I were a citizen behind the iron curtain. Nicole Morgan was the culmination of every fear I have ever had about the government come true. There were now secret police operating within the United States and investigating me for smoking and selling an organic herb.

Chapter 9— Almost Famous

"The Force is what gives a Jedi his power. It is an energy field created by all living things. It surrounds us. It penetrates us. It binds the galaxy together."
—Obi-Wan (Ben) Kenobi, *Star Wars*

Three days after Granny Annie died, my brother and I moved out of our tiny bachelor pad on Smokehurst. I had wanted to own my own hemp store, and I decided to devote all my energy to making that dream a reality. I found and leased a building on Melrose Avenue, just outside the city limits of Beverly Hills, and I moved what little stuff I had from the apartment into a back room of the building—my possible living quarters for the next few years.

In 1993, my brother and I had come up with the store name. We were talking about how in the coming decade, many things were going to be named "2000 something-or-other." Then we discussed how, after the year 2000 passed, the name would be real retro. We tried to come up with a name that incorporated *our* names, Brian and Craig. The thought "B.C." came to our minds, and in the same instant, we said it together: "2000 B.C." The name couldn't become retro after the Millennium because it was already retro, from the "stoned age," I commented. From that moment on, it was a done deal. It was perfect: "2000 B.C. *The Stoned Age Hemp Shop*."

I imagined ads on television with King Kong climbing a giant bong and playing on the idea of King of Bongs. Setting 2000 B.C. apart from the competition was my main goal when I first opened the store. I hardly had any money. The one thing I had going for me was that I knew how to market on a budget, and people always gave me great deals because they believed in my cause. The pro-pot employee at Kinko's gave us discounts on printing. One restaurant traded us bongs for meals.

At UCLA, people were always giving me free things to help with our *common cause*. There was this one student named Francois who worked in the copy center. He gave my free speech group copies at no charge to help publish our newspaper, *The Free Speech*

Occasional. It was called that because it didn't come out on a specific date; it came out whenever we could gather four stoners together to write it. It would not have existed at the level it did if it were not for Francois and people like him who believed in what we were doing. While they weren't leading the fight themselves, they were our support troops. Tactically, they ran the supply lines in the battle to end the government's phony war on *the ubiquitous evil,* drugs.

As an activist holding rallies at the Federal Building, the cops started to take notice of me. I felt a certain power because I had sold pot to the cops and somehow I had not been busted. I felt as if they could not touch me because God protected me, so I held rallies and called water pipes "bongs" in spite of all of the advice I was receiving to the contrary.

My attorney advised me against holding more rallies. Especially against doing what I had done at UCLA, publicizing and promoting a large group "smoke-out" on government property. He said that, potentially, it put me in a position to be prosecuted for conspiracy to commit a federal crime before the smoke-out even occurred. However, when he realized that he wasn't going to stop me, he advised me, "If my group were to *spontaneously* have a smoke-out that was okay." Or, at least, it wasn't conspiracy to a commit a felony.

Chapter 10— Up in Smoke

"Marijuana is rejected all over the world. Damned! In England, heroin is all right for outpatients, but marijuana? They'll put your ass in jail. I wonder why that is?"
—Lenny Bruce

By my senior year at UCLA, our Free Speech Club had a smoke-out every Friday afternoon at noon. By that time, each campus group was allowed one hour of "amplified free speech" per week. The campus began to change the rules each quarter after I started to hold daily rallies. At UCLA, there existed the possibility of one hour of amplified free speech from noon to 1 p.m.

There is not a lot of room for free speech on university grounds. The Meyerhoff Free Speech Park was turned into a mini-Amsterdam on campus. You could smoke, buy, or sell pot there. If you had no money, you could show up and someone would smoke you out. The park was a small area with a podium and speakers dedicated to free speech on campus. It was named after a professor who died in a car accident shortly after taking a stand at the school for free speech by becoming the teacher-sponsor of a Communist Club. Every club on campus needed a faculty sponsor, and the Free Speech Movement was no different.

I was the first person on campus that I knew of to use Free Speech Park except for Christian groups, which used it often in their quest to spread the word of Jesus. I was speaking the word about weed, the stuff you smoke, but I learned all about hemp. I had met Jack Herer, the author of the hemp "Bible," *The Emperor Wears No Clothes*. Jack had a hemp booth at Venice Beach, but it wasn't my thing. They were a bunch of dirty hippies preaching that hemp would save the world, which I pray it will do. I believe it will save the industrialized world from an out-of-control oil addiction, but these pro-hemp guys were slobs with long hair and they didn't shower all that often. They looked as I imagined the early Christians looked, poor of finances, but wealthy in spirit. They were proselytizing to every passerby on the boardwalk in Venice about the virtues of hemp.

When I started the free speech group on campus, it was mainly for my goal of ending marijuana prohibition and preparing me for comedy and politics by giving me experience on the microphone. The "Hempsters" (as they were referred to at UCLA) crawled out of the woodwork to inform me about the benefits of hemp, the industrial plant. I was familiar with many of the claims myself because I had purchased one of Jack's books years ago, but thought their argument fell short because they didn't have hemp products to back up their claims. The one hemp shirt they did sell at their booth in Venice cost $80 and the hemp baseball hats, which were reasonably priced, were horrifically ugly.

Few people want to spend that much money on a denim shirt, not considering it is made of marijuana, when a comparable one is available made out of cotton at the Gap, a popular nationwide chain store, for half the price. The bottom line is that no one will wear something that is unflattering. I was all for ending the prohibition of hemp, but thought that the Hempsters were sloppy and unorganized people and the clothes they were producing were not made well. even if the fabric was strong.

Jack Herer had written this great book about hemp and walked around with his belly hanging over his pants. When he spoke at the hemp rallies, my friends and I would joke, "Pull up your pants Jack…it is not a crack rally."

Jack Herer was the stereotype that Tommy Chong portrayed in the movies. His book made him famous and gave him the ability to pay for his slovenly lifestyle, but it was only attracting a certain type of convert to the "Hemp Movement," as it was lovingly referred to. The types of people that Jack attracted to the movement were known as "Deadheads" because most of them followed the Grateful Dead band.

The followers of the Dead were off-the-grid types, left over from the 60s, into the counter-culture, who didn't file taxes or have permanent homes. They didn't shower often, loved to hug and go barefoot in forests, and called each other "brother" and "sister." They lived the life that Tommy Chong portrayed in the movies, but didn't live himself.

(Prior to publishing Jack read this part of my book and his feelings were hurt, but he admitted it was true—I told him that I loved him for all of the great things he did and he reminded me, "Captain Ed and I used all of our own money, we didn't take a dime from people and we did it because we love you guys." He paused a moment gave me a grin, a wink and then said, "And we liked to smoke good weed.")

Tommy Chong is wealthy, intelligent, and ambitious. He is always thinking of what to do next and yet is relaxed in a Zen way and is grounded in the knowledge that everything happens for a reason. He eats well and takes excellent care of his body, unlike Jack Herer. The two men are two or three years apart in age, yet their bodies are years apart in wear-and-tear. Tommy is a few years older and in vastly better shape.

Not that this has anything to do with Jack and Tommy, but shows the diversity in the "Hemp Movement," it is possible to describe the difference between the camps in the hemp movement as the difference between "ropers" and "dopers." The "ropers" want to push forward with domestic hemp production because it is good for the environment. They think, based on the strength of their argument, that they will end hemp prohibition. Many of these

81

people smoke pot but don't advertise that fact, and actually some don't smoke at all. What unifies this group is that they don't care about ending the prohibition on marijuana for personal use, but demand it for industrial purposes to "save the planet."

The "dopers," on the other hand, are for the complete legalization of marijuana. They are for the rope, but feel that the best way to accomplish that goal is by ending pot prohibition on marijuana smoking because that is what the government uses as its excuse to keep domestic production of hemp from becoming a reality. The government claims that it is protecting us from this harmful plant, as if marijuana were the man-eating plant in the film *Little Shop of Horrors*. We don't live in Europe, where they breed pussies in their cradle-to-grave system that never forces humans to rely on their full set of skills to get by in the world. Why do Americans allow their government to pass obtrusive laws against consensual crimes?

If the "ropers" and "dopers" were more together, they might end marijuana prohibition more quickly. Some marijuana growers actually want the plant to remain prohibited because they, as farmers, benefit from the tax-free inflated price that prohibition brings for their crop. Therefore, the business attracts criminals and is still a shady business because of the federal prohibition. The problem is that commercial growers don't have the protection of the law.

Or they didn't until medical marijuana became so popular. The prohibition on marijuana will end. It is only a matter of time because the truth has a way of getting out, and medical marijuana clubs are popping up all over the state of California. Licensed operations can bring in huge revenues for towns small and large. People have taken to calling Oakland "Oaksterdam" because there are literally more than 50 medical pot shops, and it is all legal or quasi-legal, as in Amsterdam, where marijuana is technically illegal, but tolerated. I now have a medical marijuana card and can purchase from any one of a half dozen clubs in Los Angeles. These clubs are run similarly to how clubs are run in Amsterdam.

The "ropers'" approach is to gradually end the prohibition of marijuana by first ending the prohibition of hemp, the environmentally friendly product that, according to Jack Herer, can save the world from petrochemical pollution. Personally, I think the "dopers" have a better understanding of our government. The predicament is that the people willing to stick their necks out for marijuana often look like Jack or the characters that Tommy Chong portrays in films and on television. I would rather be the intelligent, pot-smoking Republican who uses his brain while smoking pot—not loses his brain because he smokes pot.

It might be my Republican upbringing that makes me think in terms of dollars and sense. There are millions of people making money by selling a prohibited product. This economy mirrors the way that people made a lot of money (bootlegging) during the prohibition of alcohol, the birth of organized crime. I feel confident that when prohibition is ended, I'll have the brainpower to compete for market share in the emerging pot industry. That is how I felt about hemp in college—that it had to be looked at as an industry if it were ever to be legalized. The problem is that the "Hemp Movement" wants to cling to the idea that they are fighting the government instead of trying to work with the government. I think the pot industry needs to convince the American public that ending prohibition not only makes economic sense, it makes common sense. Overnight it would turn our country around economically.

Chapter 11— Pump up the Volume

"Forty million Americans experimented with smoking marijuana in 1970s; the only ones who didn't like it were Judge Ginsberg, Clarence Thomas, and Bill Clinton."
—Jay Leno

I thought when I graduated from UCLA and joined the Hemp Industry Association that I would be a leader in the "movement"— and eventually, with 2000 B.C., I was. But in the beginning, it was all about the rally. I was a conscious capitalist with an activist agenda. I was such a master of activism that I often used natural lighting to enhance to the staging of pro-pot events.

I discovered the perfect location to set up the stage for my next big rally. When rallies had previously been held at the Federal Building, they always faced north towards Wilshire Boulevard to appeal to the drivers going by on one of the most crowded streets in the world. That spot lacked the cinematic effect that I desired.

All my plans were in place for a "spontaneous smoke-out" on Sunday, the second day of our two-day rally. It was exactly at 4:20 p.m. that the sun hit the mirrored edifice, the building across the street, with a brilliance of studio lighting. On the east side of the Federal Building was a building about the same size, with mirrored windows. One afternoon, I noticed that, for a short period of time, when the sun would set, the east-facing stage at the Federal Building lit up as if the sun were one huge spotlight. When the sun hit the building across the way, it was as if the glory of God were suddenly beaming down on the stage the way the late afternoon sunrays shine through clouds after a rain.

I decided to have the unadvertised smoke-out on Sunday because that way, the permit couldn't be pulled until the end of the event. Additionally, my attorney had advised me that a planned smoke-out on federal property was a conspiracy charge that could get me "15 to life," depending on how many people I enticed to participate in the said conspiracy, but if it were spontaneous, legally I'd be better off.

At the perfect moment, I gave Andras Jones and his band the signal to stop playing about six minutes before the sun was in position. I was planning this moment the way a director plans to shoot a sunset for a film. It seemed as if I were the only one who was aware of the coming sunbeam because when the crowd saw the light, they reacted as if they were witnessing a miracle. After making my way to the stage and thanking the band for playing, the sunlight started to get people riled up and the increased energy was palpable.

"I love the United States of America. I love the fact that we can come out here and breathe the fresh air and protest the federal government on our property without the fear of being shot or going to jail," I said. "If there is one thing that Americans love, it is the right to peacefully protest their government." With all of that pot being smoked it couldn't be anything but peaceful.

Some people were paying attention to me and others were not. There were a few cheers. There were about 100 booths, with vendors selling goods. It looked like some ancient festival, with children and adults of all colors doing business at a giant bazaar set up on the Federal Building lawn.

I was able to attract vendors on short notice because of my connection with KPFK, an FM radio station, and "She Who Remembers," Genie Erstad's on-air radio handle. Genie Erstad was a divorced mother with three young girls who was an activist running around from event to event, taping speakers. She would then sell tapes inexpensively "to spread the word" about grassroots democracy. Genie would provide free copies to public radio stations such as 90.7 FM. "Roy of Hollywood," a midnight show, played her stuff often, and she was a regular guest of his. That is how I found her.

"This is a government of the people, isn't it?" I asked the audience rhetorically. I was starting to get louder. "At least I own *my* body, right?"

It had been four years since I first addressed a crowd at the Federal Building during the Gulf War. My speaking style had improved greatly from all of the experience I had gained doing comedy and free speech at UCLA. I felt particularly confident with the microphone because I believed wholly in what I was saying.

"This is America? This is the land of the free and home of the brave? Well, I don't feel so free. I don't feel *free* to grow marijuana. I don't feel *free* to sell marijuana, and I don't feel *free* to smoke marijuana."

I was looking around the crowd—as I did when I got stuck for a moment in stand-up comedy—for something or someone to give me a clue as to what to say next. I continued looking down at the officer who was omnipresent.

"Officer Sanchez here…" I took a breath and thought of what to say next. "This fine officer is able to smoke his cigarettes. You probably smoke more than a pack a day too, huh, Officer Sanchez?"

He acknowledged that I was speaking about him and lifted his cigarette to the crowd as if to acknowledge that he was with us as a smoker.

"He is free to drink his coffee." He lifted his cup.

"And he is free to eat donuts."

The crowd laughed and Sanchez smiled. He didn't have a donut in his hand, but it was a cheap shot at cops who are famous for eating donuts; though he probably had a box of them in the office of the building.

I was starting to get rolling as more people started looking towards the stage. "We've all heard people say, 'I need a drink' or 'I need my cigarette.' If cigarettes were made illegal, I bet officer Sanchez would be out here protesting with us. He should be allowed to have his cigarettes. I hear people say every day that they just don't feel themselves until they've had their first cup of coffee. I am saying pot makes me feel better when I smoke it. What is wrong with that? I am not saying it is not addictive. I am not saying we should give it to children." I was ready for another joke. "I am simply saying that every time I run out of weed, I search my house for the roach I know I left somewhere."

I had the audience's attention because I was making them laugh, and no one wants to be left out of laughter. "If cigarettes were suddenly made illegal, 'cigarette houses' would pop up like crack houses." There was a light chuckle. "You know that it is true." Then people felt safe to laugh and the laughter grew.

I acted like a crack head. I bent my body over and looked suspicious. I knocked on the microphone. "Yo, is this a Salem house?" I said in the junky voice. Then I pretended to be the voice on the other side of the door. "No man, this is a Marlboro house, Salem is down the street next to True and More," thinking of real names for brands of cigarettes. Then back in my own cocky voice, "I want to be able to walk into Seven-Eleven and ask the dude behind the counter for some weed." This comment got some cheers.

I went into my Jeff Spicolli voice (Spicolli is the stoner character played by Sean Penn in the film *Fast Times at Ridgemont High*). "I'd say to the guy behind the counter, 'Not the Marlboros, dude, huh, I want the green box, the Marely's.'" With that, the crowd started going wild and laughing. I had their full attention. That quote was my first-ever mention in *High Times* magazine. Bob Marley (the subject of my joke, world's most famous Rastafarian and an icon of the hemp movement) was on the cover of the magazine, and I felt like a "pot star" after that. That feeling lasted a week when I realized that pot was still not legal.

As the light from the sun hit the stage, I could feel the energy of the crowd continuing to build. There had been rumors of a giant "smoke-out" for two days, but nothing had been put in writing and nothing had been spoken from stage, so there was still the possibility that it might not happen. Tension was in the air. People had been asking me about the smoke-out for nearly two days and I kept putting them off, saying, "I don't know anything about it, but I've heard rumors that it is Sunday at 4:20 p.m."

When they would say, "Well, aren't you the organizer of the event?" I would not answer, but reply with a wink and repeat the rumor that I had heard.

From the stage, I continued growing louder to compete with the screams and catcalls. "I don't feel free, but one day I will be free to grow my herb. One day, I will be a pot farmer living off the land close to the earth. One day, with the hard work of all these good people here today"—I pointed out at the growing crowd—"I am going to be a pot farmer."

Then I started to mimic Dr. Martin Luther King Junior's style of speaking. "I, too, have a dream—a dream that one day we here in America will be free like our brothers in Holland to grow, smoke, and sell the herb that we love. I not only have a dream, but I have a vision that, on that day when marijuana is no longer prohibited, I will be a marijuana farmer. On that glorious day when pot is about to be harvested, I will get naked." I don't know why I said "naked." It just came out. "I'll run through the fields with my arms spread wide, yelling, 'Free at last! Free at last!'"

There was a big laugh at that last comment and now I had the full attention of everyone at the entire assembly, and there were thousands.

I continued, "And when I get back to the house, I am going to scrape the resins, tri-combs, and crystals off my naked body, throw them in the bong, and get high as a kite, like I've never been high before, because finally, I'll be free at last! God Almighty, I'll be free at last."

At this, the crowd was euphoric. For that moment, I was their rock star and they were my crowd.

I took a moment for a dramatic pause, and now the stage was fully engulfed in light as I had planned. "Well, let me tell you right now

that freedom comes with responsibility. I am taking the first
responsible step by showing our government that we are not afraid.
Bill Clinton, I know that you can hear all of us. The government
can beat marijuana smokers, the government can jail pot dealers,
and the government can steal the children of hemp growers."

I began the long drive home, the place in the speech at which I
could insert some knowledge, leading to the climactic smoke-out by
introducing a sad but true story. "The fact is, people working for
the government killed Donald Scott with impunity." (The Donald
Scott case was famous in Los Angeles at the time because the
government said that he was growing marijuana even when there
was no pot found on his property.)

Mr. Scott was not a paranoid pot activist. He was simply a man
who didn't want to sell his land for a state park. He was killed in a
"no-knock" search of his property at 5 a.m. I explained the "no-
knock" principle to people. I was learning more and more about the
law and still considering law school, but was finding the more I
learned about law, the more inconsistent I found it.

THC and coffee, *Everyone's Gotta Dream*

.. CHAPter 2..
! aM ruN1ng n@kED thro
tH£ pOT f!eLd$, !N 10Ve
w!Th $pr1nG..

kevinpearson

"President Nixon, a mild alcoholic with fits of paranoia, so hated pot smokers and the counter-culture that he allowed the first federal provisions for 'no-knock' drug raids. This allowed militarized SWAT teams and basically anyone with a badge the authority—basically, it gave *Johnny Law* the go-ahead to kick down your front door."

"No-knock" was a departure from the normal warrant service in the United States. Previously, according to U.S. constitutional interpretation, this practice had been considered illegal. Typically, there was a "knock-and-notice" standard. "No-knock" power allows law enforcement to run amok and abuse Americans' hard-fought constitutional rights. With the abuse of our nation's laws for the supposed benefit of society, it makes me wonder: Who is really benefiting? Our forefathers put these rules in place to prevent the very abuse of power that I am now fighting—the type of thing that is common in Third World countries.

"The founders of this nation gave us the right to bear arms to protect our homes. When Donald Scott went armed to see who was kicking in his front door (according to our Constitution's Second Amendment, he was lawfully armed, ready to defend his family and home), he was shot dead. Allegedly, the 'no-knock' warrant for his arrest was issued because Donald had six pot plants potentially growing on his several-hundred-acre property." I paused for the drama. "However, none were ever found."

I then shared with everyone: "The rumor that I heard is that the government wanted Donald's land for a park, and after his death, the government took it. That is right. They can kill you for pot even if you *are not an activist*, so don't be afraid because you are standing up for your rights. Be afraid because our government is lying to us and telling us what we can and can't put in our bodies—*our* bodies."

While everyone was still in shock about the Donald Scott story, I finished with, "Oh yeah, by the way, no one was ever prosecuted for Mr. Scott's murder. It is justifiable homicide when you kill an alleged pot grower. Is this my country or not? I am not afraid! The truth is on our side and I am not afraid. In time, we will win because we are right. Marijuana is good. It is not only benign; it is benevolent! That means it is good!"

"I am not afraid," I continued, and took out a big fat joint of some *indica* that I had been holding all day. "I am willing to go to jail if that is what it takes. I am not afraid, Mr. Clinton. This joint is going to be smoked in honor of Donald Scott." Officer Sanchez had mysteriously disappeared at this moment, and no federal officers were to be seen anywhere. But they could watch us on closed-circuit television, and I saw the cameras pointing right at me, as I held up the Bob Marley sized joint.

I held up the joint in full view of the cameras watching us. "I am going to smoke this joint right here and right now on federal property because I am not afraid. If you want to change the world," I challenged the audience, "then come up here with me and peacefully protest."

A few people started to come towards the stage. "Mr. Clinton," I said, taunting the president as if he were inside the Federal Building rather than in Washington D.C., fooling around with a chubby intern. "Come get us. We are not afraid because freedom starts right here and right now...with us. We are going to be free. This is our city. This is our country. We own our bodies, not you, the federal government, and we are not afraid. I am going to smoke this marijuana right here and be free because when I smoke pot, I am free. I don't care what you have to say, Mr. Clinton. I love my country and I love this plant, and if anyone is willing to risk their freedom to make us all free, come up and join me." Little did we know, at that very moment, Mr. Clinton may have been getting busy with an intern across the country and not fully paying attention to our needs as a tribe.

However, in Los Angeles at that moment, thousands of people began rushing towards the stage. I lit the joint, took a few tokes for the cameras and crowd, and then passed it to the person next to me. It was as if everyone had been waiting for the moment. Bongs and pipes came out of backpacks. A huge cloud began to rise as the band played and everyone smoked on stage. People were hugging and dancing for joy.

It was a joy that felt revolutionary. The Founding Fathers declared America's independence from an oppressive and tyrannical government. We weren't going back to the days of tyranny without a fight. This was a sign of our freedom. This was our postcard to the federal government that said, "We are here to stay, and we won't go away." The cloud of smoke that left the park that day blew East with the wind across our country and is still making a difference today.

The stage was completely bathed in light from the reflection from the mirrored building. Bill Bridges, the local reporter for *High Times* magazine, snapped photos while the light lasted. Our group picture made it into the magazine.

The moment lasted as long as the lighting effect. In about 10 minutes, my joint had come back to me as a finger-burning roach and the light had slowly moved from the stage. Andras and the band played their now famous song, "Drug War," with the line, "Everyone's a commie in a Drug War and we've been running low on commies since the Cold War."

God was our lighting director and the show went off perfectly on that day. Anyone who was there will never forget it.

George and Laura Bush reading about their twin daughters smoking pot with Ashton Kutcher in *Rolling Stone* magazine (5/03).

Chapter 12— Mississippi Burning

"Hope is this deep and powerful sense, not the same as joy that things are going well, but rather an ability to work for something because it is good, not just because it stands a chance at success. Hope is definitely not the same thing as optimism. It is not the conviction that something will turn out well, but the certainty that something makes sense, regardless of how it turns out."
—Vaclav Havel

A turning point in the civil rights movement came when black people began to see themselves differently. They began to see that they were just one more immigrant group that came to America, albeit unwillingly. They were here and they were American— African-American. Native Americans experienced this with the standoff at Wounded Knee in the 1970s. More than one Indian elder has told me that this was a big turning point in how the Natives saw themselves. Once a community sees itself in a new light, it is possible to do wondrous and inspiring things.

I see myself as a leader of a great tribe of *cannabis* explorers. We experiment and use a natural medicine provided by the Creator to improve our health, both mental and physical. The 420 Tribe is vibrant and growing. "420" was originated by a few guys in Northern California. The number refers to the time of day and their code for when to meet after school and smoke pot. The term "420" has spread throughout the underground hemp culture because of the magazine *High Times* and hemp companies that spread the term. The paranoid and secretive nature of the stoner way of life contributed to the code spreading like a grass fire, and now the numbers are used to identify members of a loosely affiliated tribal group.

The connection of the group is in their love of the herb. Typically, the tribe doesn't want anything from the government other than to be included in the "us" and doesn't think the government should tell "us" what we can and can't put in our bodies. Many of my buddies at UCLA realized that we'd never have the influence to change the destructive nature of the mainstream culture, so we thought of moving away and starting over. We'd live with our families off the grid until this society imploded on itself because of the lack of participation from brilliant minds such as ours. I suppose it is grandiose thinking, but you have to see yourself differently to make a change in the world. I saw marijuana smokers and dealers as heroes who were saving a seed that would eventually save the world. I still do, but because of the immense profits the industry attracts a criminal element as well.

2000 B.C.'s business was slow at the beginning, but our activism paid off. Word of mouth spread quickly, and soon we were making enough money to pay the rent (on time), eat, and grow the business. It felt like we were Steven Jobs or Bill Gates, early pioneers in the personal computing industry who went on to become some of America's wealthiest men, except we were pioneering legal marijuana, imported hemp. We were taking risks, but expected to be rewarded in some grand way.

Several months after the business started, my high school friend Luca lost his real estate management job. He was one of the original investors in 2000 B.C. and a supporter of my activism since my days at UCLA. Luca was my closest friend at the time and the only non-UCLA student to regularly contribute to the *Free Speech Occasional*. Sometimes, Luca would even run copies of the paper for students at his work and not charge us. I asked him if he were interested in helping my business. I needed someone to help me manage the store's finances because the store had been steadily growing in its popularity. Luca took the job. The two of us worked well together, and 2000 B.C. was coming into its own.

Our store stood out amongst other boutique and specialty shops. We were different, and the "location, location, location" principle didn't hurt either. 2000 B.C. was in the heart of the Hollywood scene on Melrose Avenue. Pauly Shore's brother, Peter, was producing and directing segments for tabloid television, so Luca and I hired him to direct our first commercial. The commercials ran on CNN, MTV, and Comedy Central through our local cable provider.

Peter did a great job directing the commercial we had written, and it was loaded with talent. We hired some of our hot female customers to be actresses as well as some trained actresses. We also used some of my friends at the Comedy Store (when they heard that Peter Shore was directing the commercial, it helped to convince them to be in it). The commercial featured me behind the counter, trying to help different customers. We were making fun of the fact that you can't call a bong a "bong" in the majority of pipe shops (except ours). In most shops that sell bongs, they won't sell a bong to you if you actually call it a "bong." Shop owners prefer that you call it a "water pipe."

According to the authorities, if it is called a "bong," that implies that it is going to be used for an illegal purpose—namely, the consumption of pot. In addition, authorities claim that the use of the word "bong" implies that a shop owner is knowingly selling something that will later be used as drug paraphernalia. (I guess the wording "water pipe" is the ultimate disguise.)

We chose to make fun of this situation of referring to a bong by another name. We filmed close to 30 actors in the same place, standing where a customer would, in front of our counter, they were all saying relatively the same thing, then we cut it all together. During the filming, each actor would ask for a bong from a sales person. Luca and I clipped the images together so that it looked as if every customer coming to buy a bong had the same dilemma: "How do I ask for what I want without saying the word 'bong'?" Something bong buyers could relate to.

The actors asked in eight million different ways for a "bong," not using the taboo word. The camera then cut to me asking, "Do you mean a bong?" The screen then cut to their reaction of relief as they said, "Yeah." A graphic filled page with our address, directions, phone number, and store hours, then popped up while a voice-over said, "Can't we all just get a bong? You can at 2000 B.C."

The commercial was so funny that our business increased overnight. Our customers told us that they were taping our ads off the television to watch again and again and share with friends. The other thing that set us apart was that we didn't sell drug paraphernalia. We sold herbal smoke accessories only. What that means is that we didn't sell crack pipes, vials, or other non-herbal smoking paraphernalia.

It wasn't peaches and cream from the beginning because, even before we had the commercial, we still had to deal with the police over the not-so-little matter of free speech. Eventually, after the success of our rallies at the Federal Building and our business reputation growing quickly in the community, the police had to come pay us a visit. Apparently, they were only responding to a "complaint" from an anonymous source. They came to visit my store and to warn me of an impending arrest for calling *it* (a water pipe) "a bong."

They had come in with the warning that someone had complained about me, and they had a copy of my advertisements in the *LA Weekly* with them. They said that they had heard of my rallies in Westwood and that they "couldn't help but notice the eight-foot sign in my store window, 'Bongs,' over the image of a pot leaf."

The police felt as if that was all the evidence they needed to put me away as a major felon for a long time and that they were being polite by warning me of the consequences ahead of time and by giving me an opportunity to simply shut my doors and say good-bye before my impending arrest.

But, I asked politely with a straight face, "Can I call them 'water-fuckers' instead of 'bongs'?"

"Yes," was all the main police officer said, and his partner smiled and let out a little air, recognizing the absurdity of the law.

Then I had to be a smart-ass. "So I can call it a 'water-fucker,' or a 'water-pipe,' but calling it a 'bong' makes it illegal?"

100

"We are just following orders," one of the officers said.

"Just like the Nazis," I thought, but didn't articulate. I knew better than to be a smart-ass with cops. They don't have long fuses.

The cops came in a second time to actually arrest me. There were four of them. Each one of them wore a mustache and Hawaiian shirt. I was getting busted by a bunch of Magnum P.I. lookalikes. The pot leaf was still on the window with the word "bong," and the police took Polaroid photos of the window before coming into the shop. That was their evidence that I was calling them "bongs." That and the fact that I *admitted* to calling them "bongs" because I feel it is my right to call a glass tube whatever I feel like calling it. I am free to abort a child. I am free to change religions on a daily basis. And yet, I am not free to call something I own what it is. This is outrageous and not a sign of living in a free country.

I continued speaking to the officers calmly and politely. "We are at a constitutional crisis here, guys. I bought plastic units, 'bongs' as I like to call them, 'water pipes' or whatever *you* want to call them, and I think under my First Amendment right, I can call them whatever I want. I guess you are going to have to arrest me because I am going to continue to call them what I want."

Seconds later, the cops put me in hand-cuffs and put me into the back of their car that had been waiting right in front of the store. I chatted with the cops on the way to the police station about hemp, but they didn't seem too interested in anything I had to say. They reminded me that it was my right to keep my mouth shut and that I should exercise that right.

Then one of them called me "prisoner" and I flashed back to San Francisco and decided to sit back with my mouth shut. I didn't want to get beat up. They took all of the store's smoking accessories (including a "chip clip"—used to seal a bag of potato chips—which they mistook for a roach clip because I had placed it in there intentionally, hoping it would be seized so I could show a jury the ridiculousness of this arbitrary seizure of property).

After I was arrested, my brother and our friend Mecca scraped the painted word "bongs" off the window without my permission. She and my brother didn't want to egg on the cops any further. They warned me and I was given one week to change my ways. Earlier, the cops had told me that, if I didn't stop selling bongs, they were going "to drive me out of business," and now they were simply keeping their word. I had told them that I would fight back and now I was keeping *my* word.

After their warning, I didn't lift a finger. I wasn't going to be intimidated by them. The police had come in the week before to "warn me." They had given me one week's notice that if I wasn't out of town by sundown in a week (my store), they'd be back. During the warning, they brought in a copy of the H&S Code that gave them authority to arrest me. It was Health and Safety Code 11364.7 that stated that it was illegal to sell a "bong" because doing so implied that the user was going to smoke an illegal substance, marijuana. (This event occurred before Proposition 215 passed, allowing medical marijuana in the state.)

I took a copy of the Health and Safety Code that the cops gave me to Eric Shevin, a pro-pot attorney who was working with LA NORML (NORML is the National Organization to Reform Marijuana Laws). He read all of the H&S codes in that section and found a discrepancy in two parts of Code 11364. One part—the part the cops showed me—stated, "the selling of *any* 'bong' is prohibited"; and in another part of the code, it clearly stated, "only people of majority age, over 18 years old, are able to purchase bongs because they are a smoking accessory." Shevin noted to the judge that there was a discrepancy in the H&S code. 2000 B.C. only wanted its day in court to clear up the misunderstanding in the law.

We wanted to test the case and go to court. Eric Shevin was working with Bruce Margolin at the time. (Mr. Margolin is the pot-attorney who ran for California governor, losing to Arnold Schwarzenegger.) We went to court and the judge gave the police more time to produce evidence that our product was being used to smoke marijuana since their only proof was the fact that I was calling it a "bong," which in some states, I am sure is enough.

I was sure through my own experience that marijuana was being smoked out of the pipes that we were selling, but we weren't selling marijuana (not yet, anyway), so there was no way to be absolutely sure beyond a reasonable doubt without invading people's privacy. Basically, the only way the police could have gotten evidence would have been to follow our clientele home and see if they used our products in an illegal manner *in the privacy of their homes.* The LAPD, *thank God,* had more important things to do with their time.

Another thing that I found really funny was that one of the narcotics officers made a comment about people smoking crack out of bongs. How can narcotics officers be so naïve about what they are doing full-time with their lives? Crack smokers don't use bongs. I've never seen crack in my life, but I know it isn't smoked out of a bong. I know the types of pipes used to smoke crack, and they are usually referred to as "oil pipes" or "incense burners" in the head shops.

The police were never able—or never tried—to produce any evidence that we were doing anything wrong other than calling something we owned a "bong" instead of a "water pipe." The judge didn't see a crime in the word and neither did Eric or I. So, the judge dismissed the case on the grounds that the police didn't have enough evidence to prosecute. The case is highlighted on Shevin's web site.

One of the funnier statements to come out of the case was the fact that the judge told my attorney, "This could be a tougher jury to empanel than the O.J. Simpson case."

Shevin then asked the judge, "How so?"

The judge replied, "We are going to have to find 12 people from Hollywood to say they have never smoked marijuana."

However, before I had all my merchandise returned to me, the police still managed to accomplish what they had set out to do. They were putting us out of business because the majority of our revenue came from selling bongs and not hemp products. The police held onto our goods for months after the case was dismissed. They thought they could just keep our property. That is the mentality of law enforcement. They come and take what they want and then try to keep it.

Challenging a Health and Safety Code discrepancy in the U.S. court of law isn't exactly a speedy process. Shevin eventually got me back my bongs by threatening the city with an Action of Replevin. The action would have forced the cops to explain why they were holding my property even though the judge said it was no longer evidence. The cops were in disbelief that they had to hand the bongs back over to me. Most normal people would have packed up and called it a day and gone into some other business, but I couldn't. My brother and I were living in the back of the store. We didn't have other jobs or any money to move, so we fought back and won.

When you have nothing to lose, it makes sense to hold your ground and fight back. If I had had to go to jail I would have, but we were losing anyway because we couldn't pay the rent. Shevin loved *our cause* and we had become friends after months of working on this case. Eric was working for us for free and we hadn't received any publicity yet, but the arrest was about to change that. A person, especially a storeowner on Melrose, getting arrested is news. Why is bad news always "newsworthy"?

A few weeks after the arrest and bong fiasco, Bill Bridges, a local photographer for *High Times*, was in the shop taking photographs of the store in the aftermath and interviewing me. He was writing a story for *High Times* about my arrest. The article came out in the same issue that I was in for being the most successful dealer selling legal pot at Super Bowl XXX. With my Arizona Cannabis Dealer's License I sold $2,000 worth or pot in one hour, legally.

Bill and I were musing over old times when in walked a customer from Japan. He was our third Japanese customer that week. I suppose the yen was strong at the time. He came in looking for weed. I told the guy we couldn't help him, but I bowed at him. He bowed back. I did it four times more and he bowed back each time.

I calculated in my head that he was genuinely Japanese and not a Japanese-American undercover police officer trying to bust me. After Nicole Morgan, I was very cautious about situations like this, especially now that I had just been arrested for a felony count of drug paraphernalia.

This could be the perfect set-up—getting busted by an undercover officer while the cops still had my bongs. They had decided not to prosecute me for lack of evidence, but they still had my bongs and I was having difficulty coming up with the rent that month and continuing to pay for the seized merchandise. After my experience with Nicole, I became much more careful about whom I would deal with on every level of my life, so I was extremely cautious.

What is the likelihood that an American undercover cop of Japanese descent would be as clever as to pose as a foreign person? They certainly wouldn't bow over and over again.

"How much weed did you want?" I asked him.

"Not much...four ounces," he said in a thick Japanese accent, using international sign language by holding up his hand with four fingers extended to make sure I understood the four.

"How much do you want to pay?" I asked, making sure we were speaking the same language. He may have been confusing ounces with grams.

With a heavy Japanese accent, he replied, "I heard it was cheaper in America...how about $2,000?" Nope, he was talking ounces.

"Two thousand dollars?" I questioned.

He nodded affirmatively. "Can I take you some traveler's checks?" He asked in broken English, meaning, "Will you take traveler's checks?"

"Oh yeah," I thought, "This guy is not a cop."

I questioned the short, stony looking guy with the hemp necklace. "American Express?" American Express was exactly what he had. "Dude, you're on. Don't leave home without 'em. Go cash them anywhere. There is a bank down the street. Go to the bank and then come right back and I'll go grab the weed."

He looked puzzled, but smiled and said, "Yes."

"I can't buy the weed with traveler's checks," I explained to him, "so you'll have to cash them first." I repeated myself twice, not sure if he understood the subtly of "cash only" in this business, but he smiled and returned shortly. There is an international stoner code that exists and I felt confident he'd return with money.

Bill watched the store for me for a minute. I ran next door to one of my neighbors who sold pot. I scored the weed, and 30 minutes later I made the exchange with Takashi. Four ounces for $2,000 meant that the dealer got paid immediately, and the following day, the rent was paid on time in full. I made more profit in 15 minutes than I had all week without my bongs.

The yen, the Japanese currency, was strong compared to the dollar at the time, so two grand seemed like nothing to the guy. In addition, I heard they paid up to $800 an ounce for weed in Japan.

Bill couldn't believe what I had just done. I told him I was never going to do it again, but when Takashi, my first Japanese pot-buying customer, got back to Japan, he told every one of his friends, and apparently we became one of the favorite stops on the American tour. Yoshiro was our next Japanese client, and some of these tourists eventually moved to the United States.

106

When Yoshiro walked in, he just smiled and said he was a friend of Takashi's. (One of our friends went to jail in Japan for six months because he was caught mailing himself 3.5 grams of Californian weed back to Japan.) Slowly, I built up a following in Japan. Eventually, the tour buses stopped right in front of our store. Japanese girls wanted to be photographed with me and sent me letters. They knew I was the "Weed Star," soon to be dubbed "The Wizard of Weed" in a later *High Times* article.

When Bill wondered how I knew the guy was okay, I told him, "No undercover officer would keep bowing like that. That is how I knew he wasn't an undercover officer. The guy had to really be from Japan, and not an undercover officer. It is impossible to fake that kind of cultural training."

Bill thought I was crazy for taking such a risk while the cops had my stuff.

Luca and I started to learn Japanese since we had so many Japanese customers. When we decided to produce the second 2000 B.C. commercial, we decided it would be smart to appeal to our new market segment. The second commercial was extremely similar to the first. Again, we filmed several actors asking for a bong without using the word. One of the actors was Tony Barbieri the voice of Niles Standish on Crank Yankers. The commercial began with Tony saying, "Hey man, have you got one of those smoky things? You know, about this tall, put your mouth on it, suck back, and whoa! Yahoo! Whoa! Got one of those?"

Two of our Japanese customers had become personal friends of Luca and mine. In the commercial, they approached our store counter, and for ten seconds, Hitoshi and Kyo spoke entirely in Japanese, asking for a water pipe without saying "bong." We had no idea what they said because we don't know much Japanese, but it was funny.

The second commercial ended with the tag line, "Racial tension? Can't we all just get a bong? You can at 2000 B.C.!" It only aired on local cable, but that did a lot to increase our Japanese clientele, as well.

A couple of New York advertising executives for Pepsi Company saw both of our commercials in their hotel room and came in to speak with us. They were very impressed with our advertising skills (plus they liked to puff). I ended up being their L.A. connection. Humor sells, and it really sells hemp-related items. The whole subject was so taboo that we attempted to make people feel more comfortable talking about pot in a lighthearted, humorous way.

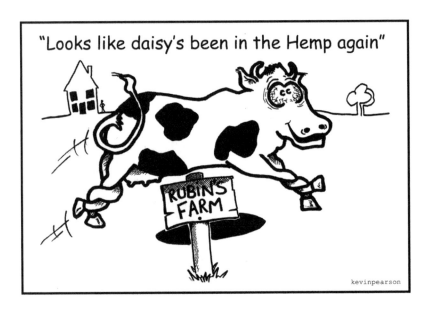

Chapter 13—Wonder Boys

"The greatest thing to come out of this for the world economy, if you could put it that way, would be $20 a barrel for oil. That's bigger than any tax cut in any country."
—Rupert Murdoch

Not only do I want to legalize marijuana for personal use, I want to absolutely and permanently alter its public image. That was part of the inspiration for starting the store. My idea was to change the way pot smokers thought of themselves. The new image I wanted to create for them was a clean look—sophisticated and intelligent. My store, 2000 B.C., showed pot for what it was, "the modern-day martini." It *is* the way people who are cool and clever commune with their friends. Under this new image, I am helping to create, my hope is that pot will be perceived as a smart alternative to wine or beer, and as a medicine that is efficacious for a wide variety of complaints.

Hemp should be perceived as a renewable resource for making paper, saving trees, and reclaiming ravaged and wasted environments. As edible crops go, *cannabis* produces four times the weight in seed (where the protein comes from) per acre than soy. The hemp seed is an inexpensive, cheap source of edible

109

protein. Hemp also stands as an alternative to the cotton industry, an industry that accounts for more chemicals and pesticides in the environment than any other agricultural product. People associated with marijuana, under the new image, would be looked at as insightful, wise, and intuitive. They are 420 Elders and warriors for *our cause.*

Looking back to 1995, Luca and I had been working full-time together for less than a year when we embarked on the construction of Bong Canyon. Luca had formerly been a property manager at a huge mall on La Cienega Boulevard called the Beverly Connection. Luca was the ex-son-in-law of hair products mogul Vidal Sassoon. He was charming, witty, and full of good, stylistic ideas. One of his ideas that appealed to me personally was Bong Canyon, but I didn't think it was going to be worth the money at first, but I was wrong. It was an idea to build a franchise around.

Our company's goal was to sell franchised hemp stores. It was my dream to be the McDonalds or Starbucks of weed, with 2000 B.C. shops everywhere. Instead of restaurants or coffee shops, my franchise would be hemp shops. Each franchise location would sell hemp products and other environmentally friendly goods, and once legal, 2000 B.C. would sell marijuana to anyone 18 years or older.

Bong Canyon was only supposed to cost $600 and take two weeks. The final project cost $3,500. I used to tease Luca constantly with his own words, "only going to cost $600 and take a couple of weeks to build."

Six months later, it was incredible, and I no longer doubted Luca's vision for retail. The project converted a small room we were not utilizing into a mini-replica of a section of the Grand Canyon that the Havasupai tribe still occupies in real life today. This famous region of the store included the *wi-ga-leeva* (Supai for "stone pillars") that hovered over the village like two sentries. It was the Grand Canyon of bongs and it, along with the commercials, put our humble store on the map.

Supai was my childhood summer playground and a place that I still visit regularly. I had taken Luca there a few times, and its beauty awed him. It is never easy getting in or out of the Grand Canyon because of the isolation. I know people who have died down there. It is not like car camping in which you drive up, park, unpack, and spend the night.

Luca was a thinking man's capitalist. He thought, "Let's bring the Grand Canyon back to L.A., so that everyone may visit" because it was so difficult to get there. The arduousness of the journey acts as a filter to people who should not go. The journey is the adventure, and you never know what to expect. In Bong Canyon, we—the employees and I—would share our experiences in Supai with the customers. It is eight miles down sheer cliffs and dusty trails to reach the village and then another two miles to the campground and falls. Not many people get to this part of the canyon. The Havasupai once guarded the entire canyon, but in the past century, the U.S. government has limited them to their reservation.

Bong Canyon had eight distinct sections, with custom-made shelves of varying depths. The shelves held merchandise ranging from $500 hand-blown, heavy-walled glass bongs to a small section of plastic bongs. I didn't realize how great it was until it was done. It was a fun place to shop. Bong Canyon set 2000 B.C. apart from the competition, and it honored my favorite place in the world, Supai, at the bottom of the Grand Canyon.

David Bloom, the NBC reporter who died in Iraq, came in to interview us one night right before Christmas. Bong Canyon was the most unique way to sell bongs in America and it was featured on Tom Brokaw's "Nightly News." There is nothing like good advertising. The story about us was negative. NBC was saying we sold drug paraphernalia, but the coverage on the canyon was national and they spelled our name correctly. We could never have afforded that kind of publicity. The next five days were our largest ever.

Bong Canyon had many celebrity visitors over the years, and that is what helped contribute to some of the store's fame. 2000 B.C. was full of celebrities but, according to the publishers of *Star* magazine, Brad Pitt was our most famous customer. He was handsome, talented, famous, rich, and, most importantly, a movie star on everybody's "A" list.

Chapter 14—Reefer Madness

"Some are born great, some achieve greatness, and some have PR officers."
—Daniel J. Boorstin

"Brad Pitt is in the store," Luca shared with me as he walked back into the office at the rear of 2000 B.C.

I said back to him, "Mark K. (one of the store's managers) told me that he was in a couple of weeks ago, too."

Acting all cool that we're attracting a large celebrity clientele, I continued, "Rod Stewart was in the other night, too, you know, with his kids. Maybe one was his kid's friend. Alan Arkin was in the other day, too, but no one knew who he was except me."

Luca asked, "The guy from *The In-Laws* film?"

Then he told me to go "schmooze" Brad Pitt. "You should go out there and give him some free shit or something. You are, after all, the face of the store."

It was difficult to tell whether Luca was serious or joking, especially when he used a Yiddish word like *schmooze*. Luca always had a smirk on his face.

"Dude, he is just another dude who puffs."

I tried to treat all of our customers equally. It was our policy to give all of our better customers (meaning people who spent a lot of dough, not just celebrities) a small discount or some free goods. Part of the winning formula of 2000 B.C. was that we made everyone feel like an "A list" star.

"Dude, he is Brad 'Fucking' Pitt. There are 40-year-old ladies right now in our store pretending to read *High Times* magazine just to get a glimpse of the guy."

Luca was completely serious. He recognized the magnitude of the situation. "This guy is the shit and he is here in our little bong shop. We need to make him feel welcome and comfortable so he tells all of his friends how cool 2000 B.C. is. People want to shop where stars shop, you know?" Luca knew too well, having appeared in the pages of *People* magazine with his wife, that celebrity customers are the same thing as publicity in this town. Luca now works for Eminem, the hip-hop artist.

"I don't have a *nug* (referring to a nodule or bud of marijuana) on me or anything," I said, making an excuse. "What should I give him?"

"Dude, we don't have to give him weed or anything"—he raised an eyebrow—"*illegal*. Simply give the guy some face time. You're just the main guy. You should go and say 'hello' or something. We can give him some free shit before he leaves."

Luca usually knew what he was talking about, so I followed his advice and headed through the door.

Brad was in Bong Canyon now, and Luca was right. A couple of 40-something business chicks were pretending to read *High Times* so they could get a peek at the guy. What a loss of privacy being a movie star, but both of those hot business women would have participated in a threesome with him in a minute, so fame has a benefit as well. (Maybe a burden if you look at Kobe Bryant's situation in Colorado. By the way, the NBA doesn't test for marijuana because if they did, they would have no players for their league).

"What's up man?" I asked Brad casually, not wanting to draw more attention to him than was necessary. I was trying to treat him like any other customer. Bong Canyon was kind of small, so we were standing very close. Brad just smiled and shook his head. "I heard you came back in before, too."

He nodded his head, "yes."

"Glad you're back, man. Thanks for shopping here. Anything we can do to help you out, let us know."

I felt sort of dorky coming out to meet him just because he was some famous guy. Luca smoothly glided into the action. He planned to casually walk up and stand next to me, and he did. All of us wanted to assist Brad in any possible way. I am sure he gets a lot of attention wherever he goes. Everyone wants to say, "I sold Brad Pitt his underwear or toothpaste."

On this day, Brad was wearing a wool ski hat and sunglasses. There was a little facial hair coming in, and I noticed the rings he was wearing. He looked like all of our stony clientele, a mix of urban cool and chic. He actually looked pretty normal for Hollywood.

He paid for his goods with a credit card and we learned his real name was William B. Pitt. (Good thing he uses the name Brad because Bill or William Pitt doesn't have the same ring.) Luca gave him three little plastic bongs for free because he said he was going on a ski trip or something where he needed small and disposable paraphernalia.

The next time Brad came in, I wasn't there, but I got the update from a handyman who had been doing some work for us. "He was wearing a leather jacket with a pot leaf shirt under it."

The next time he came in, a few weeks later, it appeared that he had just rolled out of bed like the rest of us and was out doing his errands. Imagine that—Brad Pitt, a regular guy. On this day, he was out buying some gifts for a few people on the set he had been working with—a few of the cooler people, obviously, because he was buying them bongs.

Brad was buying Jerome Baker bongs to be specific, which shows the guy's got a lot of class because Jerome Baker Designs makes the best bongs in the world, hands down. (By the way, 2000 B.C. was Jerome Baker's first commercial account. We discovered the line at a show. I often spoke at hemp festivals at this time, and I was speaking at one in Oregon when we met J.B.)

Luca and I came out of the office to hang with Brad and Dave, my friend from UCLA, and our employee who was working with Mr. Pitt at the time. "We just wanted to introduce ourselves again. I am Craig and this is Luca. Dude, we know your name is Brad, but it is nice to see you again." I did the talking because Luca, "Mr. Smooth" with chicks, was suddenly shy.

Brad kind of snorted out a laugh at my comment, that we knew his name, and shook both of our hands the stony way with the solid rock, making a fist and banging your fist into the fist of the person you are greeting, at the end.

It was cool seeing Brad Pitt just popping into my regular, everyday life. It was validation that our store was successful. We were bullshitting with him, telling him about the Indians in the Grand Canyon and asking him about the chicks that must throw love at him.

He was a pretty humble guy. I've known less famous people who have more "attitude" than he was giving off. He gave off this "I like to get high, play sports, and hang out with my friends" vibe, not the "I am the biggest chick-getting star in the world" vibe, which I am sure he could easily portray if he were that kind of dude.

After talking with him for a few minutes, he started to open up to us as if we were good friends. "Hey, do you guys know Harrison Ford?" he asked.

Dave, my good friend, being comical, says, "Not personally, but who doesn't know *Hans Solo?*"

Even though no one else was in the store at the time, Brad leaned forward to tell us the secret: "I am working on a film with him." Then there was this dramatic pause. (The pause was dramatic because it was long enough for someone else to speak up.)

116

"That's cool. Is he a nice guy?" I asked.

Brad ignored my question. "Dudes, I am working with him right now." (I forget the working title he gave us, but the film was released as *The Devil's Own*.) "I've got news for you all—Hans Solo is a major puffer."

"No way!" I blurted out.

Brad broke out in a big smile. I guess Harrison Ford is a huge actor in Brad Pitt's eyes, as well. That must be why he thinks it is so cool that Harrison puffs. "I've been puffing with him every day on the set in his trailer." Brad Pitt was no different than everyone else in L.A. "Angelinos," as the people of Los Angeles are called, tend to think it is cool to say that they puffed with so-n-so famous person.

We let out a collective, "Wow."

We were all ears as Brad told us about smoking weed with one of our heroes. Now I liked him even more. I had always heard what a cool guy Harrison was that he still did carpentry between films.

"Swear to God. I've been smoking with him every day." Brad had us hanging on his every word.

I kept on with the harassing questions, according to Luca. "Well, how's the movie?"

He looked a little hesitant to answer. "It's all right. The script is a little weak."

"Are you buying a bong for Harrison?" I asked.

He took a breath and touched his chin with his hand. "No, I need to buy a few wrap gifts for some of the cool guys who are working on the set."

It is a common practice for actors, directors, and others to purchase "wrap gifts" for co-workers on the set of a film or show. "Wrap" meaning when production of a project wraps up, not that the gifts are wrapped.

"Cool." I nodded my head, about to ask him another question when Luca rescued me. He knew I was starting to talk too much and annoy Brad. So he slapped me on the shoulder and pulled me into the back office, telling me he needed my help with something or other. I got the hint and went back to my business.

Our store was now moving right along, and in the spring of 1997, we added a "munchy bar" to the store.

Chapter 15—Little Big Man

"Marijuana is 10 times more dangerous than 20 years ago."
—President Bill Clinton

The next time Brad Pitt came into the store, it was with Gwyneth Paltrow. I guess they were dating. It was before his wife Jennifer came into the picture. Our neighbor was going out of business and we wanted to expand. We utilized their space, turning it our little café. Things were going well. We were in *High Times* often, celebrities were shopping at our store, and we were advertising on cable television.

The opening of our new café within 2000 B.C. was a celebrity fest and a family gathering. Luca and I felt as if we were the Beatles of weed, the John and Paul of hemp. I was the front man. I am the rock-and-roll-looking guy with a conservative background who didn't mind committing wild acts of free speech. Luca looked conservative, but he was a little crazier than me in ways. We balanced each other out, and we knew it. That was part of the success of the store.

During the opening, my uncle ran back into the store to get me. "Drew Barrymore and Luke Wilson just pulled up in front of your store and they want to see you," he said, with a huge smile on his face.

I didn't even know Luke Wilson was an actor until that day. I knew that Drew Barrymore was dating him at the time because that is how Drew introduced him: "This is Luke, my boyfriend."

It was a coincidence that they just happened to pop in on our opening. Drew said "hi" to Andras Jones, who was performing at the opening of the café. They had starred in a film together, *Far From Home*. Jack Black wasn't very famous yet, but he also stopped by with my buddy Jono Kohan. But it was my Uncle Nick, the movie buff, who knew who everyone was. I guess he reads the tabloids and goes to the movies every weekend, so he was going crazy seeing all of these movie stars at my place.

119

Let me digress for a moment ... I knew who Drew was. I had sold her hemp beanbags and a little pot a couple of times. I used to buy a big bag of weed and break it up for a few friends, relatives, and celebrities. Occasionally, a celebrity whom I didn't know personally, but only through television, would ask if they could get some pot. I figured there weren't too many celebrity undercover cops, so I would always help them out. I figured if I were busted selling pot to a celebrity, that it would be national news and good for business. In this town, remember that bad publicity can be good for your career if they spell your name correctly and you look good in the paparazzi photos as you go in and out of the courthouse.

I had met Drew a few months earlier in the store, and she and my wife struck up a little friendship. My wife was a young woman I'd met named Genevieve. She was at my very first hemp rally at the Federal Building in Westwood, selling handmade goods of hemp. She was a hippie girl living with Lisa Bay, someone I knew from growing up in Beverly Hills. She and Lisa Bay, the sister of famous director Michael Bay, shared a place on Doheny Drive, and now Lisa is my children's godmother. We didn't start dating for a year after we met, but the relationship didn't last long. Even though it was short, it was quite productive, resulting in my three children.

Drew Barrymore had become a big supporter of hemp. It was rumored that when she was younger, she had a drug problem and then sobered up. I know of other celebrities who had heroin problems and then just substituted marijuana without going to rehab because they felt high and could still function in the world on marijuana and couldn't on heroin.

One of Drew's friends had turned her on to our shop. She loved hemp and bought quite a bit. She started by buying some hemp beanbags as gifts for people she worked with. (Then she removed all of the seats from her screening room at her house and replaced them with hemp beanbags.)

Now back to the Munchy Bar fest ... our buddy Mr. Brad Pitt made an appearance with a total hottie on his arm. Gwyneth Paltrow was her name. We did put an ad in the paper, but that was it. We hadn't been expecting an "A list" event. Brad practically had to drag Gwyneth into the store.

My Uncle Nick was freaking out at this point. "Oh my God, it's Brad Pitt and Gwyneth Paltrow." This was after he had just seen Drew and Luke.

I often saw a similar reaction from my uncle every Saturday morning at our family breakfast. The other Saturday morning, I inquired, "Don't look right now, but is that Elvis' daughter?" Without a second's delay, my uncle turned around in the most obvious fashion. Anyway, I had no idea who Gwyneth was, but Brad was a cool guy and a great customer. I didn't want my uncle to say something stupid and make him feel uncomfortable.

I happened to catch Brad's eye and we nodded at each other as he dragged his cute blonde back to Bong Canyon. "Come on, babe, this is the coolest thing you're ever going to see." Brad was talking to Gwyneth Paltrow, but he was speaking directly to my heart.

"Wow," I thought. "He feels the same way about Bong Canyon as I do."

I decided to follow them back there to see if I could be of any assistance to them. Dave was handling the tourists (or visitors)— what we called "customers"—in Bong Canyon when Brad and Gwyneth walked in.

"You don't want to be seen in here. I think... I don't think...," Gwyneth said. She had no idea that the owner of the store was right next to her. "This can't be good for your career."

She was finally able to articulate her thought to Brad. Her sentences were questions without the question mark. I dated a girl like her once and got the immediate impression she was a bitchy, persnickety type.

121

"Are you kidding?" He blew her off. "This is the coolest store in L.A. The dudes that work here are totally cool. I just want to share this place with you. Check it out—you're in Bong Canyon. Get it? Bong Canyon!" He was like a kid in a candy store.

Brad knew Luca and I were the real deal, the real 90210. We both went to Beverly Hills High and knew everyone in town. All the kids from the television show "90210" shopped at our store. Luke Perry, Tori Spelling, and Ian Ziering all used to buy stuff at our store.

Gwyneth didn't get it. I wanted to break the tension. I assumed she must be a cool girl to be dating such a cool guy, only she was insecure about what other people might think of her if they knew she smoked.

I introduced myself. "Hi, I am Craig. What is your name?"

"Gwenth," she said very flatly, as if it were a one-syllable name, and turned her head. She had her back toward me and faced her boyfriend. It was not a friendly gesture.

"Gwenth?" I repeated in a questioning tone. "Never heard that name before," I thought to myself. Then I said aloud, "That's unusual," trying to strike up some small talk. I could tell she was hard to please. I wondered if she were like that in bed.

She barely turned around at my comment and acted as if it were too much trouble to look me in the eyes. Maybe she was stoned and feeling paranoid? Would she have felt any differently if she knew I was the owner of the store? I didn't care to find out.

Brad looked at me, shaking his head and smiling. "Whatever you guys need let us know," I said to him and stepped back into the other room to let Dave handle all of the tourists, including prissy Ms. Paltrow.

Everyone I know in Hollywood smokes weed. Some are more open than others about it, but it isn't hurting anyone's career. The only people whose careers are hurt by prohibition are the working class. The point being, rich and famous guys like Brad Pitt and Harrison Ford are never going to experience losing a job because they smoke pot.

Chapter 16— Koyaanisqatsi

"We'd like to know a little bit about you for our file. We'd like to help you learn to help yourself."
—Simon and Garfunkel

The Drug War is not supporting the preamble to the U.S. Constitution. It is not forming a more perfect union, establishing justice, ensuring domestic tranquility, providing for the common defense, promoting the general welfare, or securing the blessings of liberty for our posterity. I can agree with the government that abusing tobacco, drugs, and alcohol is bad, but I still think that prohibiting their use is worse for our country.

There are many problems with prohibitions. For one, the punishments in the War on Drugs can be administered unfairly. If the same percentage of black and white people use drugs, and the police search black people's cars more often per stop than the cars of white people, the result will be a higher percentage of black people being arrested for possession of drugs. I believe this is a form of institutionalized racism.

I don't think pot smokers pose a national security threat to the federal government. Where is the harm in simply smoking flowers? Yet, that is the level of response that weed smokers are treated with. The Drug War is destroying the African-American community as much as drugs are. I am not saying that drugs are good. I have seen first-hand the crime, neglect, poverty, and fear created in a drug-infested neighborhood. Drugs on the street are not the answer, but neither is the Drug War that was started as a political war. The fact is, in neighborhoods with poverty, neglect, and crime, drugs may be a symptom as much as a cause of the crisis.

Domestic terrorism is real. Look what happened to the Oklahoma City Federal Building. Timothy McVeigh believed what he was doing was good for his bigger plan—to the point that he was willing to use violence and sacrifice his life for his objective. What is the difference between him and a Palestinian homicide bomber?

125

One difference is that if McVeigh had gotten away with it, he might have lived to do it again. In his mind, when the state executed him, he died a hero. The maniacal men who flew airplanes into those American buildings in New York City imagined heroism for themselves, too. Everyone is wired with an internal drive to be a hero. Our society's present-day civilization doesn't always support those feelings in a gratifying way. As a result, we end up with juveniles worshiping death and creating tragedies like Columbine High School in their pathetic attempt at heroism.

To battle real domestic terrorism, not the contrived threat, we need to recognize what is really in our national interest. Americans shouldn't want to pay to lock up *consensual* drug users. A more useful way to expend police resources would be to focus on violent and non-consensual crimes. People who commit violence on others should be locked away. That is a proper use of our money because it prevents further violence by removing an actual threat to order. People who smoke pot should be taxed. We are allowing thousands of violent criminals to wander the streets because we focus our resources on consensual crimes instead of non-consensual ones. In my opinion, it doesn't make sense and is leading our nation to ruin.

Why should a natural product that is consumed by millions upon millions of Americans go onto the black market when it could fuel a legitimate economy? Ending the War on Drugs would help solve many of our society's problems and immediately help our economic situation. For example, with the legal sale, cultivation, marketing, and distribution of marijuana, the end of prohibition would turn an economic siphon into an economic boom. If we took all the money we have invested in the Drug War (it currently amounts to approximately $40 billion per year) and put it in an account, we could provide a free college education to every young American who deserved one. (My education policy is listed in the back of the book).

I can't say it enough that the Drug War is a dismal failure and is tearing apart the fabric of our society. The people who smoke pot feel a common bond of awareness and typically have less faith in the government because they choose to oppose this particular regulation and think independently. The majority of pot smokers don't believe they are doing anything wrong. If the government is going to lie and exaggerate about the negative effects of marijuana and industrial hemp, how are they going to be trusted when it comes to other issues such as nuclear power or war and peace?

One of the strongest slogans of the American Revolution was "no taxation without representation." I feel as if marijuana smokers are taxed, like the colonists, without proper or sufficient representation. We should revolt at the polls and vote the bums out of office who are wasting our money on the War on Drugs.

The fact is, according to our own government, marijuana is the number one cash crop in all 50 states. Hence, pot smokers make up a significant portion of America's population. Moreover, these are individuals with jobs—working people. (Pot is more expensive than gold per ounce. If you don't have a job, usually, you don't get to smoke, except through the good graces of others.) Pot smokers pay taxes and play a role in fueling the economy.

Portions of those taxes paid by pot smokers are allocated towards areas beneficial to all Americans (smokers and non-smokers); however, the taxes also support marijuana prohibition and prosecute marijuana consumers. Revenue from pot smokers' taxes go right back into the hands of the people who are trying to prosecute them. Why, for example, should the entire population of pot smokers pay tax dollars to support locking themselves up?

Currently, there are several organizations working to reform drug laws. These groups include the Drug Reform Policy Project, the National Organization to Reform Marijuana Laws (NORML), and the Hemp Industry Association. Yet, even though all of these organizations are lobbyists for *the cause* (ending prohibition), it is impossible for these groups to grow to their potential size and strength because of the surrounding climate of fear perpetuated by the government. People are afraid to join. As a collective group, it is difficult for marijuana smokers to organize and collaborate because *our cause* is prohibited. There is no strong lobby for marijuana smokers' rights. Simple possession of marijuana is presently deemed illegal.

Poor Tommy Chong, just released from jail (July, 2004), spent nine months locked up for selling unused glass tubes, not even marijuana; that is how outrageous this prohibition has become. I'm sure these tubes were mostly sold for marijuana use (Tommy even admitted to that), but the tubular pipes could just as easily have been sold for tobacco use. The government didn't prove that a single pipe was used for marijuana because they didn't have to. A strong lobby could have helped prevent the injustice that Tommy and others are undergoing on a daily basis. Every 45 seconds, someone is arrested for marijuana in the United States.

An important first step would be to support politicians such as the former governors of Minnesota and New Mexico, who are both pro-hemp. In addition, Bruce Margolin, who lost to Arnold Schwarzenegger in the latest election for governor of California, conducted a successful campaign with the theme, "I am a pro-marijuana attorney." Bruce won among all of the no-name candidates, but his candidacy was not legitimized because the issue of marijuana use is marginalized. Major media ignores the political positions concerning hemp, exclaiming, "It is only pot. How important can it be?"

In contrast, it would be nice to see the major media objectively publicize efforts to end prohibition. It is a dream of mine that politicians in favor of marijuana use would feel as if their pro-marijuana agendas could help them succeed in elections rather than draw federal scrutiny. I am quite sure that more than one member of the Senate smokes weed and doesn't want his colleagues to know that fact.

I know there are thousands of men and women in the armed forces risking their lives for our freedom. Does that not include the freedom to smoke an unadulterated herb? What if it makes that veteran feel better? Should they have the right to smoke when they retire from the military? At least Governor Arnold admitted to smoking pot and pro-medical marijuana.

I recently tried to get on the reality show "The American Candidate," which is airing on Showtime. I was the "pro-pot Republican," but the show didn't seem to have room for my candidacy. I wasn't chosen to be on the show. The show changed quite a bit from the executive producer's original idea, but that is Hollywood. The fact that I didn't get on the show has not deterred me in my quest for the White House. I told my children that I'd be running for president, and I am continuing my campaign with the release of this book.

I was asked to be the "director of communications" for one of the guys who did make it on the show. The candidate that I befriended is Bob Vanech. We met while auditioning for the show and both of us recognized each other as potential competition. At first he was not pro-pot, but to get my support, we met and he looked closely at the issue and decided to come out for marijuana. Now he has my full support on the show, but I was only able to help him during the first few days and then the producers put the cast in seclusion. All of the applicants were nice, thoughtful people who truly believed that they could do a better job than George W. Bush if given the chance. I felt Bob didn't stand for anything though. He wanted to do what the people wanted. His concept was too vague. People want a leader with a vision. A guy who looks good on television, as

Bob did, but doesn't have a particular vision isn't going to make it as leader of the free world.

The reason I voted for Bush was that he articulated a clear vision. You knew where he stood. Kerry bored voters to death by talking. I heard him speak on medical marijuana, an issue that I cared deeply about, if Kerry was clearly for it I may have considered voting for him, but he wasn't. Oh, he was for it, until the Federal government decides it is a bad idea then he'll be against it. Could he take a stand and fight for anything? It reminded me of his Vietnam experience. He is for the war, so he volunteers, then is awarded medals, then is against the war, and then candidate wants to be looked upon as a war hero.

Chapter 17— The Insider

"Everybody today seems to be in such a terrible rush; anxious for greater developments and greater wishes and so on; so that children have very little time for their parents; parents have very little time for each other; and the home begins the disruption of the peace of the world."
—Mother Teresa

In 1994, at the rally at the Federal Building where I met my wife, I became interested in portable vending. I couldn't stop thinking of the economics of the transportable retailers. It reminded me of how ancient bazaars must have operated in the Mediterranean in Roman or Greek times. Setting up on a daily basis and then breaking down at night.

My wife was a cute hippie girl who made hemp purses. She was gorgeous in my mind. A mix of ethnicities, she called herself Puerto Rican, but she was from New York. We lived together for a while, and when she became pregnant, we married in Supai in front of Havasu Falls. Our wedding was beautiful, but the marriage was not happy and didn't last long.

My wife left me while we were transitioning to living at our ranch in Northern Arizona on a full-time basis. She was pregnant with our littlest girl, Olivia. She wanted to be back in L.A., so I rented an apartment in Hollywood, but I had not consulted Genevieve and she was not satisfied with the location or the building. She was a lot like the fastidious Gwyneth. She wanted to live with her friend, Lisa Bay, the girl she was living with when I met her. (Lisa, coincidentally, was a good friend of Luca's ex-wife, Catya Sassoon, before she died at 30 years old; Catya had married Luca when she was only 15 years old).

When Genevieve left me, I closed the store because of all the issues at the time. The lease was up, the landlord and his partner wanted a 40 percent increase in rent, saying, "Six years is too long of a lease." They were complaining that they had missed the boom that occurred in the economy after we moved in. The landlords only wanted to sign a one-year lease with 2000 B.C. I had fired Luca and was sad about it; my marriage was ending, which was devastating; and I was just tired of dealing with retail customers. I had caught several people stealing from our store and I took it personally. My brother offered to have his company, THC, buy the business, but I chose to just close it instead. I wanted to spend more time with Genevieve and the kids, but by this point, our marriage was broken and she didn't want to work it out; and to be frank, neither did I.

Once I no longer had 2000 B.C. to go to every day, I began to leave the Hollywood lifestyle behind, but as Al Pacino says in the *Godfather* series, "It keeps pulling me back." People quote movies in modern speech the way the Bible and classic literature were quoted one-hundred years ago.

I was driving around Los Angeles, looking for pipe shops to which I could sell my hand-blown glass pipes, when I received a phone call.

"Is this Craig Rubin?" the female voice asked hesitantly.

When I'm not sure who's on the other end of the phone, I usually assume the person is about to try to sell me something. "Yeah, who is this?" I asked distrustfully.

"Is this the same Craig Rubin who owned 2000 B.C. on Melrose Avenue?" she asked a little more confidently, ensuring she had the right person. I hadn't been asked that question in a few years, so I was curious. I closed the store when Genevieve left so I could stay home and take care of our three kids.

"Who is this?" I demanded.

"My name is Jill Ishkanian and I am a reporter with *Star* magazine."

"You mean the celebrity rag, that *Star* magazine?" I didn't want to sound insulting. "I mean one of the best-selling paper magazines in the country? Is that the magazine you are speaking of?"

"That's the one," she answered.

Why are the tabloids so successful? Is it that people want to know about the lives of others in the excruciating detail that tabloids provide? Does it make people feel better to know that famous people have problems? Everyone has issues and experiences the "human condition."

Do tabloids give people something safe to talk about with others? "Did you hear about so-and-so going out with so-and-so?" How many people are shocked that the sexy Demi Moore is dating Aston Kutcher, a man 15 years her junior? I live in Hollywood; I know women can still be hot in their 50s. More importantly, why is it common knowledge around the world? The media, the fourth estate, is more powerful than politicians—at times—and this is one of them.

I was acting a little cocky. "I read the headlines at the checkout lines in the market, but I am not a reader of the inside of the magazine. How in the world did you get my number? You are not calling to sell me a subscription, I gather? I haven't had this number a whole week yet. How long did it take you to get in touch with me?" I was rattling off questions faster than she could answer.

However, she was quick to answer. "You'd be surprised. We have our ways. Actually, I only started trying to reach you since this morning and it is now four hours later." She sounded as if she were telling the truth and I was amazed by her answer.

"And you were able to get my number that fast? How did you do that? Is *Star* magazine connected with the CIA or the government in any way? How can you guys do that?" I was almost speechless, which is not easy for me.

Jill continued to be coy and still, to this day, she has not told me who gave her my name. "No," she laughed, "we are not connected to the CIA, but our sources are just as good."

Now, I was the one laughing. I didn't think half of what the tabloids wrote was true, but here was a person who actually made her living as a writer, calling me to do fact-checking on a story. I always dreamed of being a professional writer. When I sold my first article to *High Times*, I photographed myself with the check. It was impressive that she was able to get my number so quickly. I was interested in meeting with her, a professional writer with a go-getter attitude. She sounded sexy.

Jill continued, "My sources tell me that 2000 B.C., your hemp store on Melrose, was a real hot spot for celebrities. Is that true?" She was sort of flirting to get me to give up information for free and blurt out, "Yeah, Brad Pitt shopped there every day."

I said, "Look, I'd like to meet with you and tell you about an idea I have for a book about 2000 B.C., pot, Native American prophecy, and famous people."

"Well, I am in Los Angeles. You have 602 as your area code," she said, just stating the facts. "Are you back in Phoenix? Is that where you are living now?"

"No." I took note of the fact that she asked if I was *back* in Phoenix. Did she know that I was in Los Angeles the day before? "I live in the White Mountains about three hours northeast of Phoenix, but I am in Los Angeles right now."

"Oh, the area code is Phoenix."

I wasn't sure if it was a statement or a question.

"Illusion," I stated, "just like Hollywood. I want the stores that do business with me to think I am in the city so they will call me. Most of my clients are in Phoenix."

"So, you are in L.A., right now?" You could tell she was happy that I was interested in talking with her in person; however, she didn't sound too surprised to hear that I was in L.A. "Our offices are near the corner of Wilshire and Bundy. Can you come by this afternoon?"

"Oh," I said, "not far from where Nicole Simpson and Ron Goldman were murdered." I was being morbid, showing off that I knew the area.

"Yeah, wow, you know the area well." She was impressed with the celebrity reference.

"I grew up on the Westside." Enough with the small talk, I thought. "So, why exactly is it that you are calling me?" I was excited to meet with her, but I had no idea what she wanted.

"One of my sources tells me Brad Pitt used to frequently visit your store and we are doing a story on his and Jennifer's pot smoking habit." She was direct and to the point. That is how reporters should operate to gain people's confidence.

"I don't know if I know about his habit. Are you going to pay me for this information?"

I knew that *Star* magazine had a history of paying for information. This can lead to sources lying for money, but I had something they wanted. I imagined that they would pay thousands for pot information about Brad Pitt.

"Yeah, we could give you $150 for confirming some information for us. We already have the story," she insisted. "We just need to confirm some information that we think you might have on Brad Pitt. For starters, was he a customer of yours?"

"Yeah, he used to come in quite often." Then I added, "I met him a few times, and he seemed like a very cool guy. I don't really know what I could add other than that."

"Did he buy bongs from you?" Jill was direct.

135

"Look, I think we should meet, too, but I am busy this afternoon," I told Jill, avoiding the question like a politician. "Why don't we meet after work when you are not so rushed?" I wanted to share my idea with her for *9021Grow*, the book.

"Well, when can we meet?" she asked, eager to meet me as well.

Jill and I were in agreement on a place and time. I parked in the lot across the street from Jill's offices. My traveling friend from Arizona went for a walk and I went alone to meet Jill Ishkanian. It was like meeting in public for a drug deal and there was a tension in the air. We were meeting for the first time.

She was already sitting in the coffee house with her paper and pen in front of her. She was glad to see me right on time. I asked her a few questions about herself—how and why she became a writer for the *Star*. I found out that it had been her goal to be a celebrity gossip columnist since she was 12 years old, the same age I decided to end marijuana prohibition. She and I were the same age.

We talked again about the content of the story. The story, as Jill explained it to me, was "that Brad Pitt smokes pot," and I was able to confirm the story that "he bought bongs at our place, 2000 B.C." I thought this was great that Brad was about to be outed as a pothead. I wasn't the person who called *Star* magazine, and *Star* really already had a story on Brad, regardless of my contribution (or so they said).

I thought it was cool that it was going to become common knowledge that a Hollywood legend-in-the-making was a big pot smoker. In my mind, the "movement" to end hemp prohibition in America could use another "outed" celebrity besides Woody Harrelson to promote marijuana. Maybe Brad Pitt would become a spokesman for terminating prohibition. Potentially, he could even be more effective than Woody because he is a bigger star, I think. Well, you don't see Woody on the cover of *Star* every other week.

When I was speaking with Jill, trying to get her to commit to helping me with my book project, I mentioned something about

136

Martha Stewart being a pot smoker. The point I was driving home was that if more people knew successful folks smoked, the prohibition wouldn't stand up to the scrutiny of the public eye.

I knew that I would one day write a book since I was sick on summer vacation in Supai as a teenager and had that vision. The vision occurred when I was running a slight fever and didn't go hiking down Mooney Falls with my family. I stayed back at camp and smoked a little pot and then fell asleep swinging in the hammock. I had a dream that I still remember to this day. It was of an old man with a white beard and he was controlling the earth like a puppet with strings from space. He was wearing a red robe.

I have started writing this book six times. Each time, the story is different, but the same. The story always reflects the current time of my life during which I am writing. I am the hero, and I always save the world in the end, usually at the last minute in typical Hollywood fashion. The War on Drugs is a giant waste of money. There are millions of people who recognize that, but nothing is ever done. So, I have painted myself in real life and in my book as the hero who brings pot to the world. Well, it is there already, but I help to end its bad reputation, which will terminate the prohibition and allow people to use it.

The government is forced to use Enron-like accounting tactics to justify the incredible wasting of tax dollars on the drug war. It is simply alarming that our nation recklessly spends the wealth of the nation and is accomplishing so little. The people on top know that throwing more and more money at the problem hasn't helped. In fact, it is just as easy, if not easier for me, to score a bag a pot today than it was 20 years ago. Probably easier because now I am known as, "Craig X: The Wizard of Weed."

The financial incentives for more unsuccessful law enforcement are there, so we continue to fight a losing battle that drains our economy. That is why I am the pro-pot Republican running for president. I think the government should be small and stay out of people's lives. The Drug War gets the government involved in individuals' lives in a negative way and undermines the credibility of our nation's leadership.

Chapter 18— Saving Grace

"I'm for legalizing marijuana. Why pick on that drug?
Valium is legal. You just go to a doctor and get it and
overdose on it—what's the difference? Prozac is legal, so
why not marijuana? Who cares? It's something that grows
naturally out of the ground. Smoke a head of cabbage, I
don't care. I don't care what you smoke."
—Howard Stern

I had a nice meeting with Jill. We bonded; in the end, however, Jill
didn't commit to anything. I gave her a tremendous amount of
information, and it seemed that we related to each other. There
was a "big sister" feel to meeting her. The article came out, and in
my opinion, it was horrible. I directly attributed 16 paragraphs in
her article to things I had told her for the book. I was disillusioned.

No book deal. Who was I going to get to work with me at the future
2000 B.C. now? What celebrities would shop at our store after Jill
basically stated my name by saying "the owner of 2000 B.C.," after
promising not to identify me? I have since simply accepted my
involvement as a fact and now am open about it, but first I was
embarrassed by it.

Jill had said she would just use my comments to confirm Brad's
bong purchase. She even used a comment by me, which I
attributed to Genevieve, without paying Genevieve for it. The
comment I had shared with Jill was that my wife and I speculated
"Brad and Jennifer's relationship had a stronger chance of survival
than Brad and Gwyneth's relationship because they were both avid
potheads." I know people in Arizona who are actually hoping, as if
they know them, that Brad and Jen can work it out. Back in the
day, Genevieve, my ex-wife, and Jennifer were in acting class
together in New York and were both part of a circle, group of pot-
smoking *friends*, who smoked weed after classes.

Jill had only wanted me to confirm that Brad had purchased bongs
at our store. I communicated with her that I knew tons of
celebrities and other rich and famous people who smoke pot and

that I wanted to publish my story. She had not been with the magazine all that long. I didn't know that at the time. I was trying to get a book deal back then because I realized that if I were ever going to end pot prohibition, I needed to make the topic popular enough to get major media coverage. What better way to do that in "pop culture" than with a "celebrity stoner" bestseller?

My hope was that the *Star* would do a pro-pot article on Brad and Jennifer that said, "Hooked on Chronics" as a headline, not "Hooked on Drugs" with the slant in the article that they can't have kids because of their pot use. I know that marijuana smoking "lowering your chances of conception" is not true. Genevieve and I made three babies and my stoner friends are more prolific than non-pot smoking friends as far as childbearing goes. People who smoke pot make millions of healthy babies every year and probably better parents. I don't even think it diminishes your sperm count or sex drive as the government claims because every time my ex-wife and I had sex, I had to give that squirt a name.

I called Jill, upset that she used so much of what I had told her. She sent me a check for ten times the amount of money she promised me earlier. She realized how pissed I was and money was what I needed at the time, so she made it up to me. Jill wanted to keep a friendly source happy, and she did.

I was still bummed that the article wasn't a great piece on pot, the type you would see in *High Times*. I understood that *Star* writers didn't know elaborate details about pot the way I did. There are not many people in the world who recognize the way I do how hemp will save our environment from destruction. I am a true expert in the field.

The *Star* article was actually extremely negative, claiming that Brad and Jennifer couldn't have children because they were potheads. The money was so little compared to what Brad and Jennifer make that, for a moment, I was embarrassed for myself. Then I remembered to just be grateful. The government had their connections in the media and now I had mine, Jill Ishkanian.

When *Star* magazine sent me the check, I cashed it and gave my ex-wife, Genevieve, the money. I didn't take a photograph with this check. I simply gave the money to Genevieve. I justified talking to Jill by thinking that the money helped my ex-wife. That check was my saving grace because it was just enough to help Gen move out of our house and into her own place. She was saying, "I just need some space."

Shortly after the Brad and Jennifer Pitt article appeared, Jill called me back to offer me $10,000. She wanted me to tell her what I knew about Martha Stewart smoking pot. This was before Martha had been charged for lying to the government. In my first meeting with Jill, I mentioned that I knew Martha Stewart was a closet pothead. I had two sources for this information and felt confident about it. I was so eager to find someone to help me write my own story that I told Jill more than I had originally intended.

Chapter 19—Wag the Dog

"A bookstore is one of the only pieces of evidence we have that people are still thinking."
—Jerry Seinfeld

The very first time Jill called me from *Star* magazine, I knew that it was a big deal because nothing happens by accident. I am not a frequent or thorough reader of the tabloids; at most, I'll read headlines while waiting at the checkout line in the supermarket. I always know the headlines because the papers are very good at catching your attention with sensational claims.

Even after I thought she dogged me, my hope in continuing a relationship with Jill Ishkanian was to have a friendly connection in the publishing industry. I know how important it is to have access to the media in this modern world. As a child, my dad was always dispensing advice to me, and some of that advice was about the media. My dad said, "You can't believe everything you read, and you can only believe half of what you see."

I realize how powerful the media is because most people believe what they read and more than half of what they see. It is interesting not having television in my house because I can tell what is on by what people are talking about in public and on talk radio. There are certain catch phrases that people use that clue me in to the fact that they are repeating something and not articulating an original idea.

By running my free speech group in college, I learned that media in the modern world is essential for credibility. Even if *Star* magazine wasn't the most credible source of news in the world, it had credibility because of its economic success, and now I had a connection, but would she help me get a book deal? That was another question altogether.

My other goal in continuing my relationship with Jill and *Star* was that if she could find me, she could find anyone. I thought she would help me prove that I had sold pot to an officer from the LAPD. I had never mentioned to anyone that I had sold pot to the LAPD because I could not prove it was true. I thought that Nicole Morgan was a cop, but how do you prove something like that? I didn't want to sound like a paranoid idiot. Once I confirmed she was an officer, I still find it hard to believe that I was never arrested. Did God protect me? Was it just luck that I wasn't incarcerated?

I told Jill about the relationship I had with an undercover LAPD officer, whom I was selling pot to. I mentioned to Jill that she had given her name as Nicole Morgan. I figured it was her real name. Undercover officers have to invent entire backgrounds for themselves. They are forced to become full-time liars. So, why go through the added burden of using a new fake name, especially if the people you are investigating are going to end up in jail anyway?

Nicole probably thought I would end up in jail, so she gave me her real name. I knew that if Jill could get my number in one day, when I had only had that number for less than one week, she could find out if Nicole Morgan was a police officer when she stole my weed. I encouraged Jill by telling her she was as good as the CIA.

Jill agreed to help me when I told her the "full" story about Nicole. I didn't tell her the *whole* story, but enough to pique her interest. Jill had Nicole's name and the dates that she would have been an undercover narcotics officer for the LAPD. Sure enough, Jill found her. I later double-checked Jill's confirmation with a friend of mine who had become a police officer. Like a good journalist, I also looked for a second source before going public with the information that she really was a cop and that I wasn't crazy. Why hadn't they arrested me? Did God really look out for me as I had assumed? Why would the LAPD look out for me? They wouldn't.

I wanted to call Nicole with Jill so that Nicole could tell Jill how I had predicted the 1994 Northridge earthquake and we could ask her together why the police didn't arrest me for selling marijuana even though I sold it to Nicole, an undercover officer, many times. Jill called without me and Nicole told Jill that she was working as

144

an insurance fraud investigator. She confirmed that she knew me, but Jill described her as "very evasive and hard to pin down." The following day, after Jill had spoken with her, Nicole's phone number was changed to an unlisted number.

Jill only told me the number one time and I still recall it years later. That is the kind of memory that I have for numbers. It was one of the other ways I caught Nicole in a lie. I asked for her Social Security number just to show her my knack for memorizing numbers, and she gave me one number and later gave me a different one. I can still recall the one she gave me the first time. I'll bet that was her real one. She had said it rather quickly and not knowing at that time my gift for numbers. I can memorize numbers easily, even when I only hear them quickly one time.

In addition, I told Nicole what state in the country she was born in and she tripped out because she hadn't told me that information about herself. At the time, this served as a good "ice breaker." I could tell by the first three numbers of anyone's Social Security number where they were born. Usually, it was just a section of the country, but I was a good guesser and often got people's city or state by recognizing their accent, as well. No one had ever taught me how to do that, but I just have a knack for recognizing patterns and realized that numbers and accents are like zip codes and they create a pattern that reflects the geography of the country.

I had gotten the main thing that I wanted from Jill, confirmation that Nicole was a cop and that my Granny's intuition was correct. Nicole wasn't responsible for my grandmother's death, but in my mind, Nicole was the reason my grandmother didn't die at home. She was also the confirmation that I needed to prove to myself that my own sixth sense was often accurate.

Jill would occasionally call, wanting to show me a photo or ask me to verify this or that. One time, she had me look at a photo of someone unknown with Brad Pitt, and I just happened to know whom she was inquiring about. It was a girl I had gone to high school with who was now a personal assistant to a big movie star. So I was able to give her information about this unknown person's identity. She would pay me a small sum of money for information like that—a very small sum—but I didn't say "no." I have an incredible memory for names and faces, as well, that always surprises people because I am a "pothead" and we are presumed to have no memory.

My hope was that if a credible person, such as a police officer, would verify that I had predicted the Northridge earthquake people might believe me if I had a premonition of another pending disaster. The earth is facing, I think, the perils that the Hopi Indians have predicted and that were foretold in the Bible.

THC and coffee,
KEEP IT COMING

kevinpearson

Chapter 20— L.A. Confidential

"Someone told me long ago, 'there's a calm before the storm.' I know it's been coming for some time."
—Creedence Clearwater Revival

I called my media connection the day after Tommy Chong was arrested in "Operation Pipe Dreams." I called Jill at *Star* magazine again to pitch her on 9021Grow, the book idea, one more time and realized that she had moved.

Jill was now with *US*, another celebrity gossip magazine with a similar character to the *Star*. However, the new magazine was known for being slightly less scandalous than her previous employer, but the reality is it is not. She once called me to confirm a nice story about my friend Esai Morales. The magazine had received an anonymous call from someone who recognized Esai at an airport on the East Coast and she knew he was a friend of mine. Apparently the anonymous caller wanted the magazine to write something good about a celebrity.

The story was that a woman didn't have enough money for a flight and Esai gave her $100 to cover the difference. Apparently, the lady missed her flight and that was the charge to update her ticket. I put Jill on the phone with Esai who gave her his side of the story, but US magazine never ran with the positive story because it was not gossipy enough. Having sex with a seventeen-year-old girl at the airport while helping the lady with $100 would have been news, but a celebrity just helping someone was not. They are just expected to do that.

It had been two years since I first confirmed the "Brad Pitt buying bongs" story with Jill. For two years now, I had been thinking of Jill helping me to write this book. If it were left up to me, it might never get finished, and since she was a professional, she came to mind. When I got her on the phone, I asked if she knew of someone in the publishing industry who might be interested in a story like mine. She called me the next day and said she had someone who was interested, but would not give me his name.

Jill had told me how a "publisher guy" was interested in meeting me. This "publisher guy," Tony, invited me to dinner three nights later with Jill.

According to Jill, Tony Frost was the "top dog" at American Media Incorporated, which owned *Star* magazine. He looked young for his likely age; I didn't ask how old he was. The touch of gray gave it away that he was at least in his forties and possibly fifties, but I have known young people who have gone gray at an early age.

Thus far, American Media has only published books with subject-material about people like Michael Jackson, Jon Benet Ramsey, Heidi Fleiss, and Robert Blake. I could tell from the outset that my story was different and not as easily exploitable as a murder or selling sex in Hollywood. I am "Hollywood's Wizard of Weed," the Beverly Hills pothead with aspirations of grandeur.

Tony explained to me that American Media was not going to risk the money or image of the company on what might be some far-flung pot prophecy story with links to terrorism. If I wanted to sell him my book, it was going to "have to be loaded with celebrities" and, as far as I was concerned, cheesy tabloid stories. It was hard for me to get behind that, but I was considering it for several reasons. It still fit in with my long-term goal of ending prohibition, but I had my concerns that they would hack my entire story into something that looked like the headline, "Brad and Jen on Drugs."

A pro-pot story was my objective, but I need to follow the advice I had given Eddie Griffin years earlier and become famous as an expert in the hemp industry. What was I going to do?

I had my concerns, but what were the concerns of *Star* and American Media? There are two main reasons they saw my story as a bit too risky to touch. First, *Star* is in the celebrity scandal business and isn't looking to change its business model to include both celebrities and a message to end prohibition. Secondly, American Media was attacked after 9-11 (I am using the term the way it is popularly used in speech today, as a reference to the

150

airplane attack on the World Trade Center) in an unsolved terror attack in which anthrax was sent through the mail. One of American Media's employees died as a result of the attack, and here I am trying to sell them a story with major political implications.

Employees at American Media were sensitive to the connection the president had made between the War on Drugs and the War on Terror. George Bush and John Ashcroft have said on national TV, through government-sponsored commercials, "The act of smoking marijuana is an action that supports terrorism at home and abroad." Therefore, using their logic, I am a terrorist, albeit an accidental and unwilling terrorist. So, it makes sense for American Media not to publish my book and yet still want to serialize the celebrity stuff for their own magazine's sales.

Mr. Frost said that there was the option of publishing "instant books," designed to come out in paperback and be sold in supermarkets across the country. "Wow," I thought. "Even if the 'instant book' idea is a little cheesy, the exposure is incredible. I'd be in every checkout line in America with my message. Even I read the headlines while standing in line at the market."

The catch was that *Star* was going to serialize the book before releasing it to "build an interest." As far as I was concerned, as long as it helps sell the book, why not allow for the serializing of the book? But, that was about all *Star* was willing to do. I was starting to get excited, but a few days later, Tony called, saying that for sure he could not publish the book through American Media. It was not a surprise to me, but when it *was* published, he wanted to serialize it for *Star*. He then told me that he had a friend in England who might be able to handle a project like this. Tony was going to call him and let me know if the guy was interested.

I told him, "If the book is published, I don't care in what country. I would be willing to serialize the stories."

England was just as good as any other country. The bottom line for me was that I wanted to have a book out on the stands to legitimize me as an expert, but I didn't want to write it. I was still waiting for Jill or now Tony to find me a ghostwriter.

If Tony could help me get published in England, I thought, "Great, because they speak English, which I happen to write in." Once the book was published, I told him that it would be okay to serialize it in *Star*, which is what he really wanted to do anyway.

I had the feeling they wanted to exploit me as the Hollywood pot dealer reformed, and I'd be forced out of the business and probably have a hard time scoring a bag. They didn't understand that I wanted to use my book to launch an even greater career in the pot world; I didn't want it to be the final hurrah in an illegal pot-dealing career. I had quit selling pot the minute my first daughter was born. I had never gotten in trouble for selling pot even though I sold it to the LAPD, but the dream of becoming the world's biggest legal pot seller has never left my vision. I want to be the Phillip Morris of pot.

It was days later, but I finally received the call I was expecting from Tony Frost. He called with incredible news. He informed me that he was no longer going to be in the same role with American Media, the publishers of *Star* magazine.

"What does that mean for my deal and this book?" I thought. I was always thinking about myself. Doesn't everybody?

I had started writing, and it was going well. I finally got tired of waiting for Tony or Jill to find me a ghostwriter, and Tony had suggested that I write at least the first few chapters myself, so a writer could capture my style. I was now worried, but I still wondered if he were going to be able to serialize my story in his magazine, having left American Media. I thought serializing it might be one good way to make some money.

"Wow," I commented on his job loss, "that sure is big news and quite a change. Are you okay?" You never know how someone is going to take that kind of news. "Are you taking it as an opportunity for something new? Or are you suicidal?"

Everyone reacts differently to change of this magnitude. Will he move back to the U.K.? Will he stay here in the States? How is this going to affect him helping me? The questions were running through my head faster than I could articulate them.

"Always positive, mate." Tony had a positive attitude that was comforting. "I am looking at this as an opportunity to try something new. I've been here a long time, so we are working on my departure."

It sounded like some kind of coded language, "working on my departure." Tony spoke double-talk like a politician when they sound as if they are taking a position, but really they are agreeing with both sides of an argument at once. "I want to do everything *right*." He emphasized "right." Maybe I was being over-analytical? He was still working there for the time being.

"And you still want to work with me?" I eked out.

"That's right." He was so confident-sounding. "That's why I am calling you, mate."

"Well," I said, trying to stay positive myself, "this could be a great opportunity for you."

I made my comment not knowing where it left me. I didn't want to put pressure on a guy who was just fired. I didn't know for sure that he was fired, but I was getting that impression and I am usually fairly astute when it comes to things of this nature.

"I sure hope so, Craig. They just want to give the magazine a new look." Tony had a very gentle way of speaking that put me at ease. "Again, that is why I am calling you." I trusted him. I guess that is important in his business.

What could he mean? I repeated back his words to myself. "That is why I am calling you." In a moment of self-delusion, I thought, "Does he think that I can help to give the magazine a new look? Oh great, *Star* is going to focus on weed and going to compete against *High Times*." Then I came back to reality. What was Tony talking about?

I decided to shut up and listen after one question. "Tony, do you still have an interest in helping me find a publisher?" I said, trying not to sound too desperate, but excited as hell that he was calling. My thoughts were racing forward to interviews on Jay Leno. I continued, "Because you know, I have been working on the book since I sent you those first chapters." I was hoping that my enthusiasm would play well with him, and I really *was* on a roll as far as the writing was going.

"A mate of mine back in England has a publishing company. I think he might be able to do something with your story. I think you definitely have something. You have a nice style of writing, too. You are easy to read." He had read the first few chapters that I had written at this point. He was saying this very coolly, without making any commitments. I am a very good listener, and when I finally decide to keep quiet and listen, I actually notice every detail of speech and innuendoes.

I still didn't understand what kind of a role Tony would want in publishing the book. Basically, I was wondering, how he was going to make money on the deal? Why did he want to help if there wasn't something in it for him?

"Well, what are you going to do?" I asked. "Do you still want to serialize the book with *Star* magazine?"

"We are certainly going to try and do something in that direction. What direction are we taking the book?" he asked. And it didn't get by me, the fact that he used "we" when referring to my book.

"Uh-huh," I said affirmatively to Tony's answer that "we" are going to go in the direction of selling my story to the tabloids. "That sounds good to me."

"You've got to give me as much material as you can. I am heading back to London [It was 2003, before we knew Tommy Chong would soon be put in jail for nine months]. If you can put together everything you've written so far, I'll take it with me and give it to my friend. We've been chums since way back." He sounded so convincing that I could already see myself famous in the U.K. I've been to England only once, but it was so small compared to America that it seemed like being big in Japan, but maybe that is just my American way of thinking about it. Heck, I think they have finally accepted Madonna as one of their own.

"Will do," I said, confirming that I had heard his comment and would get the job done.

Tony told me how lucky I was to have him and Jill as my contacts in the publishing business. He said, "Less scrupulous people could have already gleaned tabloid stories from what you have written so far. You don't want that because it will dilute the value of your story." I am old enough now not to trust anyone, especially when they tell me how lucky I am to know them. Suddenly, I felt suspicious of him.

I had known Jill Ishkanian for two years now, but didn't know much about her business. My interest, now that she had introduced me to Tony Frost, was to know more about the tabloids. Who owned them? What were their origins? What were the politics and financial interests of the owners and managers? Thank God for Google.

The first thing I did was go to the Internet and look up everything I could find on Tony. Then I learned the history of tabloid-style press in the United States. *Star* magazine, while American-owned, was a copy of tabloid papers in England, which are aimed at working-class readers. The British acknowledge a separation of classes that exists here in the States but that is never discussed.

155

That is probably why an American company would recruit a British editor like Tony Frost.

I had followed my father's advice when dealing with Tony Frost. I gave him my best, which meant more than he was expecting, with a smile. I called when I said I would, and material was always completed and to him on time. I didn't feel as if I owed him anything at that point. He was starting to give me a headache.

Chapter 21— Collateral Damage

"Emancipate yourself from mental slavery. None but ourselves can free our minds. Have no fear of atomic energy. None of them can stop the time. How long must they kill our prophets while we stand aside and look? Some say, 'it is just a part of it, we've got to fulfill the Book.'"
—Bob Marley

Tony received the updated chapters. He left a message on my machine; he didn't sound too happy. Not only was he not happy, he was really upset—ticked-off and threatening. Tony was angry because I had included him in one of the chapters of the book that I had sent him.

I had found this out from Jill when she called me. He didn't want to have his name out there, or according to Jill, "to have the practices of the tabloids exposed in my book." At least, that is what Jill told me. It is so ironic that a person who made their living writing about others would be so sensitive when it came to someone writing about them.

I didn't want to believe it. The irony was too much, yet I understood why he was upset. I didn't like being written about without my permission either. The only things ever written about me that I liked were in the *L.A. Weekly* and *High Times*. When people write about you, it rarely lives up to what you think is the truth. I have just learned to accept that and know that everyone sees what they want to see and hears what they want to hear.

I didn't piss him off intentionally, but that was the result of my actions. "I've never written a book before," was my only defense to him when we spoke. "I told you I wanted a ghostwriter." I felt like a little kid making excuses, but at the same time, I was glad. I was an adult, yet I found the irony funny that he was angry at being written about.

Now, Tony was threatening not to work with me. He was acting like an upset father yelling at a child. He did not go as far as to say, "I am going to sue you," but I could hear that in his thoughts. He had become a true American living here in the States. Americans are the most litigious people in the world. I am glad that the two of us were located in different states.

I felt as if Tony Frost were experimenting with my patience. At first, he wanted one chapter, then another, and I sent him five more than he asked for. I couldn't stop writing and was up to Chapter 15 when he told me he was no longer in charge of American Media but that he still wanted to work with me. Now, he was saying he was only working with me as a favor to Jill Ishkanian. What was the truth?

"I am a great crusader, and you're a Herman Munster"
—"This Land"

Chapter 22— Indecent Proposal

"America is a country where you buy a life's time supply of aspirin and use it up in two weeks."
—John Barrymore

I had emailed Tony without consulting my father first. I am a man, and I am old enough to deal with business decisions on my own, but it is always a comfort knowing that my parents are both alive, caring, and brilliant enough to check my work even now. My dad has always been there with advice for me, requested or not, mostly not, so after the email I called to request some this time before I responded again.

I sent my father a copy of the email that I sent off to Tony, and he was looking at it as I spoke to him on the phone.

"Dad, it felt like I was telling Tony Frost to piss off. That I am not going to take him out of the book unless he has a solid offer to get the book published. I feel nervous about calling him back."

"You didn't tell him to piss off. You didn't write exactly what he wanted to hear, but you basically told him that you would exclude his name in exchange for helping you to get a deal." My dad was a good businessman.

"I certainly didn't kiss his ass like he wanted me to," I said to my dad. It was a blessing to have a father to be able to turn to for advice in business. "It is my story."

"You don't need to kiss his ass. You have something that he wants. He wants to help you sell your book." My dad always sounds like a businessman. I used to imagine him dating after my parents divorced listing the benefits of sleeping with him, overcoming the "No," as if he were a salesman, which he was. He had a few hot chicks in years before shacking up with my stepmother.

My dad's only hope was that I could sell my story and become financially successful. He cared that I had sold pot years before and was disappointed, but if I could sell the story and make big bucks, he would be thrilled. More than thrilled, he'd actually sleep at night.

"Yeah, but dad, I have already written nearly the whole book and he's in it." I was whining like a child. Sometimes that still happens when I speak to my parents. We adopted these roles long ago, and after years, the patterns are so well established that they are hard to shake. I try to be aware of weird personal habits such as that. I definitely make an effort to change.

My dad said, "Well, you've already told him if he gets you a deal, you are going to take his name out." My dad wanted me to get a deal and thought if Tony were for real, he was my best chance. "Why don't you stop guessing at what he wants and call him back to find out what he wants?"

My dad was on the phone all day at work and would rarely talk for more than three minutes at a time at home, so I knew our conversation would be coming to an end in a moment. I am the same way and rarely talk for more than four minute on the phone, but love to ramble on in person.

I called Tony back after getting off the phone with my dad. This time, he was calm, his voice was overly accommodating, and he approached me from another angle. "You go off on tangents about your aunts and uncles." Tony was right. My book, like my life, was unfocused. I had written nearly 300 pages and it was loaded with gems, but they were far and few between. The book needed some editing.

Tony went on, "I am not trying to take that out of the book, but I am hoping to give you more focus. The story that is going to sell is about celebrities smoking pot, but you need to do more. This is what I see for your book: a popular history of marijuana. You have to come off as the American pot expert."

"I am," I said. I wanted to say, "I am a fucking expert," but stayed in control of my foul mouth.

164

In my head, I was listening to my dad as Tony spoke. I needed to sell my story. I said, "Uh-huh," but I wasn't necessarily agreeing with him. I was just acknowledging that I was listening to him. I had found an agent in Manhattan. He was the agent on a book that I had read years ago about pot. It was called *The Death and Life of Bobby Z* and was written by Don Winslow. It was an action adventure story of a dude from Southern California that became a big time pot dealer and I enjoyed it.

I really *am* a pot expert. I went to what I call a "pot-mafia" party the other night and I knew everyone. It would be scary except that they were cancer patients, stroke victims, and people in wheelchairs. I felt like the feds were eyeing the place down and I was with people suffering from AIDS. Where is George Bush's compassion that he spoke of? These are the warriors on the front lines, risking their lives and bodies for the plant.

I know the pot industry as well, if not better, than anyone in the world. I could work for the government to inform them of what is up or I could work for you, the reader. Working with the agent and publishing houses, I felt as if I were working with the government, so I decided to publish the book myself and not take Tony's name out of it. He is part of the story and so is Jill, and now so are you, the reader of my story.

There was only one course of action that I saw available to me. I need to run this country and wake people up to the truth about pot. I am the right person to get this important job done. I should be President of the United States of America. George Bush will have his eight years. Many people like his values, but think his family is too tied in with Saudi Arabia, the defense industry, and the oil business, but like his stance for traditional values. Those are values that America shares. I like his "compassionate conservative" ideals, but we need to put the conserve back into conservative action and policy.

PARENTAL PARANOIA

Chapter 23— The Emerald Forest

"We had an episode where Bud asks his dad, 'I was named after the beer, right, Dad?' And Ed O'Neill, who played my dad, says, 'Uh . . . right, son!' My theory is that Bud Bundy was named after marijuana."
—David Faustino

My memoir briefly reflects on another "pot and celebrity" story. There are so many stories to choose from. I know some celebrities may feel left out because they are not mentioned in the book. Either I have smoked some pot with them or sold them a bag. Sorry, if I don't mention your name (to all you stony *celebs* who smoke weed), but thanks for keeping the seed alive.

I was out to dinner one night. I was stoned, as usual, with a young woman. We went to the restaurant, Pace, which is Italian for "peace," and at the table next to us was Spiderman's girlfriend, Kirsten Dunst. She was with three girls, all her age. When the bill came, she picked up the check and paid for everyone. That is one of the downsides of being famous—everyone knows you have money and expects you to pay.

During dinner, my girlfriend and I started talking to them. I knew Kirsten looked familiar, but I didn't know where from. She was too young to have gone to Beverly High with me, so I thought she might have been an actress. She had her hair up in some Heidi-ish, braided German hairdo.

When I mentioned to my date that Kirsten looked familiar, I was told, "That is Kirsten Dunst, Spiderman's girlfriend, Mary Jane. That is why she looks familiar."

Kirsten Dunst was also the star of *Dick*, one of my favorite comedies about Richard Nixon and the Watergate scandal, but I didn't realize it until later or I would have commented on the film. I love politics so much that I even love comedies about politics. By looking at her, I could tell she was not even old enough to know anything about the scandal, and most people in Hollywood are very liberal in their thinking.

Kirsten overheard me telling my date that I had the munchies and I hoped the food arrived soon. I could not stop eating the almonds and olives that came before the meal. When Kirsten heard that I had the munchies, she sweetly giggled and reached into her purse and pulled out the baggy holding her weed. She handed over her plastic lunch bag to me.

"Is yours better than that?" she asked.

I took my bag of weed out of my pocket and passed it to her. She took a little bud out of my bag in full view of everyone in the restaurant (it was dimly lit), and then she pinched the bud, put it closer to her nose, and drew in a breath. The restaurant was fairly dark, so it was impossible to get a good look at the bud, but by pinching it, the smell was released. She lifted her head, smiled, and said, "I think mine is a little better. What do you think?"

I reached into her bag, performed the same ritual she had just done with my bud, and told her, "I agree. You have better Mary Jane." She laughed at the comment.

We then exchanged bags back again and proceeded to finish our dinners. My girlfriend and I chatted with the girls at their table for our entire dinner. They were all very pleasant. Most stoners are.

It doesn't matter where I go in Los Angeles, I run into celebrities and I always steer the conversation towards pot. One night at Baja Fresh, I saw the foreign kid, Fez (Wilmer) from "That 70s Show," with two of his high school buddies, Blair and Jason. We started talking about weed and how Tommy Chong had given everyone on the set a "Chong Bong" with their characters' names written in the glass. Tommy was a regular co-star or guest-star on the show way before his arrest.

The other night, David Faustino, the actor who played Bud Bundy on the Fox Network's "Married with Children" series, was over at my house, hanging out. He was recently married to a beautiful young actress named Andrea. They got married in Las Vegas at the Little White Chapel where Britney Spears and countless other celebrities have tied the knot.

He was telling me how they were running late for the wedding ceremony. "We were scheduled to be there at 3:30 p.m. Las Vegas time, but as usual, the woman was slow." He smiled, blaming his new wife for the delay. He smiles the same sly Bud Bundy smile he is famous for on the television show. "But it all worked out because when the preacher finished, she said, 'I pronounce you man and wife,' blah, blah, blah. Then she looked at her watch and said, 'at 4:20 p.m. local Nevada time.' All of our friends started screaming. We were man and wife at exactly 4:20. It was great, man."

At times, as I listen to these "Inside Hollywood" pot stories, I'll think to myself, "Wow, I really *am* Hollywood's Wizard of Weed!"

I know Hollywood. I have dragged a few celebrities into my story to show the rest of America, outside of Hollywood, that American entertainers who citizens feel they know, enjoy marijuana as much as the rest of the country. In the USA everyone, from ambulance drivers to super-models, smokes weed. I have smoked with people in every state of this union to which I have traveled. Americans smoke pot and we are not free to do so even in the privacy of our own homes. This is simply ridiculous and needs to change!

Chapter 24—The Patriot

"Government exists to protect us from each other. Where government has gone beyond its limits is in deciding to protect us from ourselves."
—Ronald Reagan

My feeling is that pot is good for me. I don't care what the government says. I know my own body. I know what makes me fell better. I know more about myself than either George Bush or Attorney General Gonzales. I am telling the truth when I say marijuana makes me feel better at times. I'll be 40 years old this year and I know the difference between right and wrong. I don't want to break the law, but when I know the truth and I am facing a mountain of lies, I will no longer restrain myself from shouting and screaming the truth from every mountaintop.

Even in the middle of this ridiculous prohibition, most American pot dealers don't long to leave their country, the land they love. Most simply wish to be respected as businessmen. That is how pot entrepreneurs are looked at in Vancouver, British Columbia, or Amsterdam, Holland. Pot dealers in these cities are wealthy, well-respected capitalists who employ thousands of workers.

American family members of mine have left this country because marijuana prohibition is draconian to live under. One of my relatives who sold pot in America decided to move to Holland, a country that tolerates marijuana cultivation and sales in coffee houses, so he could grow pot without fear of persecution. I am not going to join them because I love America too much to leave. I would rather stay and fight for what is right.

I know celebrities from television, movies and music who have grown or grow, and or sell or have sold pot. The marijuana industry can attract anyone because people don't feel as if they are committing a crime. The guy I purchase my marijuana from is a minor celebrity in town. I imagine that local pot dealers are minor celebrities in any town they live in. They are on the edge of fame

171

and infamy. I am not sure what it was like during alcohol prohibition, but some gangsters from that period are still famous.

"Dude," I said seriously, although I am a grown man. The word "dude" had many meanings, and he knew exactly what I meant.

It is the middle of the day. My dealer arrives in a black corvette about an hour after our phone conversation. "Chirp, chirp." I hear him set his remote alarm on the car.

"Dude, it's American-made," he says, as I eye down his car as I stand in front of my house. He loves talking about America, his car, and the price of gas. He invests in the markets and always knows the price of major commodities such as oil. As he walks into my office in the garage of my house, I can smell him. He smells like a skunk.

He stands six foot two with long hair, "rocker hair." He looks as if he is straight out of *Wayne's World*. He is thin and dyes his hair because it would normally be gray. He is over 40 years old and used to be the lead singer of a fairly well-known punk band in town. Now "the dude" is an art collector and bud dealer, living in his own pad in the nice part of Santa Monica. He is single, has never been married, but dates many women as is the style in Los Angeles for wealthy men. I have heard some men refer to this as their harem. A girlfriend of Bill Maher's calls the other girls, "The Ho-Chi Min trail" that arrives with every new show. One such girl is currently suing Bill, but the case doesn't have much merit. Bill and other celebrities are known to attract, "The Ho-Chi Min trail."

The funny thing is that my pot dealer doesn't stand out in Hollywood. He would stand out in a crowd if he lived in Ohio, (I am only guessing) but in the greater Los Angeles area, he blends into a crowd nicely. Service and quality are everything to the man. He has awesome season tickets to the Lakers, and some of his better clients are invited to games occasionally. His new thing is real estate school.

"Dude," he'll say. "I am going to make millions in the real estate market and I am going to start by saving on sales commissions on my properties."

He is a real entrepreneur, and he somehow credits me with getting him started in the marijuana business because before he met me, he was afraid to sell pot, but somehow I alleviated his fear. Therefore, he always charges me a reasonable rate for weed. When the rest of my friends pay $350-400 per ounce, he sells it to me for $300.

When I returned to Los Angeles, after a few years of living on my ranch, he knew that I didn't have a lot of money. He has attended every rally I've coordinated at the Federal Building and wishes he knew me when I was at UCLA. Not only was he there, he jumped on stage. He only wishes that he was at every smoke-out in the past and says he won't miss any in the future. When I say, "I am truly grateful," he replies, "Brother, you're the Wizard of Weed, and I can't see the Wizard without the best weed in town." He has been one of the biggest supporters of my writing, emotionally speaking.

My family has been skeptical about my writing. My brother calls my book a "kiss-and-tell." A trucker on FM radio called me, "Smokey the Tattle-tale," but my dealer keeps telling me, "Dude, everyone is going to want to read your story. I've seen you speak. I know. When I saw you at the Federal Building, telling people to grow bud and sell bud, I was blown away. But when you sold a bag for $20 in front of the Federal Building cameras and they didn't do anything and then you smoked out 3,000 people, it was insane, dude. Bottom line—it changed my life. Before that, I was just into the bud a little, but I was shy and thought everyone was a cop. After seeing you, I felt emboldened."

"That is so funny, dude," I said, reminiscing about UCLA and not knowing if I should be flattered or feel bad. "I convinced this girl at UCLA to start selling bud in the dorms when she heard me give a casual speech at our Free Speech Club. Her name was Jenny."

"No way! Brother, that is the kind of power you have to influence people." He just smiled and shook his head, looking at me.

"I didn't do it on purpose," I responded. "I was giving the speech on how to deal weed safely and what a great job it was when you looked at it like a job."

"I would have never thought of going to Holland before I heard you speak, and now look at me." That was the one thing about my bud dealer he did seem to have a mild case of ADHD, attention deficit and hyperactive disorder, and often skip subjects mid sentence. "I have been there five times. You can convince people to do things." It was nice having him puff up my ego like that. I didn't feel as if I had much influence, but it felt good hearing him say that I did. I just hoped that people would buy the book.

When I was at UCLA, I tried to push free speech to its limits to see what would happen. The campus police once held and ticketed me for trying to start a riot and for smoking pot, but the police dropped the riot part of the charge and, eventually, asked me to plead guilty to a pot possession charge. I fought them for months on the matter and finally decided I simply didn't have the time to fight the Babylon system, so I took a plea in which I paid nothing and my record was cleared.

I risked arrest for exercising free speech just to know how much free speech I actually had. Could I promote a revolution on campus? We did declare our park an independent country. My goal wasn't to say radical things, but trying to end the prohibition of pot is fairly radical for some people. The penalty for illegal aliens, people not wanted in our country, was not to use violence. We simply pointed our finger at them and made them feel real bad.

"Marijuana is good," I would say. "I like it and I am not afraid to say I smoke it and grow it, and one day, I want to sell it legally for a living."

When I started the Free Speech Club, I was incredibly young and naïve. I thought if the Free Speech Movement of the 60s at the

174

University of California at Berkeley could help end the Vietnam conflict with a Free Speech Club, then maybe I could do the same with the Drug War. Maybe our little Free Speech Club could be influential in ending the War on Drugs I realize now, however, how green I was at the time; but I was sincere. I had a revelation once I opened the hemp store. As a business owner and capitalist, I was able to buy free speech in newspapers, magazines, and on television in the form of advertising. There is no greater exercise of free speech than commercial advertising, and I created some memorable ads.

I felt a sense of reward now that my marijuana distributor feels great about his job rather than guilty. He even told his mother how much he loves marijuana and why he was going to Amsterdam, to judge marijuana in a *cannabis* cup. Whenever I speak to crowds, I praise "dealers" as heroes, and yet warn them not to be involved with anything but cannabis and to act ethically. In my mind, pot dealers truly are the ones saving the seed that will save the planet. My dealer's conservative mother even voted for medical marijuana and now thinks all pot should be legalized. Confronting one's family can be an enormous test, but the reward when the subject is raised can be equally gargantuan. The result could lead to a cleaner and healthier world. Don't be afraid to speak with your grandfather. He probably knows more about hemp than your parents.

Chapter 25— Dances with Wolves

"There is a house in Hopi waiting for the Havasupai. Our
prophecy will be fulfilled. The Hopi are holding our power
songs for us, but soon the time is coming when the songs
will return to the Canyon, to Supai. We are the true
Guardians of the Canyon. That is why the Creator put us
here. The other tribes know that and look to us for
leadership. Even though we are a small tribe, we are
spiritually powerful and the other nations know that."
—Roland Manakaja

Smoking pot changes the way people think and see the world, but
not as much as movies influence the way one sees the world.
Moving images are extremely powerful and absolutely have the
power to influence people. I have heard it said, "Sex and violence
in entertainment do *not* have an effect on individuals watching it."
The people who say that are lying. In my opinion, the moving
picture media is extremely powerful, and that is why a corporation
will pay millions of dollars to put a 30-second commercial in front
of billions of viewers during the Super Bowl. Corporations
wouldn't waste the money if it were not effective.

Marijuana can influence people in a different manner than the way
they are influenced by the media. Smoking marijuana doesn't
make the user want to run out and buy a new car, own a new
computer, or find a better mousetrap. Marijuana smoking makes a
potential consumer more open to new experiences—being grateful
for what they have rather than wanting more. In my experience, it
gives the user an interest in their immediate environment, the
environment (both internal and external), and mostly, unlike
alcohol, it stimulates thinking rather than shutting down that
faculty.

I recently read that Senator Orrin Hatch of Utah used to warn
parents on his Web site (http://hatch.senate.gov/), "A sure sign your
children are smoking pot: if they become *overly* concerned about the
environment, civil rights and/or race relations." Obviously,
cannabis influences your consciousness. Maybe this plant is illegal

because it is bad for productivity? Or maybe it is prohibited because it makes you more compassionate to the plight of others?

Marijuana smoking gives the smoker a feeling of being connected to others outside of their own group. One of the ways slaves were controlled in the past was by keeping them pitted against each other: old versus young, field worker versus domestic, male versus female, and so on. Do workers in the modern economy, voluntary slaves to a system, have their best interests represented? Is the prohibition of marijuana simply one more way to divide Americans? To keep "us" divided from "them"?

Looking from a historical point of view, American workers' ancestors are the peasants and serfs of feudal Europe, the surviving Africans (of the genocide that occurred as a result of trans-Atlantic slavery), and Native Americans from above and below the U.S./Mexican border. Has the dominant culture ever looked out for these people's interests?

Here is what I have discovered after years of hitting the bong and thinking about the big picture. There are currently two classes of people in the world. They can be distinguished easily by asking one simple question: How much fossil fuel energy do they use in a year? One group, on average, uses a whole lot more energy than the other group. If you are reading this book, you are most likely part of the energy-intensive group. The other group survives in this world with a lot less energy—a whole lot less.

Within America, there are two distinct groups: workers and owners. I have heard people call workers "wage slaves," but that is not fair to say because people in the bondage of slavery were not free to quit their jobs if they didn't like them. American workers sometimes feel like slaves as a result of their treatment by bosses and managers, but they are welcome to leave if they aren't happy; slaves are not. Slaves have to suffer through whatever maltreatment may come their way because their lives are truly dependent on the whims of the master. In slavery, it is clear that the masters didn't have the slaves' best interests in mind when making decisions.

178

In my opinion, there is a colossal deceit being perpetrated by leaders, owners, in the industrialized societies and the lives of workers are dependent on this system. They are free to leave it, but they have chosen instead to become dependant. The fact remains that in America workers and owners are *all* slaves to something that no one talks about. It is a group addiction that has lead to dependency, and in this society, we are all living as addicts—in denial. The master that has enslaved us all is our dependency on cheap oil. Our economic system is in need of an overhaul because it is based on the infinite availability of a limited, finite resource. At the moment, our economy runs on petroleum. Cheap energy is the principal fuel of our current industrialized economy and even at three dollars a gallon gas is cheap and works hard.

Supai, Arizona, is the one place in America where gas prices don't seem to directly matter to people. There is not one paved road in the village. There is not a gas station for 70 miles. The Havasupai live in an isolated village at the bottom of the canyon on their reservation. They don't witness the daily fluctuation of gas prices going up and down like the stock market as most people living in cities experience.

Even though there are no cars, gas prices affect their isolated way of life. The most reliable source of transportation to Supai village is horses or on foot, walking, the foremost modes of transport for nearly 500 years in North America. Two days a week, weather permitting, a helicopter flies from the top of the canyon down to their village. The isolation of the tribe means that commodities are trucked to the hilltop above the canyon and then flown or packed down on the back of a mule or horse. When the price of gas goes up in the outside world, the price of commodities goes up even in Supai. Marijuana, as well as commodity prices, are both influenced by basic laws of supply and demand.

The point I am trying to make is that, in our modern industrialized global society, we are all connected, even the most isolated village, whether we like it or not. One of the main things joining our seemingly different societies together is a common need to use the earth's natural resources—*global economics.*

I know that a lot of pro-hemp individuals think that our society would be better off if we all went back to the time of horses and gave up on cars, but I am going to respectfully disagree. It is not as if there are only two options: polluting, Middle-East-oil-dependency or living in the Dark Ages. In my opinion, these Luddites are missing one big point.

People have been deluded into thinking that life was easy, clean, and romantic in previous eras without technologic advances. Movies falsely reinforce this view. Many films acknowledge the frustration of the Luddite mentality. "Man versus machine" is a common theme in film these days. Having gotten to know real Indian people on the Havasupai reservation, and having lived on my own ranch, I have unique insights into the realities of low-energy societies that movies tend to gloss over. Since many people form their worldview based on film images rather than real-life experience, I think it is important to dispel this illusion.

Large numbers of Americans have been fooled into believing that they could survive better without our modern conveniences. I am not burdened with such an illusion. I know that it would be difficult for me to survive on my own and live "like the Indians" off what I could trap or grow. I am happy to be a member of our modern technologic world. I like going to the movies and getting lost in the illusion. I do think that we could have all of this technology without all of the pollution and violence currently associated with the machinery.

When I first when to Supai at six years old, in 1972, there wasn't much interaction between my family and the Havasupai. They still lived in traditional homes and shacks heated with wood-burning stoves. Many didn't have running water. There were Havasupai children at the falls, my mom and aunt bought baskets from the elderly women, and we paid young men to ride us out of the canyon on their horses, but we didn't talk to them much. In the early 1970s, most Havasupai tribal members didn't speak English well.

180

Additionally, they were too shy to speak it poorly. Their experience with white people hadn't always been positive. As a result of this, our interaction was limited.

As I return over the years, I have noticed the people of Supai change, from an outsider's perspective. Not only have I been a witness to Mother Nature's awesome force and ability to alter the canyon through wind, rain, and flood, but I have also noticed changes in the people and culture. Fewer and fewer people from Supai enjoy the falls nowadays. I also have noticed that, over the past 30 years, the tribe has become, generally, extremely overweight. Their language is changing, too. The children who now have television in their homes (probably in the past 10 years, it has become common) have begun to speak English more often and with confidence. They are more connected to my world, the industrial way of life, than that of their grandparents.

The same year that the cops in San Francisco beat me up, there was a flood in Havasupai. The two events are related in my mind and my life. I recount the two events together because, as my world was changing, so was Supai, the place of my dreams. News of the flood appeared on television. My friends alerted me, and I immediately called down to the village to see if I could help. I called the Tribal Council offices to volunteer. I wasn't sure what was needed, but I wanted to help out. It turned out, parts of the trail, homes, and horses had washed away in the disaster. I ended up on a trail crew rebuilding the trail. The area of the trail is called the "ladder" as people walk down the canyon on their way to Supai.

Since I was working as a volunteer all week, I was hiking on the trail out of Supai. I was a little disappointed not to have befriended anyone from the village. I had a vision of that before I left Los Angeles, but it had been a strange week and I was treated with suspicion.

Then someone said, "Hey, spark it."

I looked at two guys sitting in a ditch. They were taking a break from working. I wasn't sure which of them had spoken, but I replied, "I am all out." I then shrugged my shoulders. "Smoked it all with the guys on the trail crew."

I felt sort of distressed, not knowing whom I was talking to. I hadn't really seen these guys the whole week and I didn't know who they were, but they both had friendly smiles. It is not that the Havasupai were mean to me, just skeptical. *Dances with Wolves* had recently come out, and I am sure that a lot of white people wanted to be "Indians for a day." That means white people coming down to the Rez, acting "Indian," with beads and feathers. Arizona is a Mecca for white men practicing shamanism, the art of tribal healers. I didn't want to be an Indian. I just loved Supai. It was the place of my dreams. I just wanted to be able to visit without paying a camping fee because I was poor. I thought if I were helpful to the tribe, no one would ask if I paid to visit.

Before that week, I had never used a wheelbarrow, so I was a little clumsy and dropped a load or two of rocks while repairing the trail. I had never worked as hard, slept so well, or felt better about myself than I did that week. It was my chance to give back to a place that had given me so much, including my nightly dreams, but I didn't feel *truly* welcome.

That is until Roland and his friend, Armando, talked to me. "Sit down and join us, and *we'll smoke you out*," Roland said, inviting me to join them in the ditch where they were taking an afternoon break. Roland was recently out of jail and learning to change his ways. He had married, had a son and baby girl, given up drinking, began learning traditional songs, and started keeping his ancestors' traditional sweat lodge ceremony.

"I heard you worked hard all week." He said it as if he had been watching me with a spy-cam, although I imagine it was through others' reports. I hesitated answering for a moment.

Then Roland offered me his hand with an unlit joint in it. It was the act of him sharing his smoke that made me feel as if I had just made a friend. "Join us, brother, we've got some. We want to thank you, smoke with you, and find out about your story." Those words were never so welcoming. "Why did you come down and work for free?" he asked, handing me a plastic disposable lighter.

It was nice being acknowledged for my hard work, and I liked him right away. Roland, like many Supai people, also loves marijuana. Marijuana is a powerful aid when it comes to enabling people of dissimilar cultures to communicate with each other. It is what broke the ice between us.

When I came to volunteer, I smoked my weed with everyone and word got out that I had some good stuff, *gwev-gwa-chi* ("the thing that you smoke" in their language). The Havasupai working with me constantly said "Spark it," and we did. Consequently, my herb didn't last long, and now I was going home empty-handed. Roland and Armando were working on the irrigation system, making sure that the water flowed to everyone's gardens. After jumping in the ditch with them, they smoked me out with one joint after another. It was bunk weed that I wouldn't normally smoke, but just to smoke with some nice guys was great. We talked about all sorts of things. Roland told me about the path that he was on to becoming leader of his people and his mission to protect to the canyon from reckless development.

I told them how I tried to volunteer on the phone, but I was told by the elderly tribal chairman, "Stay away; we don't need anyone's help." But I came anyway, and when I got to the blocked off road that said, "Supai Is Closed," I went around it, figuring I could be helpful. They both appreciated my tenacity.

"When I am a member on the council, I won't let that happen," Roland said, knowing it would be many years before he was ever on the council. "The old people are still leery of getting any help from outsiders."

Then, in a moment of true friendship, Roland invited me to join them at their traditional sweat lodge. He decided that he had worked enough and that it was time for a sweat.

At the sweat lodge, there were guys who I had worked with all week on the trail. I didn't learn their real names until that night. Havasupai don't like to give their names to strangers. That is the story of how I became friends with the traditional leader of the Havasupai, Roland Manakaja.

One day, years later, Roland was explaining the traditional Havasupai religion to me and how marijuana fit into that worldview. "Every day we live our lives, according to our ancestors, each day lived is another page in our Bible, a living Bible."

It is always strange to me when people talk about the Bible because the book is so famous and it is all about my people, the Jews. Even Jesus and the disciples were Jewish (in the Bible II, the New Testament, the sequel to the Old Covenant).

He continued, "Traditional Supai don't write the words down, but we value the Creator's creation just as much as the Christians do. All of us are God's children, and we pray for everyone in our prayers." His explanation sounded very Christian to me. "We are all related, even the four-legged, so we pray for them, too."

"See that cottonwood tree?" He pointed with his lips because traditional people find it rude to point with your fingers. I nodded my head that I saw it. "It is sacred to my people." There were tears welling up in his eyes for a moment. "It tells us when it is time to plant, it provides heat for cooking, and wood for building homes...I could think of 20 different uses right off the top of my head. This is beneficial knowledge passed down from my ancestors, but to white people, it is just a tree."

I didn't take the "white people" comment personally.

"With satellite television down here now," Roland continued, "many Supai residents, especially the kids, see the tree like white people do, not as something sacred."

184

I read the Bible to my children and think it is true. I don't use my time to spread a biblical message, but I enjoy discussing and debating stories of the Bible with friends. I was grateful for Roland's insights into the Havasupai traditional religion. I know that Native people don't often speak about their traditional religion to outsiders. They don't have the story of their people codified into a written history the way the Jewish people do.

My friends and I often discuss and debate the Bible. I am always interested in what others think. Esai, my daughter's godfather, claims that he is a Christian, but doesn't think that Jesus is a historical figure. He thinks the New Testament is using old famous stories in a morality play rather than it being true history. We debate this point all of the time. The Bible is a source for debate among my friends and me as it has been for my ancestors for generations. I love to talk about the scriptures, and I realize sincere honest people can have differences of opinion. Even though I live in an extremely secular world, my relationship with the Bible stories is a personal one. These are stories for my family, friends, and me to talk about.

The fact is, everything changes or influences your mind: the food you eat, the medicines you choose to use, the television and movies you watch, and the books you read, even the particular newspapers or magazines you choose to read. In my opinion, marijuana is a good counter-balance to the negative influences in the media. Marijuana helps people to read between the lines. To remember even though 24-Hour cable news is selling famine, death and gloom night and day, if you just remember to open the windows and step outside God is still at work making the trees grow, the sun shine and babies laugh.

Chapter 26—Rising Sun

**"My point of view, while extremely cogent, is unpopular...
The repressive nature of the legalities vis-à-vis drugs are
destroying the legal system and corrupting the police
system."**
—Jack Nicholson

My life is a dream and I never know where it will take a turn in the
road. For instance, my family and I were in Laughlin with my
girlfriend for a Memorial Day weekend in Southern Nevada. We
were in the car at the station, filling up, and we were heading to
Vegas right then. Vegas and Laughlin are both relatively short
drives from Los Angeles. Relative to the Southwest because they
are five-and six-hour drives, respectively. While I was inside the
gas station, a police officer brought in a young Japanese tourist
needing to go to Las Vegas. Knowing that there are no
coincidences in the world, I invited the young man to join us.

All of his worldly possessions in America had been stolen. Las
Vegas was the nearest place he could access money from Japan or
get a duplicate passport to get back on his journey. I heard the
police officer explaining to the cashier at the station what had
happened to this guy. He agreed to ride to Vegas with us. In the
car with me were my girlfriend and my three children, but we
squeezed him in on top of the luggage.

Ando was a 27-year-old schoolteacher from a small town north of
Hon Shu seeking adventure in America. He rode his bicycle from
Seattle to Los Angeles, not an easy feat. Then he traveled to the
Colorado River along Interstate 10, also through an incredibly hot
desert. Laughlin, Nevada, was on the Colorado River north of the
"10" closer to Interstate 40. Ando was not the typical tourist; he
was a man in search of adventure.

Six hours earlier, Ando had stopped in the blazing sun for a bath in
the Colorado River and to wash his clothes. He found a shaded
spot where he seemed safe from the mid-day sun, so he took a nap.
He put a lock on his bicycle, but did not lock it to anything solid.

He was only a few feet from it when he laid down for a nap. His saddlebag with his clothes and daily journal were both stolen, along with the bicycle. As a fellow international traveler, I understood the gravity of his loss.

On the car ride over to Las Vegas, he told us that he planned to go the Grand Canyon. It happened that I knew the Grand Canyon well and was just telling Tara, my girlfriend, about it because we were in the land of the Coconino, the ancestors of the Havasupai.

I explained, "There was a large Coconino culture before the Europeans came into contact with the Havasupai, whose ancestors were part of that vast culture."

I had been telling her a little about my experiences in Supai, the history of the people in the area, and my unique familiarity with the tribe. As the sun was setting, we drove out of Laughlin, a small Nevada gambling town along the Colorado River, through the rugged terrain. As I spoke about Supai, I missed the canyon. It had been a few years since I had been down there even though I still dreamed of the place nearly every night.

I advised the passengers in the car to keep an eye out for the Big Horn sheep that roam the area. The animal is sacred to the Havasupai. I have seen giant herds of them in the area. Big Horn sheep roam in the desert between Laughlin and Vegas. They look like goats with giant horns. They seem bigger on television than they are in real life. Actors and animals both have that same effect. The first time I saw Sylvester Stallone in real life, I couldn't believe how short he was. But the first time I saw a bald eagle in real life, it was more amazing than the ones I'd seen on television. Television has a way of distorting reality even more than marijuana. My description of Supai was so detailed and intriguing that Ando dreamed of going there.

Ando and my girlfriend had been influenced by the media and asked if the Havasupai still lived in teepees. I let them both know that Native cultures of Arizona never had teepees. Teepees were the housing style of the Plains Indians because buffalo was the

188

major natural resource and therefore people in that region had plenty of leather for teepees. Many people have that misconception about modern Native Americans because their only experience with American Indians is from films.

Roland's wife told me that it only took one week for Ando to learn many Havasupai words because Japanese is similar to the Havasupai language. Ando did the "sweat lodge" when he was in Supai. The sweat lodge is a traditional Native place of worship; it is a house of prayer. The building itself is made of an earthen substance. The sweat lodge at the *hetch kema* (the Little Falls), along Havasu Creek is one that I have helped to build several times.

Roland Manakaja gave me a call when Ando arrived at the bottom of the Grand Canyon with my CraigX.com business card. I should have guessed that Ando would make it there, despite it being a difficult location to get to, because the guy road his bike from Seattle to Los Angeles and then across Death Valley. I didn't call Roland ahead of time, as I told Ando I would. Roland had gotten the number off my business card. He made it clear that he was unhappy and asked me never to do that again. If I were going to send someone down the canyon from now on, I needed to call personally. I apologized and agreed to call first in the future.

Roland went on to explain that he feared for his life. He is an activist, standing up against the government by asserting tribal rights over uranium mining and ski resort development (moneyed interests) in the region. He felt that he could be a target of violence. Historically, Natives in America who stand in the way of "progress" have been neutralized, and that is what he was calling to let me know.

Roland then invited me to come down for the "Healing the Nations" gathering in Supai where he was speaking. My girlfriend happened to be there when Roland called me about Ando arriving unannounced. She was excited to hear that Ando had made it there safely. When she heard that we were invited down there, she said, "yes" before I did. Immediately, she was off planning and buying stuff for the trip.

Even though Supai is called the "Shangri-La of the Southwest," the place is not perfect. There are conflicts that exist among the Havasupai that are similar in origin to the conflicts that exist in mainstream society. The group supporting marijuana prohibition in Supai (a microcosm of America) is made up of the types of people who think they know what is better for other people.

The role of our government is not to protect citizens from their own stupidity. That is the role of natural selection. Traditionalists in Supai think that each person should have the right to decide what goes in their own bodies. The individual's bodily reactions let that person know what foods and medicines are okay and which are not. The Creator gave each of us the power to discern for ourselves what is fruitful and what is not in own lives. To not use this human faculty would be an insult to the Designer who created humans to think independently.

Traditional peoples of Native America (unaffiliated 420 Tribe members), especially the Havasupai of the Grand Canyon, smoke pot and simply want the BIA (Bureau of Indian Affairs) to leave them alone. Smoking is a tradition of America that Europeans wrote about when they first arrived here. More than half of the Havasupai tribe is committed to reggae music and marijuana, but the power and money of the tribe is more in the hands of non-traditionalists at the moment.

In America, as in the rest of the world, power follows money, and it is no different in this isolated little village. While other tribes exploit gambling as a source of income, I have always dreamed of the Havasupai growing weed on their reservation for medical marijuana clubs. If tribes are considered independent enough from statutory authority and regulation to allow gambling, they should be equally liberated to grow marijuana.

Washington D.C., August 6, 2004—(C-SPAN)
President Bush is on the campaign trail, trying to win

Native American votes. States that are loaded with
Native Americans had tight election races in the last
presidential election. A few Native votes could make
a large difference in another tight election.
Addressing the UNITY Conference, an association of
international journalists of color that meets every five
years, the president made some interesting
comments. After he gave a speech, he took a few
questions from panel members. Mark Trahant, an
editorial page editor *of The Seattle Post-Intelligencer*,
asked live.

Reporter: Mr. President you've been a governor and
a president, so you have a unique experience looking
at it from two directions. What do you think "tribal
sovereignty" means in the 21st Century? And how do
we resolve conflicts between tribes and federal and
state governments?

George W. Bush: "Tribal sovereignty" means that.
It's sovereign. You're a...You're a... You have been
given sovereignty and you're viewed as a sovereign
entity. And therefore, the relationship between the
federal government and tribes is one between
sovereign entities.

Bush then goes on...

I think that one of the most promising areas of all is
to help with economic development and that means
helping people understand what it means to start a
small business...encouraging capital flows.

He then goes on to talk about the importance of entrepreneurship.

There are not many economic opportunities for young Havasupai,
and most of them love marijuana. Why is the government keeping
them from growing? There are many problems on the reservation,
and drugs and alcohol cause some of them, but pot is not a problem.

If anything, it brings people together as the leaves of this plant are used for healing their nation. Many former alcoholics now only smoke pot in Supai. These "Rasta People of the Grand Canyon" have been featured in *High Times* magazine. It is my belief that remote tribes should force the president in his final four years to keep his word and allow hemp farming if a Native nation chooses that route for economic growth.

I have smoked pot with Havasupai as young as 12 (with their parents) and as old as 80 years old. It seems to be a big part of their culture, and they even have a creation story about marijuana, which I have been told "means that it is part of our traditional culture."

I know the Supai story of marijuana. I don't want to say too much because Havasupai is not my culture and stories in their culture are mostly told in the winter. In their culture, you are considered lazy if you are caught telling stories in the summer months when tribal members should be working. The winter is the ideal time for storytelling because it gets dark early and is too cold outside for every type of work.

What I can say is that the plant was a woman who was hated. She wanted badly to be loved, so the Creator turned her into the thing that is smoked, marijuana, and now all people love her. The Havasupai traditionalists nearly all smoke pot and even some of the "Christians" do too. The problem is that the majority of authority figures on the tribal council, the ones with money and power, don't smoke, or if they do, they aren't willing to take a stand against the federal government to end prohibition on the Rez.

It is similar to conflicts that exist between the federal government wanting to respect states' rights when it comes to abortion and not medical marijuana. Ashcroft doesn't think the states know what they are voting for when they overwhelmingly vote for the right to use medical marijuana again and again, but he believes that individual states should have the right to ban abortion and jail doctors for murder if they perform the procedure.

192

Marijuana is illegal down in Supai (one gram of pot in Arizona is a felony). People who smoke at home or at the sweat lodge are not bothered for smoking pot by tribal police or the BIA. These pot smokers are contributing members of the tribe and arresting them would create a greater conflict. That is the compromise that is worked out in their village, and the pot smokers are growing in numbers while prohibitionists are declining in numbers. It won't be long before weed is legal in Supai or there will be revolution from the current order.

We arrived for the "Healing of the Nations" concert only to find that we were the only outsiders there, the only white people. There was one other member of my tribe there, a Jewish man and his wife (Robert Roskind and his wife, Julia; the Indians call the two of them the "Ras-kind family, as in Ras-ta), who were guest speakers and co-organizers of the event. He and his wife thought the spirit of "One Love" as professed in reggae music had healing properties, and they were advocates of this message. They were in Supai because of the tribe's unique relationship with reggae music and the "One Love" message.

John's Book of Revelation speaks of a plant that will be used for the healing of the nations. Bob Marley took much of his music from the Holy Bible, so Rastafarians are extremely devout. Damon, the Rasta tribal member produced the show, "Healing the Nations" (a teach-in and reggae concert), named for the Rasta marijuana philosophy that the Supai traditionalists espouse, namely that marijuana is a healing plant. It was co-sponsored by the tribe and the Roskinds.

Roland, my friend, was speaking at the event because he is the director of tribal resources for the Havasupai. He is more like the traditional chief of the nation because he takes his role as guardian of the Grand Canyon seriously. He is looked up to among 13 tribes in the area, who claim some affiliation with the Grand Canyon, but he knows it is the Havasupai who are its guardians, and he takes the lead role for the tribe in outside affairs relating to its protection.

There is a *raison d'être* for everything, especially if you believe in chaos theory, sometimes called the "butterfly effect." For me, the explanation for chaos theory states that small variables in a complex system can lead to wildly different results. This theory is the reason that accurate weather predictions can only be done in the short term. I know it sounds unreasonable to some who don't think Lorenz's Curve is sound, but if you think there are no accidents and that all things are connected as I do, then you have to consider that possibility because if Ando's stuff hadn't been stolen, I would not have been in Supai for the gathering called "Healing the Nations."

At the gathering, we learned from a Hopi snake priest named Radford that the Hopi had just turned down a guaranteed $20 million a year in tribal gaming revenue. Roland realized that if someone were a target in his tribe, it was he. The influence of traditional leaders like Roland and Radford helped turn the tide against the casino. Sometimes it can be one or two people in a large community that turn the tide for or against something, they are the small variables in these complex systems. I am a variable in the system.

Life seems safe when you are a normal person, but when you are a "variable" or as I like to say a "warrior," your life is constantly on the line, and you know it. Roland is actually much more than his title, director of tribal resources, would suggest. He is a warrior for his people as I imagine myself a warrior for the millions of pot smokers who don't stand up for the herb as I do. Roland knows about the history of his people and the canyon. I know about the history of hemp and the culture surrounding it. He is truly the protector of the Grand Canyon as I am an advocate for cannabis.

The name "Manakaja" means, "Leader of the People." As his name suggests in his language, he is a leader among his people. "The government tries to give other tribes authority over the canyon, but it is the Havasupai who lived there, where the park now is," Roland explains.

194

"What if historians, years from now, come to America and, say after the year 2000, it looks as if the Chinese people seemed to have taken over because everything, all of the artifacts, are made in China?" Roland goes on, explaining why different tribes' relics are in Supai territory. "We traded with people all the way down into Southern Mexico. That doesn't mean they lived here or should have any claim over our land."

He laughed, "Unless the Chinese can claim America because their goods are here; people trade."

Disconnection with the outside world as a result of their geographic isolation has caused the Havasupai to retain their culture more than other tribes have. Supai village is the most isolated village in the entire United States, still receiving mail by mule train. Maintaining their traditional culture more than most other indigenous people of North America has caused the Havasupai to be looked up to among tribes in the region and nationally. Yet, with all of their seclusion, there are many goods made in China in Supai village.

This fact highlights the reality of this current material global economy; we are all connected and interdependent. When the price of gas goes up in the outside world (there are no gas stations in Supai), they feel it down there. I can't stress enough the fact that, as isolated as they are, they are not completely self-sufficient or autonomous. The tiny village of Supai is part—albeit a small part—of the global economy.

One of the other ways in which the outside world encroaches on this little paradise at the bottom of the Grand Canyon is by restricting their use of the beneficial and valuable marijuana. Marijuana is smoked outside the sweat lodge between rounds when it is available, not inside. The only herbs burned in the sweat lodge are put on the hot rocks prior to the water being poured on them. The Havasupai taught me that the hemp plant is beneficial and good medicine for the earth.

My favorite place in the world to attend church and worship God is in the sweat lodge along Havasu Creek. As I sit there in my shorts on the mud floor, surrounded by all of the things God put on the earth to help humans survive, I am thankful to be alive. In the sweat lodge, we give thanks for the water to drink, the wood and living things that provide shelter and food, the spirit of life, the air that we need to breathe, and the rocks and earth and fire. It feels good to feel so blessed.

It is in Supai that I realize that the Creator has provided me with all I'll ever need. Life is a dream, and I am a warrior smoking this beneficial herb with my fellow warriors, the Havasupai traditionalists. Nothing happens by chance, and there is a reason for my being.

I am, and that is all I need to know.

Chapter 27— The Little Buddha

"Reefer makes darkies think they're as good as white men."
—Harry J. Anslinger

My dad said, "If you think pot is good for you, then you have been brainwashed by the counter-culture and the hippies you're hanging out with." I know pot is good for the world. The fact is, mainstream society has been programmed to think that caffeine, nicotine, and alcohol are not drugs when they are. Once people realize that all human consumables create chemical reactions, then it is only a matter of semantics.

My father takes drugs daily only a doctor prescribes them. Forty percent of all Americans take legal drugs daily. Women in this country eat Midol, a drug to relieve cramping associated with monthly menstrual pains, as if it were candy. What if marijuana were a more efficacious medicine for cramps? What if it were safer for your system? It was the number one prescribed medicine for that purpose 100 years ago. Why should our mothers and sisters not be allowed to use whatever works best for them? I want what is best for our society, whether it is a pill or a natural plant.

I am one of the few people who recognize the needs of the future. That is why I think that I could be a better president than anyone else who is going to follow George W. Bush. I understand more than most that the world we live in is changing. The world climate is changing, both mentally and physically. More than ever, the world needs stability and direction. The Hopi believe that we are living in the End Times, as do some Christians. This was the focus of the Hopi snake priest's speech at the "Healing of the Nations."

The Hopi are not one people, but a group of Pueblo dwelling clans and tribes that subscribe to a peaceful way of life and share connecting mesas. Their nation is circumscribed by the largest of all Native nations, the Dine, or as they are known to whites, "the Navajo." The Hopi legends, as I understand them, state that the world has reached this level of "global civilization" four times. We are currently living in the Fourth World, according to their creation myths, and about to enter into the Fifth World. A great flood destroyed the last global culture, as the Bible states also. I've learned these stories from books, white Indian experts, and the Havasupai. When I heard Radford speaking, that was the first time I heard with my own ears a Hopi elder speaking about prophecy.

We are living in an interesting time of history. People around the globe are in movement. One of my cousins flies all around the world for his work. He doesn't have a permanent home, and his only phone is cellular. The best way to reach him is via the World Wide Web. The Hopi prophecies are not based on dates, but on events, such as "people will communicate over spider webs." Prophecy is always vague, but many who know about the Hopi prophecy believe that this is the Internet. I am not sure who is brainwashed: the people who live in denial of the fact that oil is a finite resource or the Hopi who believe this global civilization will commit suicide.

Whether you believe in prophecy or not, the fact is that large numbers of people in the past 100 years have left rural areas and have moved to cities where they earn more money. However, while earning more money, they become dependents of the global industrialized society—as opposed to being more self-reliant, living in the rural areas—for basic necessities such as food and water. Nowhere more so than in American, for the first time in recorded history, the majority of earthlings are living in urban centers. By the billions, humans have voluntarily made themselves dependent on the global economy. People are only connected to the food-producing locations of the earth by this global system. Nearly every country on earth is rushing towards this world system, as well. How long will it be before RFID chips are implanted in people? Is this part of the future of industrialized societies because we wouldn't want to feed terrorist?

The Hopi don't give a reason for the sudden collapse of industrial man; they just predict its occurrence. I know the reason for the misfortune about to befall humankind and it won't be from a collapse in the value of money.

That is a byproduct. The sad truth is that technologic society has not yet figured out how to create something from nothing. It seems as if the laws of physics apply to all societies and on all planets. The first law of thermodynamic states that energy is neither created nor destroyed; it just changes forms. This means that there is so much energy in the universe and that this number, whatever it is, never changes. The same is true of the planet earth. The significance is that our culture is currently addicted and dependent upon a limited resource. The resource is finite. Once the cheap, poisonous, efficient, highly combustible, easy-to-use crude oil reaches a global peak in production, our way of life will come to an unexpected end, and that time is fast approaching, oil prices will skyrocket breaking new records everyday as they did in October of 2004. Economist will play it off as normal market fluctuations, but they don't realize that we don't eat without that oil, especially in America.

Our technologic society has citizens that can truly call the entire earth their home. Yet, rather than focus on the planet there is renewed interest and spending in traveling and living in space. The irony didn't get past the Havasupai either. Outside the sweat lodge, smoking weed and joking, more than one Supai person made a joke about white people in space. Mostly about white people wanting to return home to the stars where they came from, because the week we were in the canyon was the week that the first private successful test flight to space occurred. By now, there have been three private flights to space. Sir Richard Branson, owner of Virgin Airways, bought the company to do it and now they are Virgin Galactic and in their on-line site show an image of one of their craft in space over California.

The Havasupai may have been joking about white people going back to space, *their home*, but modern industrial people do act as if they are not of this planet. It is easy to say that because inhabitants of earth from "developed" societies don't care for the planet that gave birth to them the way a child should care for a parent. Thoughtless citizens of the industrialized world treat the earth as a trash dump rather than as a home.

Our president needs to have an understanding of the current mindset of the world population in order to interact with other global leaders, but must also act in America's best interests rather than for the supposed "world good." As far as I am concerned, a world government is bad. I'd rather have our system, with all of its faults, because it was designed to protect the minority. A world system will be designed to protect business interests and not individual rights as the U.S. system is supposed to do.

The Founding Fathers realized that they, the moneyed-elite, slave-owning ruling-class, were a minority and that their rights needed to be protected. In a pure democracy ("mob rule," as they called it), the majority would strip the elite of all of their property. In the United States of America, minority rights have slowly been expanded to protect more people than originally envisioned when the Constitution was penned. Even though similar forces, as when the nation was founded, currently still run our country (a wealthy, privileged, business-owning, ruling-class), there is room for change in our society without tearing down the basic structure of our society, the Constitution. That is the foresight that the Founders had. The ability to create a document that would protect the minority and yet still be flexible enough to change in the future, once they were dead.

There is a reason that refugees risk their lives to come to our country. Refugees go to other countries, but they risk their lives to come to America. Immigrants from around the world know that they will be protected in the United States. No other country in the world allows minorities to have the economic freedom and social mobility as America, and that freedom is extended to more and more people as time goes on. The democratic principles that this country was founded on were based in the Founders' Christian morals. Examples of this can be found in their writings and journals. These were moral, God-fearing people, albeit slave owners.

There is an alternative to the anarchy of the Luddites. The alternative is to lessen our dependence on foreign oil by exploring hemp as a renewable resource for fuel. Let's not throw away all that we have and start over. If we do that, we'll end up in some biblical world-government hell. As Americans, we should cherish our individual freedoms, realizing that they come with a responsibility to maintain that independence. The United States is the city upon the hill that lights the way in the world. As citizens of this great nation, we must be vigilant to protect our hard-won rights and freedoms, especially from citizens of our own nation who would seek to subvert the ideals of this nation for their own profit.

Watching Michael Moore's film *Fahrenheit 911* made me think that he wishes he were born in Europe rather than America. The Europeans, in my opinion, gave up their freedoms for safety long ago, and we should not follow their example. They are neither safer nor more secure in their quasi-socialist state. Do the Chinese have freedom of thought, speech, and religion? It is a crime to spread Jesus' message of peace and love in China. Why do we do business with a country that kills its university students for standing up for freedom of religion and speech? Under Bush and Clinton, foreign investment in China has grown out of control and we are undermining our own security for money. This is just one of the small things that lead to unpredictability in a complex system.

What is the value of paper money? The value of paper money is the faith people place in the government that issues it. That is the value of the American dollar. Shortly after Bush took office, the euro was $.85 ($9 trillion) to the dollar; and now it is $1.33 to one dollar. America lost money (Trillions dollars in value) as the European economy grew and the Europeans didn't do a thing. Why is our nation suddenly less valuable on the world market? The difference is that people now have more faith in the euro than the dollar. That small shift in faith led to a drastic adjustment in value. People of the industrialized world place enormous faith in money, something that can't be eaten or drunk, whose only value is the faith people have in it.

I am a pro-American, pro-pot Republican at war with my government at the same time. The irony doesn't get past me. The War on Terror is real, and it is not a war against Mexicans. Muslims are the ethnic profile of the fighters fighting our Judeo-

Christian way of life. Yet, I've been strip-searched at the airport. I've been pulled over by the police and forced to allow a dog to smell my things to make sure I wasn't a "terrorist." As I said, I feel as if my own government is terrorizing me because I smoke pot. The War on Drugs is real. In America, there are millions of prisoners of war, people in jail, for marijuana.

Since I am dealing in reality, it must be admitted that terrorists sell illegal drugs to finance their illicit activities. Why, then, does our society falsely inflate the value of those drugs by fighting a losing Drug War?

There are several reasons for world's interest in the Middle East, but I would have to say, the number one reason is that industrialized nations are interested in oil. There are a handful of countries sitting on the largest reserves in the world of cheap and easy-to-get oil. Europe and China need the oil of the Middle East as much as the U.S. does, so their leaders welcome Muslims into their nations as brothers. Most countries wanting cheap oil accept Islam's hatred of Jews. They deny Islam's hatred of Christianity, and their actions actually encourage Arabs to ethnically cleanse Jews from the face of the earth. I am a Jewish pot warrior; I put my life on the line every day, protecting the freedoms of millions of pot smokers around the world, so I recognize the realities of war. The U.S. is one of the few nations standing up for what is right in the Middle East rather than what is expedient. It makes me thankful to be American. Technologic society is itself a global empire. America, the biggest fish in the pond, is forced to secure access to cheap oil for that empire. If it didn't high oil prices would send the world economy into a tailspin.

Ending the prohibition of hemp would allow domestic industries to create hemp fuel. Currently, it is cost-prohibitive to import hemp for biomass or to import hemp fuel. Henry Ford built a car out of hemp that was stronger than steel. I think people have been brainwashed by a corporate-controlled media that easily influences popular opinion. No matter where we go in the country, the same media is there. These corporations need an effective method of marketing, so they have taken over our public information

202

distribution networks to deliver their message: "Buy me! Eat me! Wear me!" The same corporations are everywhere, in every little town, with the same songs, the same shows, and the same food. That is why the Internet is so important for the free flow of information.

I have learned the importance of the freedom of information by traveling to other countries where liberty is lacking or nonexistent. Part of the reason anyone goes on an "adventure" to somewhere new is to come back and tell others about it. It is the same reason people try new things like marijuana. Experimenters want to go where others have gone so they can test the results for themselves. I like to take an adventure partly to come back and share my personal stories. *9021Grow* is sharing my story of this adventure called "life" as it relates to the prohibited marijuana plant.

What is it that makes this plant so dangerous to the social order that society has banned it? Our government currently says, "Marijuana has no medical benefits." Marijuana has been classified as more dangerous than alcohol, tobacco, cocaine, heroin, and many other drugs that I know from personal experience are more dangerous, and yet are legal for recreational and medical purposes. Anyone who has smoked pot can attest to the "munchie" effect. That is why marijuana is helpful for cancer patients. Cancer patients die of starvation because the medicines taken to fight the cancer cause the patient to be so sick that they are unable to keep their food down. Marijuana smoke stimulates the appetite and reduces nausea, allowing these ill people to get the nutrition that is needed for a possible recovery.

When I was younger, I was often asked the question traditionally asked of children, "What do you want to be when you grow up?" My answer was always the same: "A hippie." I don't recall why, but I always wanted to be a hippie. To many in our country in the early 1970s, it seemed as if we were on the brink of political revolution that never materialized. A *societal* revolution did occur, and I remember hearing about it from Bruce Grakal, Chris' father, as he dined at my parents' house one night. He was drunk, rambling on about how the Beatles changed the world. Of course, he considered himself a player in that change as Ringo's lawyer. Everyone imagines themselves heroes and changers of world events, and in some way, it is true. Within us each one of us, there is the power to change the world.

Native American Indians were the world's first hippies, with long hair, beads, and feathers; they shared symbols with the hippies. Maybe that is why I wanted to grow up to be a hippie, American Native. Indians became icons of the hippie movement and marijuana the official flower of the new, emerging tribe. This new culture or tribe was partly inspired by psychedelics, anti-war demonstrations, a "back to the earth" movement, and partly by a religious revival all occurring at the same time in the late 1960s and early 1970s.

Native Americans became the symbolic ideal of how to live in harmony with the earth; whether or not it was historically true didn't matter. Indians were promoted to the position of icon and emblem for this new culture. There was even a commercial that featured an Indian crying about pollution on his native land, the city. A single tear rolled gently down his face. It was a powerful image when I was a child. I later met and spoke with that actor at a medical marijuana benefit where he played music and I was a speaker.

Through the use of psychedelics, hippies came to believe that everyone was brainwashed; it simply became a matter of what you used to wash your brain. At this point, the "counter-culture" adopted Natives as their idols because it gave the new culture a sense of what they felt was sacred and connected them with something from America's prehistoric past. Indians knew how to live on this land. At least, more in harmony than the industrialized society, which only in recent history had taken over the land of the United States.

This was obvious at the time to young people who were joining communes and refusing to live in the mainstream industrialized culture. The emerging way of life was not a shock to Native elders. It had been expected and these elders had been warning for years of things that were now coming to pass. To many young people in the counter-culture, it seemed as if the answers had been in the Native traditions all along and that the industrialized world simply missed the evidence. Hopi Indians were even influential at the famous Woodstock concert, where they spoke of ancient prophecies and a coming world catastrophe.

As a child, I became fascinated with Native Americans and their culture's stories. For some kids, it is dinosaurs and volcanoes, but for me, I wanted to live in nature with the Indians. I've read books about Natives and visited historical sites, but my personal knowledge of Supai and its people was limited until I met Roland. As I got older, fascination with Native cultures never diminished.

I now have a less romantic view of their societies. It has been replaced by a more realistic view. One of the most distinct things about traditional people when compared to modern technological people is the opposite outlook on physical objects. The technologic view all over the world, regardless of nationality, is that the world and its essential parts are basically lifeless, dead. Human beings happened by accident in a puddle of mud as a result of some cosmic mishap. People with this view think the "natural world," humans included, can be understood simply as chemicals in a tube or a chemical reaction that occurred by chance.

Havasupai traditionalists don't believe in chance. They know that everything happens for a reason. In their world, God is alive and well.

"Who makes the grass grow and the water flow?" Roland once asked me. I wasn't sure where he was going, so I just shrugged my shoulders as if I didn't know. "In our culture, the Creator is actively working every day, making the grass grow. In Christian culture, God was killed two thousand years ago."

I am not sure Roland was making a perfect analogy, but I understood where he was going with his thinking. *Baak-iyo-Va* (the Havasupai word for "Creator" or "Almighty"—I am not sure of the exact translation, but that is how the word is used in the sweat lodge) in their worldview is, second by second, actively involved in making everything happen. This Spirit has given the people everything they need for this lifetime and beyond, from a place with water to the trees that surround them.

The function of the contemporary schooling system in the modern technologic world is to reinforce this "shit happens" worldview. Schools are paid to produce information in the form of papers that identify and classify human cultures and societies as separate from each other. In this worldview, these cultures are seen as equal and simply different methods humans have used to gain control over their individual environments to exploit them for survival purposes. The present corporate-sponsored universities teach a way of thinking as much as they teach content. The mode of thinking that is taught is "compartmentalization." Students aren't really taught to look at the big picture. If they were, more people would be aware of the coming global changes.

The basic shared worldview of indigenous peoples, regardless of nationality and despite some differences, is that the world is alive and blessed by a living Creator, God, or Great Spirit. These cultures recognize the earth and cosmos as a hallowed place and the fact that we are alive as something truly special. People living closer to the earth know that all beings are alive, related, and interconnected. Even the rocks are alive in their worldview. In the Bible Jesus even said that rocks could speak. According to the Supai way of looking at the world every tree and every leaf has a place in this world, and the Creator has put everything in its proper place.

In traditional Native culture, the individual's responsibility was, and is, to hold all life holy and to live in balance with nature. To be thankful and give back as much as is taken. This is how traditional Havasupai still live. There are still a few Hopi people carrying on the old ways too. Most however have been lured away from traditions—not by war, but by a convenient dominant culture that is insidiously material-oriented. You are not a cool Hopi if you don't have a pick-up truck, music box, and gold chain with your

206

name on it. The traditional Hopi believe their ceremonies keep the whole world in balance.

In my mind, I have come back to "civilization" from my home in Arizona on 40 acres with a message for the pot smoking "420 Tribe" living in the cities. For some reason, I believe they might listen to me, a leader in the revolution to end prohibition, and anyone else living in the industrial technological world that might recognize that what I am saying is the truth.

My message is this: The world we live in is dying because of our inner health, our collective states of mind, but we can take steps to create positive outcomes. Some people in our society are beginning to wake up to these facts. If you were drawn towards this book, you may be one of those people. The fact is, the weather is changing as a result of human impact on the biosphere. Storms and droughts are becoming more severe. Based on what I have read about oil production I predict that in 2005 oil will reach world production capacity while demand will continues to increase. Peak oil in 2005 could force the price of crude oil to skyrocket. *Cannabis* is an incredible natural resource that could limit our dependence on foreign oil. WE NEED TO USE IT!

I think our nation should plan for the future, not by sending us into another war, but by getting us off of our petrochemical addiction. We need to develop alternative forms of clean energy and use our creativity to lead the world to a better future. It is important for the world to have faith in the United States if we are to survive as a nation; the value of our dollar depends on it. It is most important for Americans to realize what it is that makes us a great and strong country, not our bombs or tanks. Our values make our nation great. We are a beacon of freedom and democracy for people around the globe. What does the EU stand for? They are held together by a common market. America is held together by an ideal.

The most important crisis that I see brewing on the horizon is an energy crisis. I think that world oil production is peaking and that in the future, it will be difficult to drive oil prices down without reducing demand. Oil is a finite resource, and that is why production is peaking. An annual renewable resource would never suffer the same fate. Hemp is an annual renewable resource that could replace some of our imported energy needs through a process of biomass. The Saudis and people in the oil industry actually profit from instability and terrorism, so what is their motivation for fighting it full force? As Europe and China grow in industrial capacity, they will be competing with America for the same oil. Let's face facts. Oil is one of the reasons we are in Iraq now. There is no greater national security issue than the development of alternative energy sources.

This is the truth: Pot can save the industrial world for two reasons. One, smoking it can give us hope and helps us to see what is really important in life—each other. Secondly, it is the greatest natural resource that God has given to man. Why do we continue to drive with an energy source that kills? If you spend one hour in a closed garage with the car running, you'll be dead as a result of the poisonous fuel that is being burned. If you ran that same car on hemp fuel, the exhaust would not be deadly. Think about that.

Hemp is an annual renewable resource. It doesn't have to be grown in the Middle East. It will grow well in the middle of America. Wake up! Our time on earth is short. This dream world that we call our life is a sacred gift from the Creator. Don't mistreat the environment or each other and you'll live healthier lives. I am not saying to worship a plant. Worship only God; it is that simple. But this plant is a gift from our Creator for the healing of the nations. That is the truth.

The Havasupai are an impressive people, not because they live off the land; they don't. They don't live off the land, even in their isolated village. These days, no one is ever completely self-sufficient unless they are stranded in some type of accident. Who would want to be that isolated? I would not. What makes the Havasupai impressive is that they have survived as a people, on their land and with their language despite the government's war against them. Like the hemp plant they have survived and thrived despite the persecution.

For a while, I thought that was the ideal, "living like the Indians." In actuality, living closer to the land is harder than it appears in the movies. In the cinema, everyone looks cool and neat. In reality, a toothache without drugs is a disaster. You don't see people dealing with humidity, bugs, freezing weather, crop failure, difficulty finding food, and all sorts of other tragedies that can happen when "living off the land." What did they use for toilet paper? Think about that reality next time you wish civilization would simply disappear.

When I decided to move to my ranch full-time, I had a fantasy that I could produce my own food. It felt as if nothing in the city was sacred, and I wanted to escape to live in the woods. I was giving up on society and going off to live like the "Indians" or how I thought the traditional Indians lived. What I realized is that traditional ancient Native Americans didn't live as I imagined them living.

Living like the Indians is not as romantic as Kevin Costner makes it seem in his award-winning film *Dances with Wolves*. I had purchased an inexpensive home in the country. It was an old church that I converted to a living space. It was in Northern Arizona that I learned to grow large amounts of food. I had hippie neighbors trying to be self-reliant by earning a living off the land. No one I knew, including the Indians in the most isolated place in America, was completely autonomous.

At the time, I was like Michael Moore, only focusing on the bad things that America has done, and there are quite a few. I could focus on all of the positive things that America has done and have a contradictory point of view. Instead, I am not so polarized. I realize that good and evil coexist within the same country. Even within each individual, there is good and bad.

The sad truth is that if we don't care for our environment and each other, our civilization will end up existing as the hunters and gathers do today. Not as well as most current hunters and gathers either, because we won't have generations of experience at perfecting it. Growing food, killing and skinning animals, making candles, sewing clothes, and living without the automobile are not easy ways to make a living. This lifestyle creates a small impact on the earth, but so does being poor.

Being poor and broke is not entertaining and causes one to actually work harder for basic survival needs. We are blessed in America with great wealth and excess because we live the way we do, providing freedom and opportunity for all of our citizens. We govern ourselves with the uniquely American and Christian principle, "In the eyes of the Creator, all men are equal." If we don't value our history and heritage, we are sure to lose it. When Albert Einstein was asked what types of weapons World War III would be fought with, he thought for a moment and said, "I don't know, but I know that World War IV will be fought with sticks and stones." We are now told by historians that World War III was the "Cold War." But, isn't World War II really just World War I continued?

As a society, it should not be our goal to destroy our magnificent civilization with all of its up-to-the-minute conveniences, whether with weapons of mass destruction, cataclysmic earth changes, or simple neglect, and yet we are creating conditions to allow for all of those possibilities. By simply accepting the fact that you, the reader of my story, were put here on earth for a reason, you can make a difference and change the world.

Your reason could be to help enlighten the world to this great resource, *cannabis*. Hemp is a natural plant that can save our industrial way of life and get us off our petroleum dependency. Even though I am a registered Republican and support many of the current president's policies, the film *Fahrenheit 911* illustrates that we are in the Middle East for oil as much as we are there for helping our fellow humans escape the tyranny of a dictator.

Oil is important to our current industrial technological society at the moment, but we cannot and should not continue to be as dependent on it as we are now. If we remain dependent on Middle East oil, we'll never get out of the Middle East. Did you know that

210

Henry Ford built a car that ran on domestically grown hemp fuel in 1937?

Ford's technology did not disappear and it needs to be revived. Hemp is a divine gift that is being kept from our society. Join the warriors and 420 Elders in making a difference on this planet! There is a reason you read this story. God wanted you to know about hemp.

Now, go do the right thing! Grab a seed, grow some weed, and together we can save the world.

kevinpearson

212

Epilogue— Far Out, Man

"We shouldn't have to be burdened with all the technicalities that come up from time to time, with shrewd, smart lawyers interpreting what the laws or what the Constitution may or may not say."
—Dan Quayle

I spoke with Tommy Chong on the phone today. He is doing well and thankful for all of the support he has had since his arrest. Jay Leno treated him like the star and hero that he is last Friday night. It was Monday, two days after his Leno appearance, and I was calling him to see if he needed any help writing his new movie or *anything*. He mentioned on "The Tonight Show" that he and Cheech were making a new movie together.

When I called, Tommy said he and Cheech already had the movie written and they were starting to shoot it right away. I told him I was willing to do anything to help and gave him my new number. He was just glad to be home. His being away wasn't easy on his wife, the lovely Shelby Chong.

I didn't get to see him on Jay Leno because I don't have television reception at my house. I don't pay for cable. My family was talking about it Saturday morning at breakfast and one of my female co-workers was talking about how handsome Tommy looked with his silver beard. She told me about his great line.

Jay Leno asked, "Did you have any weed on you when you got busted?"

Tommy answered, "Of course, I had weed. I am Tommy Chong."

It is that kind of attitude that I love. Tommy is not afraid to say, "Pot is great and every American should have the right to smoke it." He is such a cool guy and has always been so nice to me.

He called his experience "going to camp," but he admitted, "It is real fucking jail because you can't leave, man, you're there." He explained that the guards were sympathetic towards him and everyone treated him with reverence. He told me that part of his sentence was living in a halfway house. "It is no different than jail. I could still get written up."

Then Tommy got serious for moment. "Shit man, I was in real jail. It's no joke. Even though I was treated well, I was a prisoner just like everyone else in there and I could still be put in the hole." I didn't know what "the hole" was, but it didn't sound good.

Even though I am a Republican, I personally believe Ashcroft is out of control and am glad that he has retired for Bush's second term. I am simply glad that my icon and mentor is out of jail, but I know he is not home-free. Many people go back to jail for probation violations. Many Americas recognize that Tommy was a "political prisoner" in the United States and that he was sentenced and jailed because of who he was, not what he did. Of the 55 people arrested in operation "Pipe Dreams," Tommy was the only figure sentenced to anything more than house arrest. Chong's arrest and incarceration were symbolic because, according to pre-trial court documents, "he made a career out of flaunting the pot laws and additionally made fun of law enforcement in his career in films and television."

He is a comedian; like court jesters of the past, his job is to point out the ridiculous in our world. In my opinion, there is no more free speech or freedom of thought in America if you can't speak out for pot, or at least joke about it as Tommy Chong has made a career doing.

Tommy continued, "Our Constitution has been gutted and cut to shreds. The government wins 97 percent of the cases it tries. That is not justice, so if they want you, they got you. You can't fight these guys because they have all of the money. Look, I am not a threat to society other than pointing out the obvious: America's pot laws are ridiculous. For God's sake, I am a comedian. That is what I am supposed to do. I make fun of society for a living." He was articulating exactly what I was thinking.

214

I told Tommy that while he was locked up, medical marijuana clubs had been popping up all over the state of California. According to the law in this state, we only need our doctor's approval, nothing more. The government tried to shut down some clubs in Oakland several weeks back and the people who ran the clubs refused to shut down. There was a guy in a wheelchair named Kenny on the local news. He ran one of the "shut down" clubs and was refusing to stay closed. He was reopening the next day.

When the news crews interviewing him asked if he were afraid of jail, he said, "This wheelchair is my jail. Pot makes me feel better and I am not going to stop smoking it or selling it to people who want it."

I don't think it looks good for politicians to be sending people in wheelchairs to jail. It is hard to convince people that paraplegics are a danger to society and need to be locked away in jail for smoking medical pot. People in California don't care what the government has to say anymore. We have overgrown the government's ability to stop marijuana production.

When I mentioned this to Tommy, he suggested a reason as to why the government can't admit defeat. "The DEA can't give this up. They are making money at both ends. Almost all drug arrests are for pot. What would all those agents do if it were suddenly legal? Those guys don't want to be out of a job. I was at a private prison. The private prisons are making money hand over fist. Do they want to stop?"

Tommy and I both knew that society's answer to the problem was being delayed because of moneyed interests gained from pot remaining illegal. There is also a problem with our justice system. The more money you have, the more justice you can afford. We all need to get off our collective butts and end the prohibition of marijuana.

Tommy said, "I hope my incarceration will show the American people that no one is safe with Ashcroft as Attorney General."

Now, a man in his mid sixties who has never hurt anyone is on prohibition for one year and citizens have to pay for it with tax dollars. Tommy Chong is a medical marijuana patient with a doctor's note, which in California allows him to smoke. Will the government allow him to use the medicine? Let's hope so. I want 420 Tribe members to pray and work towards having Tommy's name and record cleared. In my opinion, that should be a collective goal of the tribe. It is cool to me that I can just call Tommy Chong at home and rap with him on the phone for 30 minutes while driving across town. I guess I really am "Hollywood's Wizard of Weed."

He told me about some of the other people in jail with him. How an old Chinese man taught him the *I Ching* while incarcerated.

Tommy said, "I've been getting some readings that are telling me I don't have to do anything: things are going to come to me, big things." The *I Ching*, or *Book of Changes,* is an ancient Chinese divination manual, and I don't know anything about it other than that.

Ashcroft thought he was going to silence Tommy Chong, America's first 420 Elder. The Attorney General has awoken a sleeping giant. *Cannabis* will not go away. The earth needs it, and our tribe knows it. I think Ashcroft's plans are going to backfire, and more people are going to stand up to end this crazy prohibition. If the Supreme Court goes against medical marijuana it will cause a social revolution. People will not be fooled by the government's lies. Tommy survived, this plant has survived and so will our culture.

Know the truth and the truth shall set you free!

Regarding Iraq, I am glad that we are liberating people half a world away, but we are not just there to liberate out of the goodness of our hearts—we have an agenda. How unfortunate it is that the energy our society needs to run ended up under the land in the Middle East, but it did. That is just how the Creator planned it. I am sure the Bush family and friends dream of all that oil being in Texas, but it is not.

Ending the prohibition of marijuana would allow farmers to grow hemp for fuel. Hemp is the only domestic answer as an alternative source of energy for the United States. Hemp will not completely erase our dependence on foreign oil, but it will slow down our voracious appetite for fossil fuel. By lowering demand and the amount of fossil fuel consumed in this country, we will help to keep the price of oil inexpensive for some time to come. Without hemp, the industrialized world will be forced to secure this precious resource militarily. If demand continues to rise while supplies continue to diminish, prices will skyrocket and any nation with the ability to do so will be forced into sending military around the world to protect the energy.

One would think that the campaign to eradicate marijuana would have accomplished something by now, with all of the money that has been spent on it. The War on Drugs, started in 1972 under President Nixon, hasn't accomplished much towards elimination of the plant as was promised. In fact, that plant has evolved and become more widely known as a result of the prohibition. Nixon didn't understand why Jews and Leftists were smoking, but he thought that creating a war against these people was a way to save his presidency. The president dedicated the resources of the most powerful nation on earth against this weed—by all means, it really should not be here anymore, but alas, marijuana is stronger than ever, bearing fruit and being harvested 12 months a year.

I think the plant is thriving to save us from our industrial nightmare. We have polluted our living space with the overuse and abuse of petrochemicals. Hemp permits our technologic society to operate cleanly. That is why the plant is successful despite the war against it. Native prophets such as Hopi elders, Wovoka and Black Elk saw an end coming to their societies and their traditional way of living, but they also had visions of a new beginning. Many people think that we are nearing the biblical End Times of John's Book of Revelation. The Native prophets saw people of different colors and cultures coming together around a *plant of understanding*. That plant is *cannabis*.

This plant was to replace the buffalo that the prophets had seen dying. Over 60,000,000 individual buffaloes were killed, and the animal almost went extinct in North America. The U.S. government realized the best way to control the Indians of the Central Plains was to destroy their source of income. The buffalo provided food, clothing, and shelter. They were the center of the Natives' spiritual world, as well. The vision of the prophets is that there will be a plant to replace the buffalo. *Cannabis* is the only plant in the world that will provide food, clothing, and shelter. Marijuana is also a big part of peoples' spiritual life.

Hemp is a vital resource that enables mechanized communities to survive off the grid. This plant provides for so many needs. Please, if you trust my story and me, then do something about ending prohibition. Let my willingness to risk my freedom be proof that this plant has the potential to reverse the abusive path we are treading on. If we as a society unleash the healing properties of this plant, we will reap the rewards of healthier citizens and an improved planet.

218

To be Native anywhere in the world requires loving the land that you are on so much that you wouldn't think of defiling it. I consider myself a Native American because this continent is my home. It is possible to become Native anywhere you live in the world. One way to be closer to the land you live on is to grow something. Experiencing first-hand the reciprocal relationship humans have with plants is the first step in the process of going Native. What better plant to grow than marijuana—a plant that alters your awareness and helps you to realize your connection to other.

Section II

420 Guardians save the Leaves of the Tree for the Healing of Nations...

SECTION II

420 Elders: Navigation in a World Blinded by Greed

Marijuana Dealer's Guide

Growing marijuana: Marijuana is a plant, a weed, and it grows most everywhere. Growing it outside is the easiest, but indoor is not hard either. The fact is, the seed has evolved for millions of years and knows exactly what to do. When growing pot, take some advice from Bobby McFerrin: "Don't worry, be happy." The plant can feel your vibes.

If you are growing out of doors in soil, drop the seed in the ground about a quarter of an inch deep, making sure that it will receive at least five hours of direct sunlight per day. Give your plants plenty of water, and every once in a while, sing to them. Even though it may feel silly at first, the results will show.

Marijuana is a plant with two sexes. I have grown hermaphroditic plants, ones that show signs of both sexes, but for the most part, marijuana plants are either male or female. The plant has produced two sexes as part of its reproductive strategy. The trigger that turns your plant either male or female is the diminishing light caused by the changing of the seasons that occurs from spring to summer. Think of this as nature's biological time clock.

People in the Northern Hemisphere familiar with the sun's locations as it rises and sets along the horizon notice how the sun moves north until the Summer Solstice, June 21, marking the first day of summer when it begins moving south again. When the sun is moving north, the daylight hours get longer and longer. As the sun moves south, the days get shorter and shorter until the Winter Solstice on December 21 (it is the reverse in the Southern Hemisphere).

The plant, like all living organisms, seeks to reproduce itself. Part of the purpose of all life is its perpetuation. The way most flowers reproduce is through pollination, seed production, and dissemination. Some plants attract bees to help them reproduce in a system that scientists call "co-evolutionary," meaning two distinct species influence each other's development. This usually takes place when each species gains something in the process. Humans can be one of the species in this co-evolutionary process. Human intervention is the reason there are so many varieties of dogs, as well as strains of marijuana.

Marijuana has discovered a new way to reproduce itself. Part of its evolutionary strategy has been to influence human consciousness. Marijuana and other hallucinogens such as psilocybin or peyote have a way of showing the users the connectedness of the universe. This unique consciousness-altering feature within the make-up of the plant has caused humans in record numbers to cultivate pot. The inflated profit created by prohibition has induced millions of people to try their luck at growing a money tree.

Humans aid in the plant's evolution, whether starting from seed or cloning. Individuals influence the characteristics of each new generation as they choose different methods of propagation for the plant. Naturally, this plant births its next generations with seed. Marijuana seed grows in the part of the plant that is smoked, the female buds or flowers; however, the best marijuana to smoke is a female flower without seeds.

The plant starts to show its reproductive organs, sex, when it is time to reproduce. The light is reduced, and the plant feels "fall" coming on. A male plant has balls that look like bunches of grapes and the female plant has beautiful flowers that resemble little green golf balls or buds. When growing a medicinal herb, the male plant should be removed the moment it is recognized to be male. Clones are almost always the same as the "mother," the plant the clone was taken from. To make a clone, one simply cuts a branch off a mother plant and then gets the cutting to root using various stimulants. Once the plant has rooted, it is ready to vegetate and then flower.

224

Indoor growing theory: The philosophy of indoor pioneers was to recreate the outdoors, the best possible way you can, in your closet. However, because of prohibition, the goal has become to produce the highest-grade pot with larger yields in the least amount of time. New seeds and strains have been developed that make this easier.

After a short period of plant growth in the vegetative stage, during which the plant's leaves grow quickly, cut the light back from 16 hours of lights on and eight off (some growers go 24 hours lights on in the vegetative state) to 12 hours of lights on and 12 off to simulate flowering conditions since light reduction instinctively makes the plants reproduce. Remove the male plants unless you want seeds and then you are off to the races and on your way to *sin semilla*, the Spanish words for "without seed."

Smoking marijuana is easy, too. I am recommending it to anyone who has not previously tried it or to people who want to think differently than they do now. Tribal societies' and technological societies' thinking are distinct. Industrial thinking classifies species unconnectedly rather than in relation to everything. Marijuana helps you to think like a tribal member, more universal, where everyone and everything in the world is connected by the verve.

I don't want to encourage anyone to start smoking as much as I do. Inhaling smoke is not necessarily good for your body, and even though people say marijuana is not addictive, every time my bag runs low, I always seem to call my local dealer. When the dealer arrives to collect my money and drops off the best bud in the city of Hollywood, I am grateful to give him my money. If I am not medically addicted, let's just say that I have a strong desire not to run out.

Jack Herer claims that people who smoke marijuana actually live longer because they have less stress, or at least have a way of coping with life's stresses better. If you are going to smoke for

225

recreation, the way I have found best is to smoke pot through a bong. I enjoy the snapping sounds as the ash goes crashing into the water, the red ball of flaming herb shooting down the female down-stem, and sizzling into the water. Man, that is cool. If you are a medical patient with a compromised immune system, I recommend a vaporizer. It doesn't create smoke and leaves behind no ash. This is the cleanest way to medicate one's self because the herb is not combusted.

It is possible to smoke marijuana rolled in a cigarette. This is usually called a "joint" or "doobie," and is great for traveling. The first several times I tried smoking pot, it was rolled in a joint. The bong was a little scary to me at first because it was so foreign. The bong is an ancient smoking device that filters the smoke through water. Smoking a joint is a more mellowing experience than taking bong hits. The trick to rolling a joint well is to lick your fingers and then wipe them. This allows your fingers to grab the paper for a good roll.

Then there is the pipe. Wood, metal, stone, glass, bone, or antlers are just a few of the pipe materials I have used in my lifetime. My favorite is hand-blown, change-color, heavy-walled pipes, but I have even smoked out of tin cans, toilet paper rolls, and believe it or not, apples. There is no end to the creativity when you have some weed and no pipe handy. I even rolled a dollar bill into a joint once.

Selling marijuana: Selling marijuana is life's coolest and yet trickiest jobs, and it is quite profitable. The reason for the great profit is the great risk—it is illegal. Many people sell marijuana, and it is possibly America's largest multi-level marketed business, so even though there are dangers involved, the risk and profit entice many to try anyway.

Here is my advice for anyone willing to try his or her hand at dealing marijuana. Number one, don't keep your beeper in your name (Use a pre-paid cell phone) and *only* sell to "friends." "Friends" are people who have an actual long-term interest in not seeing you go to jail for selling pot. Anyone else is not a friend.

226

You should know your "friends" for a while, their families, and the two of you should have at least two other friends in common.

If you are among those risk-takers keeping alive the seed that will save the environment, I hope you are safely putting some money away as well. This is my counsel for you dealers: Your health and family are the most important objects in the game, so take care of them first. Secondly, always count your money and weigh your pot. Trust no one! That is the unfortunate side of selling something illegal; you can't go to court or call the cops if things go wrong, so know whom you are dealing with.

It is a business, so run it well. Be honest! Make sure the bag weighs what you claim it weighs. Have the money you are supposed to have, for the people you are supposed to get it to, on time. The way to get ahead in any business is to have integrity, but it is especially important that you can trust the people you are working with in an industry where you can't trust anyone.

Don't smoke all of your profit. Be realistic, set up a business model, and stick to it. Greed is what gets everyone in trouble. Don't be greedy. If you have food, shelter, smoke, and clothes to wear, then the Creator has done His job; be thankful and realize that everything else is a bonus. We live in a "free" and capitalistic society. It has benefits and drawbacks, but the benefits outweigh the drawbacks.

One of the drawbacks is that life in this type of "Democratic American" society can be brutally hard. We are not Europe, which is practically a socialist state. Life in America is more brutal than in Europe, but freedom comes with responsibility. Not everyone can be well off in our society, but the great thing about our social order is that if you start a business, it doesn't matter who you are—rainbow-colored, rich, or poor—you are supported by a legal system that historically has been pro-entrepreneur and pro-business. Our society provides a greater degree of mobility in class ranking, while in Europe one remains in the caste into which he or she was born for life, regardless of skill or ambition.

My advice to you pot dealers reading this book in the early days of this new millennium is to realize that you are warriors. You are engaged in an epic battle of good versus evil. Please, continue to fight and use the capital generated from your covert enterprise to invest in our country and your community. My story has shown you a world of possibility. Where you go from here is up to you, but consider investing in long-term sustainable infrastructure. My personal plan is to build a vacation resort in the four corners region of our country. The concept of the resort will be based on the ideal of self-sufficiency.

Our culture: The 420 Tribe is a culture I have inherited, as much as I have helped to create. It is my culture from my family, blood relations, and spirituality. The majority of my friends, my mom, and, for crying out loud, even my little old Granny puffed herb when she was alive. Who in Southern California or the whole Southwest, for that matter, doesn't know at least one person who puffs herb?

Despite the mass numbers of marijuana smokers in this country, the government continues to choose to prosecute. Even though this is the most popular smoking herb in the world, smokers are at war with governments around the world. At first, I was an accidental warrior, not realizing I was part of a long tradition of people practicing civil disobedience in America. After several years of research and a few run-ins with the law, I realized the federal regime had declared war on me. "We need a regime change" here in the United States as President Bush was so fond of saying about Iraq prior to the war. Our next president must commit, not to bringing home the troops, but to bringing back the American farms—with hemp.

I chose to be a marijuana smoker, grower, and dealer of *cannabis* flowers, but the American government chose to make me a criminal. Contrastingly, the governments of Holland and Canada now make marijuana dealers successful business leaders. In those countries (now in Spain and other EU countries, pot smoking is no longer a crime), individuals have the freedom to smoke marijuana or not, and fewer citizens choose to smoke when it is legal. In Canada, according to *Forbes* magazine, "the government all but looks the other way because marijuana exportation provides for such a large part of British Columbia's economy."

Marijuana, Earth's medicine: In fact, marijuana can help save our forests and replace wood pulp for a majority of paper products. If drugs are the great menace to American citizens that the government claims they are, the technique being applied to fight the problem is flawed. The current government stratagem ignores the reality that *cannabis* is an important natural resource for industry.

Both illegal drugs and legal drugs, when misused, can have harmful effects on society. Any medicine that is abused can be harmful. The main problem arises when these negative effects spread beyond the individuals abusing the substances and begin to harm the family and/or community these folks live in. This has stood as the reasoning behind the Drug War, and it does have some validity. However, the criminalizing of non-violent, consensual crime erodes the legitimacy of a democratic and (supposedly) free government. I even had a hard time trying to find a credit card processing company to sell my book online because the book has a controversial political message; it is pro-pot.

When I smoke marijuana and realize the effect is rather benign when compared to some over-the-counter, controlled substances such as tobacco and alcohol, it makes me question our government's reasoning. I think, "Why am I being lied to about the effects of smoking marijuana?" When more people question the authorities on this issue, they begin to see the thinness of the argument used to continue prohibition. What might the authorities lie about next? The safety of our skies?

I know with every fiber in my body that what I am doing is right. I think the government is wrong, and rather than passively accept what the administration has dictated, I am choosing to take a stand and fight by writing this *Marijuana Dealer's Guide*. I've tried protesting, which is useful, but too slow for me, and there is no profit in it.

Dealers should not feel guilty about saving the seed that will save the planet. I love smoking pot; I don't lie about smoking *cannabis*. I don't cheat or steal to get it. I don't think God created everything on earth with the exception of this one natural plant. The bottom line for me is that all non-violent marijuana users convicted for consensual crimes should be let out of prisons right away. If I were president, this would happen. As a society, we must insist that the government stop letting violent criminals out of prison to make more room for potheads, because that is what is happening. Our justice system has become unjust.

The pipe business may only be a one billion dollar industry, according to John Ashcroft, but according to the government's own Drug Enforcement Agency, the recreational marijuana industry is larger than the television and film industry combined. It is estimated that there is over $100 billion a year transacted in marijuana trade alone. Pot smokers, stop for a moment and think. Do you spend more on books per year than pot? Is more of your money spent on weed than going to the movies? We have power in a consumer society, and we need to exercise our power.

Marijuana is the number one cash crop in all 50 states of the union. My goal is to one day be a legal multi-millionaire marijuana farmer. This goal also includes bringing back the American family farm. I take pride in America's agricultural heritage. By creating excitement for gardening, we may keep young people on their families' farms and attract new individuals to the agricultural industry. Let me tell you, from experience, growing the money tree is extremely exciting.

Every 45 seconds, another marijuana smoker is arrested in the United States. Taxpayers are paying billions of dollars to lock up users and sellers of the most popular untaxed item in the country. Eric Schlosser suggests in his book *Reefer Madness* (2003 Houghton Mifflin Company) that marijuana is a huge percentage of the Los Angeles economy (up to 20 percent), one of the largest

230

economies in the world. Marijuana most likely is the largest multi-level-marketed item in the country. I know for sure that it blows AMWAY away!

Successful people who smoke marijuana aren't standing up because they live in fear of their own government. They can afford to buy pot because they have jobs, so as long as they can get it, why protest? They don't want to risk losing their jobs or their social standing in the community for speaking out against prohibition.

My own mom, a former corporate executive, smokes weed and had to hide it from her employers. Last year, my mother was honored as the number one salesperson in her company; yet, she was hiding the fact that she enjoys smoking weed on occasion. In June 2004, my mom retired from her company and moved to Holland (Amsterdam, to be specific).

The only reason Whitney Houston sort of said "mind your own business" to America in her Barbara Walters interview was because she got busted at the airport in Hawaii with a bag of weed, so everyone knows that she puffs now. Did Whitney get in any trouble? No, she didn't get in trouble because she is rich and famous. Will anything ever come of Rush Limbaugh's drug problem? Rich and famous people don't go to jail for drugs. Only average Americans do. Whitney even fled the state after being stopped by authorities. Most Americans would wind up in jail for pulling a stunt like that, but not celebrities.

Rich and famous people don't go to jail for pot—poor and broke people do. I have known wealthy growers and dealers who were busted and did no time in jail. This is not to say that there were no consequences for their actions (they did get probation); however, they were able to avoid incarceration because they were well-to-do. The money allowed them to hire private attorneys, and that dramatically reduced the risk of serving time in a U.S. penitentiary. Unfortunately, money couldn't save Tommy Chong because the administration was intent on locking him away *as an example to people who exercise their right of free speech*. His incarceration is supposed to let future moviemakers think twice about making fun of law enforcement on film.

Our country is different than most nations in the world. This nation was established with the ethic of equality as a central theme. Money and fame have always made it possible to bend the rules or cut corners in any nation, but ours is different. Our nation has an ethos of fairness. Because of our nation's history, I have confidence that the truth will prevail.

I am taking a stand in this matter. 420 Elders will transform our society by changing the way pot smokers see themselves. I am willing to share my ideas and story, even at the risk of going to jail or alienating some important people in my life. My goal with this book is to help in this *cannabis* revolution. This is a cause I think must be championed. *The 420 Tribe is saving the world by saving the seed the world needs to survive.*

Section III

Pro-pot Republican Craig X for President...

SECTION III

Drug Warrior and Pro-Pot Republican—The Political Views of Craig X

Until pot is legal, write-in candidate **"Craig X" for president!**

March 2005

Dear Reader,

Tell your friends that you are voting for **"Craig X" for president in 2008!** To many readers, a pro-pot Republican running for president seems like a joke; well, in a way it is. I know that I can never win in the traditional system, but I do have a chance to have my message heard in this great country of ours, and that is what I am doing. In contrast to Michael Moore, I am a conservative; but like him, I am trying to make an honest buck by providing entertainment and having my political message heard at the same time.

I auditioned, but didn't make it onto the "American Candidate" reality show on Showtime, but I still think that I would make a great president. That is the great thing about America. Ordinary people still believe they can lead our country, and it is not a crime to say so. I am not sure why I was not selected for the show. I don't know if it is because I was too conservative for the producers, too droll of a character and not "electable" in their eyes, or if I was simply too cute for television. That is the horrible thing about the mainstream entertainment industry if you want to be "talent." You have absolutely no control, no say, and basically are treated like a mushroom: "kept in the dark and fed shit."

The process of selecting people for the show gave me some insight into the politics of America. I met a group of conservative people who voted for Bush in the last election who were sincerely concerned about our country, and all of them thought that they would make a better president of the United States of America than Bush. I thought I could do a better job as president than George Bush, but I voted for him this last election.

However, I am not part of the party system. Living in Hollywood, most of my friends are Democrats. I am a registered Republican, but I like to think of myself as a Republican with Libertarian Party values. I have Libertarian views like the majority of my Democratic friends, but we are divided between the two current parties with all of the money and power. Also, people tend to belong to the party their parents belonged to in a very slavish way, similar to the inclination of keeping your parents' religion without thinking about God for yourself. "I am [fill in the blank] religion because that is how I was raised."

I actually am no different. My father is a Republican, but my mom is a Democrat. Personally, I am glad Bush beat Kerry, and not because I am Republican. I believe that our nation has been in the War on Terror longer than we realize. Bush has brought that war to the surface by giving it a name. My biggest issue with Bush and his running mate are their connection to the Saudis, the weapons and oil industries, and the appearance of impropriety that it creates for our country abroad and at home.

I think that Bush is an honorable man, and I like many of his policies. I am a Reagan Republican: small government, lower taxes, and a strong defense. After seeing *Fahrenheit 911*, to the shock of my Democratic friends, I am still a Republican, and for the most part, approve of the job President Bush is doing; however, I think more than ever that I could do a better job after he is gone. One of the greatest things that the "American Candidate" show did for me was force me to take written positions on popular political topics and imagine myself as president of the United States.

I am a conservative, so if you are a "U.N. pussy," you may disagree with me, but I am open enough to share my opinions. The following pages are my answers to some of the show's application questions. My answers here represent my political views. Keep in mind that no one is paying me for my ideas or opinions except you, the reader/buyer of my book. I do have a point of view, but it is mine and not brought to you by multi-national corporations. I am grassroots and homegrown.

I am publishing my book myself, and by the way, thank you for buying it. I am trying to sell ads inside the book to make it more homegrown and to offset the self-publishing costs. Capitalism is great and I am lowering my risk by accepting ads, but the book was written before any ads were accepted or solicited, so the content of the story has not been altered to fit any advertiser's needs or demands.

Craig X Rubin

"Each time a man stands up for an ideal, or acts to improve the lot of others, or strikes out against injustice, he sends forth a tiny ripple of hope. Crossing each other from a million different centers of energy and daring those ripples build a current that can sweep down the mightiest walls of oppression and resistance."
—Robert F. Kennedy

WEDGE ISSUES

In my opinion, these are the issues that politicians use to separate themselves from their competition. This doesn't mean that these are the most important issues of the day, but they are the ones that the producers of the show asked the applicants, and they reflect what the modern media is interested in.

ABORTION: As president, I will use all of the government's moral authority to lower the rate of unwanted pregnancies. This is an extremely important issue. I would not use the issue to exploit people and divide them into separate camps for political gain as is currently being done. The reason mainstream politicians exploit small differences between themselves and their opponents is that, on most issues, they tend agree with each other. By finding and exploiting divisive issues, they are able to distinguish themselves from their opponents. With Bush and Kerry in 2004, no matter who loses, Skull and Bones (and Imperial America) win. I simply find that weird.

Getting back to the issue, I personally am not for abortion. I don't think people who are pro-choice are "for abortion." I support a woman's right to choose. I support every American's right to choose. When I am president, I will use the power of the office to make this "choice" a less attractive option without penalizing women who choose this option.

In my opinion, there are too many abortions performed in this country and something needs to be done about it. Abortion is not

238

an acceptable form of birth control. The first step I will take to reduce the number of abortions performed in this country is to use the authority of the White House to encourage good moral values.

I will publicly fund abortion clinics, giving free and safe abortions to all women asking for them. No one wants to force women to seek unsafe abortions. However, I will give pro-life advocates plenty of free speech and office space within walls of those publicly funded clinics to encourage young women not to choose the abortion option. As president, I'll commit to helping women who choose to birth their children. It is proven to be less expensive to create incentives for good behavior than to deal with the anti-social behavior of neglected children later. Our jails are full of adults who were neglected or abused as children. A poor upbringing is not an excuse for anti-social behavior, but healthier families would reduce the numbers of neglected youth in America, thereby reducing prison costs later.

I will bring pro-choice and pro-life forces together to lower the number of abortions performed in America, which is something both sides would agree is a positive step. Pro-choice people are not pro-abortion; they are mostly concerned with the health of women. Pro-life people have to admit that even when abortion was banned in this country, women still sought the procedure. If abortion were suddenly banned, women would still seek the procedure and, more than likely, in unhealthy and unsafe ways.

I will create incentives to encourage proper prenatal care and make adoption a more attractive option. Our country will be better off without abortion, but I would not prohibit it. As a nation, we should coach young pregnant women and potential fathers seeking the government's assistance how to enter the work force, how to be in healthy relationships, and how to be responsible parents. If parents of originally unwanted pregnancies choose to keep their children, they will be better able to handle that responsibility. If they choose to put their children up for adoption, hopefully, the biological parent(s) will make more responsible choices in the future.

GAY MARRIAGE: This may or may not be an important issue for the government to tackle, but it has become a national issue because homosexuals have so much money and we live in a capitalistic society in which money talks. I think that this is actually a small issue because the percentage of people who are homosexual, while significant in number, is still relatively small. On the other hand, marijuana smokers make up a huge percentage of the population. They are affected by society's laws and discriminated against more than homosexuals. The fact that pot smokers are less organized than homosexuals is the only reason "gay marriage" is a bigger issue. Pot smokers certainly have money or pot wouldn't be America's number one cash crop.

I believe in the separation of church and state. I *don't* think the government should regulate marriage. Marriage is a religious institution and should be handled by religious people. The federal government's mandate is to handle taxing and defense. The government, when I am commander-in-chief, will promote domestic partnership rights for all. These rights will be granted similar to how "corporate charters" are issued.

Americans on the "left" and "right" both recognize the benefit to society that stable family units provide. It is in our national interest to promote strong family units. The family is the foundation of our nation, or any society for that matter. The government under my leadership will not issue marriage contracts, but will support the family by issuing and regulating "domestic partnership agreements," with tax incentives that encourage stable, healthy, and happy homes.

Domestic partners will be granted tax breaks (the true authority of the federal government) because it is in the best interest of our society that people commit to long-term relationships. These tax privileges will not come cheaply. Divorce is rampant and easy in our culture, and it is not good for our nation. Therefore, the financial cost of terminating "domestic partnerships" will be high. This will force all people to think twice before entering into this type of arrangement.

This type of solution keeps the government out of people's business and out of religion. It also doesn't mix government's institutions with religious institutions. Marriage is in the Bible and is a sacred religious act. Marriage should have nothing to do with the government. However, it is in our nation's paramount interest to encourage fidelity and lasting relationships. Children raised in stable, loving environments are more likely to be healthier, secure, and happier. As a nation, we want happy, healthy, and secure children, which is true national security. Our Constitution states that discrimination is illegal, and our experience tells us this is wrong.

RACE RELATIONS: I do not support affirmative action. I do support diversity at publicly funded, higher learning institutions, but to base it on the false assumption of race is antiquated. We need to have *economic* diversity in this country and make sure that all Americans have a chance to achieve the "American Dream."

I think that there is only one race, and that is the human race. I would, however, take into consideration the top-to-bottom make-up of a large corporation that was to be awarded a significant government contract. I would not be looking for a specific quota, but I would like the companies that do business with the government to reflect the country as a whole.

THE DEATH PENALTY: I don't think the federal government should administer the death penalty except where proscribed by the Constitution. I do, however, think forced labor—just short of torture—is okay for some heinous criminals.

LEGALIZATION OF DRUGS: I think the Drug War is a dismal failure, and it has turned some law enforcement agencies dangerously close to criminal organizations themselves. I would change the focus of America's battle against drugs to a battle against drug addiction.

I would examine the level of addiction to prescription drugs as part the effort to fight drug abuse in our country. I would fund clinics rather than jails. Rush Limbaugh is a prime example of how prescription drugs are being sold illegally. "Doctor shopping" is too common, and it seems as if the drug companies know that. The profiting drug companies and manufactures don't support regulation that would curb abuse. Rush is also an example of how someone can clean up without going to jail. The government in Florida is wasting tax money that could be better spent (or not taken from taxpayers in the first place) by trying to prosecute this man.

I understand the policy of equal justice for the rich and poor. I want that principle applied, but I don't want to see poor people go to jail for drug abuse either. What forced Rush to clean up his act? In my opinion, it was public pressure and not more guns, not more police, not jail time, not monetary fines, and not George Bush or John Ashcroft. What got Rush to clean up? In my opinion, the fact that the public (his audience) knew he was using drugs (not the government). When it became public and he was embarrassed for being an addict, he decided to clean himself up, and supposedly he did. It is not my business whether or not he really did. It is his life. It is his business.

My first solution for the Drug War would be to immediately end the prohibition on hemp and its medicinal flower, marijuana. I will make the legal age to purchase marijuana 18 years old. Art Garfunkel was stopped with pot in his car last year, 2004.

Do we as a society need to send him or any other entertainer who smokes pot to jail? We would not have had all the great music of the 1960s if we had thrown every musician who smoked pot in jail. What about the guy who grew Art Garfunkel's weed...do we, as a society, need to send him or her, the grower, to jail? I don't think so. I think we need to tax and regulate the commercial production of America's admitted number one cash crop, and I am the guy to do it!

242

"Vast Right Wing Hypocrisy"

Gogue

GUN CONTROL: I think every American over the age of 13 years old should know how to control a gun. As president, I will make gun control a mandatory class in high school. Every student will know that upon their 18th birthday, they have as an inalienable right, the right to bear arms. They will know what freedom is. This great country of ours is great because it has faith in its citizens. This was unique in the world at the time our Founding Fathers wrote the Constitution. They felt this was important enough to make it second among the amendments in our Bill of Rights behind freedom of speech, the press, and religion. I will emphasize the Second Amendment to students. The reason the Founding Fathers created this amendment was to protect our country from tyrants.

The gun control education will stress that with all rights come responsibilities. I will find community leaders who will come into the schools and teach these gun classes. These community leaders will teach the students ethics and about community responsibility. These "teachers" will be sort-of-forced volunteers from the community and not on the payroll of the local school board. The teachers will be chosen at each school by a secret ballot of students. The candidates won't have to run. They will be chosen from among the parents of the students. There should be one "mentor," acting as community leader per one hundred students, and each mentor should have a paid assistant. This is not a replacement for school counseling, but in addition to. Additionally, when I am president, in order to receive a high school diploma, high school seniors will need to learn by memory the Constitution of the United States of America and the Bill of Rights.

Local police should educate the chosen community leaders on gun safety. At once, all students will be learning proper gun control, ethics, and community responsibility. This will be a mandatory class for all four years of high school. With a program like this, I don't think we would see a Columbine situation in America again or much crime.

IMMIGRATION: Immigration and guns are what made this country great. I will not ban either. As far as illegal immigration is concerned, I look at it this way: If the minimum wage in Canada were $78 dollars an hour (what American wages are in comparison and on scale to the average Mexican peasant who crosses the border), Americans would be lining the streets of the Great White North looking to rake in some of that gold. I am from California, a state built by a gold rush. People move to where there are opportunities to live better.

We need to control our borders, but we also need to grant special privileges to the Native Americans of Mexico who are migrating here illegally. Rich European Mexicans who run and own everything in Mexico are not sneaking over our borders. Poor Native American peasants are flooding into our country by the millions. "Real" politicians can't even say this because it is not politically correct, but it is the truth. If you ask the Mayans, they say they have colonies all over the United States. So do other Native American ethnicities or tribes from south of the border. Nahuatl, Zapoteco, Otomi, Yauqi, and others are consciously colonizing North America in the style and tradition of the

Europeans. The most important question the U.S. needs to ask is, "Why is our neighboring country being run so poorly that millions of its citizens want to leave?"

Our economy is demanding their blood and sweat to keep growing, and yet the nation doesn't want to pay the full bill for their services. As a nation, we should not treat these "guest workers" and their children as second-class citizens, but we are. That is a fact, and it will lead to an apartheid system similar to South Africa's or the system that exists in Mexico today if it continues. I think the path we are heading down is leading to inequality in the future and we must reset our direction if we are to maintain our values.

We need to care for the Native American children as their parents care for our homes, restaurants, businesses, and our children. But we shouldn't have to pay for them on the backs of our poor people, closing public hospitals and blaming immigration. If we create a divided system in America, we will be building a divided house. In a system like that, any nation will fall prey to petty tyrants and be terrorized by an out-of-control population. We need to rise above the racism that underlies some of the fear and look at a new way to deal with Mexico and its Native American populations.

We cannot support law-breaking (illegal immigration) and don't want terrorists sneaking into our country, so we must control the borders. The only way I see to do this is to stop letting our neighbor, Mexico, run the country so corruptly. We no longer accept that type of behavior from tyrants half a world away. Why should we accept it from the rich oiligarchy (misspelling is intentional) in Mexico?

The Mexican ruling class needs to treat its own huddled masses better so they are not flooding over our borders. Our nation should respect the treaty of Guadeloupe Hidalgo and grant the Native Americans of Mexico the ability to work and travel on both sides of the border more freely. Most Mexican immigrants want to return home after making money here, but as we tighten our borders, the cost of going back and forth becomes prohibitive. Our regulations are forcing more illegal immigration than we can handle. There is a solution, and it starts with our neighbors running their country better and it ends with Americans realizing who exactly is coming over our borders.

THE ENVIRONMENT: The environment is a wonderful place to live. We should not harm it. I am recovering right now from skin cancer on my back and shoulder. One hundred years ago, skin cancer was not as common as it is today. Since hemp was prohibited in 1937, our environment has deteriorated as a result of over-use of fossil fuels. That will end when I am POTUS (President of the United States).

THE ECONOMY: To improve the economy, I will do as Ronald Reagan did. I will lower taxes. The policy of letting Americans keep more of the money they earn is not only right, it stimulates the economy. I will bring back some of the manufacturing that was sent overseas by providing incentives to companies to bring those jobs to America and not the other way around as is the current policy.

Currently, the federal government spends about $200 per U.S. citizen fighting drugs in the Drug War, which is mostly a war on pot (80 percent of all drug arrest are for marijuana). I will end that and double George Bush's tax cut. You'll keep more of your money at home when I am president.

Cheap gas is a good way to keep our economy going smoothly, as well. I will work with oil-producing countries to keep the petroleum lines full and flowing while at the same time making a coordinated effort to end our oil-based economy with an energy source that is more compatible with the long-term health of our economy and environment. I'll work to create global cooperation among petroleum-producing countries so that they'll be involved in developing alternative energies as their limited resources begin to shrink. This will lessen the likelihood that oil-producing nations will think that they need territorial expansion to survive when their oil is gone.

I will reduce our dependency on foreign oil by ending the prohibition on hemp. This will save the federal government billions of dollars. I will change the focus of our nation's drug policy to fighting chemical dependency. I will commit government monies towards substance addiction rehabilitation and less on the costlier incarceration.

It will be my goal to build the self-esteem of our nation's youth so drugs and unwanted pregnancy become less of an issue in the future. I think many of these problems are the result of poor self-esteem and lack of self-awareness. My belief is that many children in public schools are in the wrong learning environment. The day of public education factories pumping out good workers is coming to an end. My administration would promote school vouchers and results in education. Currently, too much money is being wasted in the administration of education and not enough on the basics.

I am not going to lie and say if you elect me, all of society's ills will end as past leaders have done. I promise to make our nation a better place to live and Americans a better people. My administration's justice department will focus on criminal behavior such as driving under the influence, petty crime, grand larceny, and corporate fraud. I will not focus on the small-time users of drugs. I am aware of the harm caused by drug abuse, but I think prohibitions in a free society cause greater harm to our society. The Drug War has been especially detrimental to our economy.

I will follow the example of corporate gadfly John Gilbert and try to bring more democracy to American corporations when it comes to dealing with stockholders. There needs to be a strict code of ethics when it comes to running our nation's public companies whose stocks are traded around the world. Our nation's reputation and stability is tied to the soundness and leadership of these vast ships navigating the world's economic waters. If we are to lead the world politically, we need to raise business leaders who will represent our nation with honor and grace.

EDUCATION: All for it! I don't think the federal government should get too involved in the local education curriculum. That should be handled on a community level except for special civics classes (for example, the gun control classes talked about earlier) that promote the Constitution of the United States and create a common bond for all of America's youth.

When I am POTUS, for K-12 the federal government will provide each student with a voucher. Parents will be allowed to choose religious schools, but the voucher will be based on results of the education tested on a national level. State governments will cover additional costs. The rest of the educational budget should come from county and city governments, as well as national service performed by 11th and 12th graders.

We should not reward failure at any level, but we need to reward success at every level. I am for creating a national scholarship based on standardized tests for college-level education, thereby opening the road to higher education for more people. Education is the pathway to opportunity. I support a free education for all school-age children and think the best and most fair way to accomplish this is with a voucher program. I think that all high school upper classmen and women should perform some sort of national service for the free education that they have been provided. This service should be part of 11th and 12th grade. We should not be afraid to send our adult children (ages 16-18) to different parts of their home state. They will grow from the experience and their work will be a significant contribution to their states. Plus, they'll have the opportunity to meet their fellow citizens.

Children enrolled in private school (with the voucher program, all schools will be private) will not be exempt from national service. When I am the president, high school upper classmen and women (juniors and seniors) will perform community service before they are allowed to obtain full-privilege driver's licenses and high school diplomas.

SOCIAL SECURITY: Social Security is a good idea, but not a good safety net. I would encourage personal savings. I would keep Congress's hands out of the savings account of our nation's elderly citizens. I am not going to rely on the government for my retirement, and I don't think anyone should have to.

I will encourage people to invest in our nation's businesses by giving great rewards, in the form of tax incentives, for people who save for their own futures. I will create public housing for elderly citizens. There will be elderly homes within normal public housing projects. Old people should not be segregated to living alone. This program will be a safety net for those who didn't plan well, but it will not be free; and able seniors in these homes will be asked to assist in local schools.

I am going to use the office of the presidency to inspire compassion for old people. I cared for my grandmother as she grew old, and I was holding her hand as she gave up her spirit and passed from this world. I talked to her through her death and gave the eulogy at her funeral. We need older people in our society as much as they need us. They are an important link to our past, a living heritage, and they will have a role in my administration.

WAR ON TERRORISM: The war on terror will not end soon. There are many people who wish to destroy what the United States has built. The new Bush doctrine as I understand it is that "the U.S. will no longer support and benefit from the rule of ruthless dictators." We are washing our hands clean and starting down a new path that I think is good for the future of the world.

Cult-like ideals taking hold in the U.S. or abroad are scary and a risk one takes in a free society. One of the dangers these secret societies (small cults or occult groups) pose is terrorist violence because they don't have access to state violence. Groups that don't have access to military power fight an armed conflict with terror because it is a cheap and effective tool. Look at what the "D.C. sniper" did with $20 worth of bullets, an inexpensive car, and a pawnshop rifle.

Small extremist groups will persist in committing violent acts of terror if they are not stopped. The question is, "How much are we willing to sacrifice freedom for security?" If our nation chooses to forfeit our freedoms for "security," we will have neither. The last time I flew, August of 2004, a guy with blue rubber gloves stuck his hand down my underwear. He was searching me at the Seattle airport. Is this for terrorism or drugs? I was wearing a pot leaf shirt. I was coming from the Seattle Hempfest. Do you still think he was looking for bombs? This is one of the most important questions facing the next president. Do we lie to our own citizens or tell them the truth?

This is where President Bush has most failed us as a nation. He has allowed the War on Terror to be muddled by the War on Drugs. George Walker Bush has taken away rights from Americans while Osama Bin Laden is still free or will be for a little longer. Americans have been charged as terrorists for running strip clubs and using chemicals in the small-time production of illegal drugs, yet Bin Laden is still free as of this writing. Where is our national security apparatus?

CONNECT THE DOTS

WAR IN IRAQ: I don't think that the U.S. should be rebuilding historic Babylon. We don't want to be seen as a conquering force, but we are. As a nation, we need to accept the facts. Yes, it is true that Iraq may be better off and that Iraq under Saddam was not the great place Michael Moore paints it to be in his film. But, the fact remains: We are an empire. Part of the reason we liberated the Iraqi people is that we wanted to stabilize the availability of a necessary natural resource. There is an incredible computer game that explains our predicament. It is called "Imperialism"; other games are "Risk" and "Rise of Nations." In these games, the country that develops and controls the most oil, land and technology wins—either through conquest or negotiation—typically through a not-so-delicate combination of both. These are my favorite games. I have taken over the world countless times.

I would never turn over Iraq to a weak and confused United Nations or to a leadership there that hates us. At the moment, we are the world empire. Our empire requires economic stability, and oil is the fuel that stabilizes the global engine. That is a fact. I don't like it, but it is true, and Americans need to start quickly dealing with the truth because we no longer have the luxury of living in ignorant bliss. We have an oil addiction and if we are to overcome it we must stop living in denial.

The question then becomes, "Should we rob the Iraqi people blind for their oil?" I know $1.00 a gallon for gas sounds great, but is it realistic? Advisors to President Bush want to price oil at $182 a barrel to slow down the out-of-control world consumption, where the U.S. is the number one user of oil. I think that we should pay the nation of Iraq a fair price for their oil, and they will do business with us because we liberated them from Saddam. We should give them a government that won't jail or kill protesters, students, and journalists. But our military should occupy their country, building permanent bases there. The Romans would have. We will protect Iraq's democratically elected government as long as they continue to do business with us.

Our bases should remain outside of their main cultural centers the way our bases are in Japan and in other countries of the world. The Iraqi base and/or bases should be built to ensure the safety of our armed forces and the security of the resources we are there to protect. If we are to create a legitimate government there they must protect their own people. Our men will protect the fledgling democracy to ensure free elections. Once we have successfully converted our economy to substitute cleaner fuels, we will close these bases, leaving behind a society that will not threaten our stability. We should work with this new government, encouraging them to invest their money in alternative energy sources rather than extravagant palaces and weapons. Therefore, when the oil does run out (and it will) Iraqis will have a new source of income to support their people.

WELFARE: I am not for welfare lasting a lifetime. Any American should be able to go on welfare for no more than four years per 20 years. Only after a citizen is 18 years old should they be allowed to collect welfare. Poor children should be covered under a different system called "Well Child."

Our current welfare system, the permanent welfare state, is creating a nation of pussies. Hard times can fall upon anyone, but they should not last a lifetime. I see welfare for people who are permanently disabled only and even then it is questionable. When I am president, welfare fraud will be prosecuted vigorously. Children should not have to worry about irresponsible parents, and parents should not be rewarded for irresponsible behavior.

THE MIDDLE EAST: The Middle East is a mess, and I would get involved, trying to bring the different sides together. I would move the U.S. embassy to Jerusalem, the capital of Israel. My administration would learn from what was accomplished under former presidents. We would not turn our back on Israel's self-defense for cheaper oil from OPEC. I would make it a priority to solve the land and, more importantly, the water issues of the Middle East in as much as it threatens America's stability.

I would try to bring together U.S. Middle East allies. Saudi
Arabia, Jordan, and Egypt should be leaned on more heavily to
influence their neighbors because we have firm relationships with
these countries. We need to use our good relations with these
countries to encourage them influence their friends and allies in
the region. It is in our national interest to open up the society of
Saudi Arabia to some legitimate criticism. I heard a Saudi Arabian
commercial on the Los Angeles radio yesterday saying that their
kingdom was a great "friend" to America. The fact is, Jews are not
allowed into the country of Saudi Arabia, and Christian worship is
prohibited in the country.

In the Middle East today, the conflicts are over oil, blood, and land.
In the future, clean water will be the biggest issue. Already in the
United States, a bottle of drinking water can be more expensive per
gallon than gasoline. Water is more necessary for life than
gasoline. Our economy runs on gas, but that will change in the
future; our bodies need water to survive, and that will never
change. Our bodies will survive with no economy; the economy will
die without healthy humans; humans die without clean drinking
water. Those are the facts, and that is what I think of the Middle
East.

TAXES: I am going to significantly lower federal income taxes. It
is my priority and my commitment to the voters. President Bush
gave a pseudo tax refund because he ran up the debt from a
surplus. He borrowed money and called it "giving you back your
own money." I will run the country as the insurance company
USAA does, as a not-for-profit. Each year, USAA returns to
customers the unused monies from the previous year.

George Bush was elected because of his name recognition and his
connections to the Grand Old Party, but he spends like a socialist.
Our government under him is too large, and people are asked to
pay more than is necessary to have high-quality government.
Besides lowering taxes, as president I will create a way for people
to have a greater say in how their money is spent. I will make tax-

paying more democratic by changing tax forms. Each taxpayer will have a small say in where their money will be spent.

CAMPAIGN PROMISES: By Executive Order, I will end the prohibition of hemp and pardon Tommy Chong on my first day in office. I know that Tommy is already out of jail, but he should not be on probation; nor should his good name or record be tarnished with a felony.

I will work with the Legislative Branch to lower the federal income tax to a 20 percent maximum. Under my plan, every American would pay a tax, with a minimum of $100 per person. For this country to reach its potential, everyone must add something and have his or her voice heard in creating our nation. For example, a family of four would pay a minimum tax of $400. The maximum federal tax in my administration would be lowered to 20 percent, regardless of how high a person's income goes or what the source income is.

I will drastically reduce the number of abortions performed in this country. I feel strongly about this. I will not take away a woman's right to choose. In fact, the government, I think, should pay for the procedure for women who cannot afford it. If I were president, I'd work with pro-life forces to make healthy children and life a responsibility and not a choice. A large part of the unwanted pregnancy responsibility falls on upon a society that promotes promiscuity in every public arena and yet shuns biblical sayings and moral teaching in every public institution.

(Side note: To me, it is ridiculous that the Ten Commandments can't be posted in a judicial building. Where does our modern system of justice originate? Can we not publicly celebrate that? Why did President Bush not use his office and leadership position to stand up for this when it became a public issue?)

As a people, we must recognize that women seeking abortions are our nation's mothers, sisters, and daughters. They are women and not statistics. These women are usually in very difficult situations. It is obviously a difficult situation when they are forced to make

254

this choice of life or death for their own children. It must be our responsibility as a Christian nation to help these women. As a nation, we have great resources at our disposal. This should be a priority. As president, to solve this problem I will bring people together rather than exploit minor differences for political gain.

My next presidential action would be to let out of jail all non-violent criminals who are locked away for drug offenses. This would immediately save the federal government billions of dollars.

When I am elected president, I will extensively and quantifiably clean up the environment of our nation. Globally, I will take the lead in encouraging other countries to respect the Planet Earth that we all live on by immediately ending hemp prohibition worldwide.

"One has not only a legal but also a moral responsibility to obey just laws. Conversely, one has a moral responsibility to disobey unjust laws."
—Martin Luther King, Jr.

Legal Profile

ARE YOU A LEGAL RESIDENT OF THE UNITED STATES?
Yes, I am a legal resident of the U.S. of A.

HAVE YOU EVER BEEN ARRESTED OR HAD A RESTRAINING ORDER TAKEN OUT AGAINST YOU? Yes, I have been arrested, but not charged, for trespassing at the Nevada Nuclear test site on October 12, 1992. I was also arrested for calling a water pipe a "bong." The charge was "possession of drug paraphernalia," but the judge dropped the charges. However, it has kept me from purchasing a gun that day. I have to be "administratively delayed" every time I purchase a firearm.

In the bong incident the judge agreed with me that it was a matter of free speech and asked the police officers if they had any other evidence against me. The judge gave the officers more time to collect evidence, but they were unable to find evidence against me. The charges were dropped and my merchandise was returned. After that, I made the "Can't we all get a bong?" commercial that you can download on CraigX.com. I am starting to sound like a criminal; however, that is the just the life of a freedom fighter in our society.

A former girlfriend filed a restraining order against me. She is now an NPR commentator, and most of her commentaries are about her lying and cheating her way around the truth. Her name is Michele Serros. I think she is funny and beautiful, but the fact is she did file an order against me. She lied about what happened, but that will be for the reader to decide.

Check out her commentaries on the NPR Web site: www.npr.org/programs/theride/mserros/. I have not spoken with her in years, but I own her book and CD. The girl is hysterically funny, and I am a fan of hers, but she doesn't tell the truth (all of the time), and when she tells lies, her shoulder moves up and down like my youngest daughter's.

HAVE YOU EVER BEEN CHARGED WITH A MISDEMEANOR? I have been charged with a misdemeanor, the possession of marijuana, more than one time as well. The majority of the time, this was in connection with a political action.

HAVE YOU EVER BEEN CHARGED WITH A FELONY? I have never been charged with a felony. Actually, I was for about ten minutes. I was standing up for my rights in Orange County California by fighting a misdemeanor charge of marijuana possession when the prosecutors two months into the battle threw a felony at me in the hopes of scaring me into pleading guilty to the misdemeanor. When I asked the judge to bifurcate the two charges, she promptly dismissed the fraudulent felony charge.

"Everyone thinks of changing the world, but no one thinks of changing himself."
—Leo Nikolaevich Tolstoy

Personal Profile

WHAT IS YOUR CURRENT RELATIONSHIP STATUS? I am divorced, but have an amicable relationship with my ex-wife. We have joint custody of our three children, who are currently living with me in Hollywood. My ex-wife lives in Studio City.

IN WHAT U.S. CITY AND STATE WERE YOU BORN? I was born in the Golden State of California in the beautiful "City of the Angels," in English, but in Spanish, it is known by the name, "Ciudad de Los Angeles."

HOW WOULD YOU DESCRIBE YOUR ETHNIC OR CULTURAL BACKGROUND? My father is an Ashkenazi Jew born in Buffalo, New York, and my mother is a Gentile of German, Welsh, and Irish descent. My mom was born in Detroit, Michigan. Both of my parents' families moved to California when they were young in the 1940s. My folks were raised on the West Coast. I was raised Jewish and attended Hebrew school as a child. I still consider myself Jewish, but I know that Jesus was who He said He was.

The genetic reality as to my ethnicity is that we all have two parents, four grandparents, and eight great-grandparents, and this pattern of ancestors doubling continues forever back in history, making us all related. Culturally, I am an American first, but consider myself Jewish and am raising my kids to follow the Jewish traditions. We celebrate Passover, Hanukah, and Christmas. We are not affiliated with any group or church, but read the Bible every night (Old and New Covenants).

DO YOU LIVE ALONE? AND WHO DO YOU LIVE WITH AND WHAT IS THEIR RELATIONSHIP TO YOU? I do not live alone. I have three small children who live with me. My eldest daughter is Jessica Anne Rubin (eight years old; 3/12/96), my son is Christopher Avi Rubin (six years old; 5/29/98, Hebrew name Avi

257

ben Israel), and my youngest daughter is Olivia Rose Rubin (four years old; 6/08/00).

WHAT IS THE BEST THING ABOUT YOUR LIVING SITUATION? The best thing about my living situation is that, as Dr. Laura says, "I am my kid's dad." I am a father who is actively involved in his children's lives. Watching them grow is a joy, and I am grateful for the opportunity to be with them.

"Leadership is action, not position."
—Donald H. McGannon

Political Profile

HOW DO YOU DESCRIBE YOURSELF POLITICALLY?
I am a registered Republican, but I don't always vote with the party. I tend to agree with many Libertarian ideals, but I am a Republican. I would describe myself as being politically conservative, with strong environmental values. I'd like to put the "conserve" back into "conservative."

I would keep the U.S. engaged internationally, but not encourage American corporations to move overseas. I think it is insane that most of what we use these days is made in China. It is most upsetting to me that public money, tax dollars, is used to encourage corporations to leave America.

The reason I feel an affinity to the Republican Party is that I don't believe in "Big Brother" government. I think everyone should be responsible for himself or herself and not dependent upon the government. That independent spirit is what made America great, and our Republican president simply pays lip service to those values. He is much like his father, "Read my lips," saying one thing and doing another. "I will not be a nation-builder." That is why I'll do a better job than he is doing. I will be honest. We need to be nation builders right now.

My administration will let people know the truth and actually follow through on Republican values. Republicans have promoted African Americans by giving them a chance to serve in top offices that they are qualified for. Abraham Lincoln was a Republican. I think the government works for the people and not the other way around. Each person in our nation matters and should keep the money they've earned. Education is the responsibility of parents and not the government. School vouchers allow parents to choose the education that is best for each individual child. I think America is better at spreading freedom than the United Nations, which spends half of its time condemning Israel. I have faith that if the American people are properly informed, they can rise to the occasion, develop ways to conserve energy, and continue to be world leaders in business, culture, freedom, democracy, and an industrialized future.

HAVE YOU EVER RUN FOR OFFICE OF ANY KIND? I ran for public office in 1984 when I was only 18 years old. The office was a rotating city council seat on the Beverly Hills City Council. If elected, I would have been the youngest mayor of Beverly Hills. I was victorious in paying the least amount of money per vote, which shows that I know how to stretch a dollar.

IF YES, TELL US ABOUT IT: It was an interesting experience. I learned that it takes good organizational skills to get elected in the United States. I also learned that "free speech" isn't free. You are free to express yourself, but there is always a cost, and it is usually money.

IF YOU COULD DISTILL YOUR CANDIDACY TO ONE "BIG IDEA," WHAT WOULD IT BE? I want our country to be the leader of the next millennium because our values, our stated values, are more idealistic than any other nation in the world. Our system is not always fair to every single individual (no system is perfect), but our system is free. If we are to remain free, we must get our domestic house in order. As president, I will make clear distinctions between the Drug War and the War on Terror so that our freedom at home is not compromised in any way.

I will end the Drug War and begin to find better ways to deal with the issue of chemical dependency, including pharmaceutical drugs. With the War on Terror, I will pursue it vigorously and go after countries harboring terrorists. Our nation will save billions ending the spurious Drug War.

I would ask Rush Limbaugh to be our next Drug Tzar because he has experience quitting extremely addictive drugs; he has the experience and the ability to articulate the danger of drugs. If I am elected, Rush will be asked to join the team. I bet he would, too, because he is a patriot who values service to the nation. He seems as if he genuinely cares about America, and Americans, and his leadership could be valuable on this issue.

WHY WOULD YOU WANT TO BE PRESIDENT? I want to be POTUS because I think I can do a better job than the current president is doing leading our nation into the future. He is leading us into deep debt. He is not leading us down a path for long-term security when it comes to the economy. He is not being honest about America's energy policy.

My presidency will show people around the world that American democracy truly is the way to govern society because leaders are chosen among the most qualified and not from the best connected. In our country, average Americans really do decide who is given the privilege of leadership. In America, leadership doesn't have to come from the moneyed class. Citizens with vision and skill to communicate should be given an opportunity to serve in the highest offices of the land regardless of family connections or wealth.

Our nation has been blessed with wealth and political freedom. This country further stands above other countries is that America is not a land of royal birth. Anyone can win an election to become mayor of his or her town or even president of the United States. Of course, in this country (as in any other), it helps if you are related to the ruling class. A last name like Bush, Gore, or Kennedy helps. The same way it helps in Hollywood if your last name is

Barrymore, but it is not essential. America is great because our citizens are great. Americans as a people are great because we hold certain truths to be self-evident.

WHY WOULD YOU BE A GOOD PRESIDENT? I would not just be a good president; I will be great. I have the ability to educate and to inspire. Our greatest presidents have always encouraged great accomplishments. The great ones have also had the ability to arouse greatness in others. I will inspire our nation to do great things and Americans to be better people. I have a skill that brings out the best in others. I have leadership skills that are difficult to quantify, but somehow people are inspired by me. That is what will make me a great leader. I understand that great leaders are surrounded by good people, as well, so I will recruit the best.

My candidacy is like the first Rocky film in which Rocky goes up against the champ, Apollo Creed. If a softball player hits enough home runs, he gets to try out for the majors, and if I sell enough books the marijuana issue will be part of the next election's debate.

MY CAMPAIGN SONG: "Drug War" by Andras Jones.

MY CAMPAIGN SLOGAN: "Can't we all just get a bong?" It is thought-provoking and catchy. Plus, it sums up a major philosophy of mine.

WHO WOULD BE MY VICE PRESIDENT? For vice president, I would ask either Jesse Ventura or Newt Gingrich to join the ticket. Both of whom would make good presidents. They would also add credibility to my campaign. Jesse is an honest man and unafraid to speak his mind. My cousin worked for Newt and she respects him and from what I have seen of him on television it is obvious that he understands the issues facing America. Joe Lieberman is a loyal American and the only Democrat who I think has the integrity to be president, I might consider him as well.

These men are leaders and would lend credibility to any Executive Branch ticket. Jesse has the experience of having been a leader without belonging to a major party. Even though I am a registered Republican, I would be a party outsider, so his experience would be valuable. By choosing Lieberman, I would be bringing together a Republican and Democrat in the White House, which is not a bad thing because if elected, we'll need to work with a divided Congress. If Newt was my choice we'd be very popular because not only is he intelligent, he is likeable.

WHO SHOULD BE THE NEXT PRESIDENT OF THE UNITED STATES? If I am *not* elected president, I would like to see Jesse Ventura elected POTUS. I think he is qualified. That is why I would ask him first to be my vice president.

WHO WILL SUPPORT OR JOIN MY CAMPAIGN? The people who will be supporting my campaign fall within the demographics of typical American voters. I am a candidate for the future and will appeal to younger voters who want to hear the truth about our country.

Democrats will support me because many of them have libertarian leanings and want a rational policy on the Drug War.

Republicans will support me because I am more of a Republican than Bush. I am pro-business, for less government, lower taxes, and government-funded private education. Most importantly, I am all about keeping the government out of your personal business.

Libertarians, Independents, and Greens will as support me because I am a true outsider. I am for ending the Drug War and I am pro-environment.

Millions upon millions upon millions of marijuana smokers searching for a voice will support me. These are the people I hope will get out and work for my campaign. I am going to turn their little individual puffs of smoke into a cloud of protest that will sweep across the country. Our message will be like a giant rain cloud pouring down the truth about hemp.

IF YOU COULD PASS ANY LAW AT THIS MOMENT, WHAT WOULD IT BE? I would pass a law lowering the maximum tax bracket for all Americans. I would make the federal income tax no more than 20 percent. No one should have to work for his or her government for three months a year (20 percent is 2.4 months). We are not slaves. The people created the government, not the other way around.

Americans do not choose to enslave themselves, and that is why I'd lower taxes. As a people, we escaped the tyranny of a king when we rebelled against England. Are we going to create another tyrant, the taxman, here in the U.S.? "Thank God that we don't get the government we pay for," is what my dad says. I'd like to make the government more accountable for how money is spent and wasted.

IF YOU COULD REPEAL ANY LAW AT THIS MOMENT, WHAT WOULD IT BE? If I could repeal a law, it would be the law prohibiting the domestic cultivation of hemp. This law is holding back vital experimentation that will save our ancient forests and lead to other developments of environmentally friendly products for food, fuel, fiber, medicine, and more.

IF YOU COULD CHANGE ONE THING ABOUT OUR POLITICAL SYSTEM, WHAT WOULD IT BE? Unruly and as influenced by money as it is, it is a very good system. I would try to create more democracy for the average American citizen. It is my belief that the only true power the federal government has is the ability to tax and spend.

I would allow the taxpayers to commit a certain percentage of their tax to a specific department of government that they choose when filing and paying taxes. For example, the percentage that is of the citizen's choosing would be divided by percentage into the Department of Health, Education, Defense, and/or any other department budget. Voting with your tax dollars is direct democracy in a capitalist society. This process empowers the citizenry by involving the taxpayer.

WHAT, IF ANY, ORGANIZATIONS ARE YOU OPPOSED TO AND WHY? I am opposed to Al-Qaeda, Al-Quiada, Al-Kaida. No matter how you say it or spell it, I am opposed to them. I am also opposed to any group or organization that declares war on America and attacks us.

WHO IS YOUR HERO AND WHY? Jesus is my hero. By birth, I am only half Jewish, but culturally, I was raised Jewish. I didn't learn anything about Jesus' life (other than that He came back from the dead) until I was an adult. I am still Jewish, but Jesus is my hero. I think the way He knowingly sacrificed His life to accomplish His mission here on earth was admirable. The way He was fearless in the face of man's authority, not rebellious or revolutionary, but fearless is an example that I try to follow. He didn't come to change God's law. He came and made it simpler by pointing out the two most important laws: one, love God with all of your heart and might; and two, love each other the same way. They are pretty simple rules in my book, and I follow them.

In the USA, the power to govern comes not from God, but from the people, via the vote. The power to be heard comes from the media that is interested usually in one thing, money. Therefore, it is difficult for people without great resources (money) to practice free speech. Without the ability to practice free speech on a mass scale, it is difficult to be elected to national office. Hence, the Catch-22 position that anyone seeking office is in, so I want to say "thank you" to buyers of my book for this opportunity to run for the office of president.

I think running for president takes great courage. I think George Bush is a brave man and has done his best job and has not done too badly by America. I think I could do a better job for the American people. It is my admiration for Jesus and His fearlessness in the face of danger that gives me the courage to take on this challenge. It will be risky to my life and I will be sacrificing privacy simply by deciding to write such a controversial book. Having grown up here

264

in Hollywood surrounded by famous people, I am aware of the double-edged sword of fame.

The odds of me winning as president are extremely miniscule and to say differently would sound foolish, but I am grateful for my country and the opportunity to try. I have faith that it is possible. Stranger things have happened on this planet, so I'll put my faith in my hero's example and trust God that it is possible.

IF YOU WERE GIVEN A MILLION DOLLARS, WHAT WOULD YOU DO WITH IT? I would buy land in Northern Arizona and build infrastructure. First, I would put in a micro-solar electrical generating plant, several wells, and water storage facilities. Then I would grow a garden and raise my children where the air is clean, the water plentiful, and songs come rolling off the tongue. I would stay home, hire tutors, and teach my children myself. Maybe I would open up some of the land for camping to tourists visiting the nearby Indian reservations and local sights, eventually turning the place into a resort.

WHY I WILL BE FEARED? Honesty is why I will be feared as president. I am not going to keep things from the American people, using national security as an excuse when that is not the case. For example, why is John Lennon's FBI file still being held, edited, and blacked out? This type of behavior leads to distrust of the government. As president, I will open John Lennon's files to the public so that the public may learn the truth that our government had nothing to do with his death, if that is the truth.

If there were a political assassination that occurred, I would allow the truth to come out and declare that our country would no longer do that as a practice. I would apologize to the world on behalf of our nation and move on. There is no reason a rock star's FBI files should be blacked out with the excuse of "national security" more than 20 years after his death. I don't believe our government had anything do with it, but I, too, want to know the truth.

WHY I WILL BE LOVED? Honesty is why I will be loved, as well. I think it is the reason people like Jesse Ventura and John McCain. They don't lie to you; they tell the truth, and it shows in their popularity. I will be like them, calling it as I see it. Even when people disagree with me, they will respect me for telling them the truth on where I stand on the issue. I won't give political answers in which I agree to both sides at once, the way John Kerry does. I will be a leader who takes a position he thinks is right and then acts firmly on that belief, similar to President George W. Bush in that you know where he stands on an issue, agree or disagree with him, the President let's you know where he stands on an issue.

IN MY WHITE HOUSE, THERE WILL BE: Hemp growing in the Rose Garden.

IN MY WHITE HOUSE, THERE WILL NOT BE: There will not be lobbyist and campaign donors trying to collect favors for their contributions because I am not taking any contributions. I am a capitalist and will use whatever resources I have on my own to run for high office.

IF YOU WERE PRESIDENT, WHAT PUBLIC HOLIDAY WOULD YOU INTRODUCE? National Hemp Awareness Day, only I'd hire someone clever to come up with a fancier name.

WHO IS YOUR FAVORITE AMERICAN PRESIDENT? Ronald Reagan is my favorite American POTUS. He inspired me to care about our country and made me realize what made our country great. Our country is great because we have set high ideals for ourselves in our Constitution, and Americans are good people who have strived to live up to those values. When there is a disaster, Americans are the first to help.

This includes the fact that we are a nation of immigrants. Americans know what it is to be a stranger in a strange land. President Reagan taught me that "You can go to Germany and never become German, Japan or China and never become Japanese or Chinese, but you can come from any little country on the entire planet and become an American."

I think that is an important lesson for all Americans to remember. America is an idea as much as it is a place. Ronald Reagan understood that ideal and inspired me to reach for more in my life. I think that should be the job of an American president.

WHO IS YOUR LEAST FAVORITE AMERICAN PRESIDENT? My least favorite president is George H. W. Bush, the current president's father. He squandered the gains of Ronald Reagan. He lied to the people of the United States after promising, "Read my lips, no new taxes." He committed us to oil rather than investing in the future. I don't think he was an evil man. I think that he was guided by his beliefs and acted as such, but he is my least favorite.

WHAT CURRENT POLITICAL LEADER (ACTIVE WITHIN THE LAST FIVE YEARS) DO YOU MOST ADMIRE? I admire Colin Powell a great deal. He has managed to have an opinion and yet not be disloyal to the president. He is honest and has sacrificed much of his personal life to accomplish many great deeds in his distinguished career of service to the nation.

WHAT CURRENT POLITICAL LEADER DO YOU LEAST ADMIRE? I have the least admiration for Al Gore. I think what he did to Joe Lieberman was appalling. Al Gore showed that he has absolutely no loyalty whatsoever. Joe Lieberman didn't enter the race until he knew Gore was not going to run and then Al Gore endorsed Governor Dean without even a phone call or personal warning. This shows that he is a calculating man without class.

I think that Gore's strategist hoped Dean would win the nomination and lose the election so Al Gore would have one more chance to become president. He is a conniving political hack with no loyalty for people close to him. He is the man whom I least admire.

WHAT ROLE DO YOU THINK THE MEDIA PLAYS IN POLITICS TODAY? The role the media plays in politics today is *huge!* I would not have a chance to even dream of being president without the help of television. Television has the power, practically overnight, to turn a "literal nobody" into Clay Aiken or William Hung (WilliamHung.net if you are not familiar with him—he can't sing, and in the first week sold 95,000 albums).

WHAT MAKES YOU PROUDEST TO BE AMERICAN? I am most proud to be an American because we are a mixture of the world. America is a collection of immigrants living together in relative harmony, as an example to the world. We welcome people from all over the world to be our brothers and neighbors. What is greater than that? Americans are the most generous people on earth. I've said it before, but this makes me most proud that if there is a disaster, anywhere in the world, Americans will be the first ones to lend a helping hand.

WHAT ANGERS OR FRUSTRATES YOU ABOUT AMERICA? What frustrates me is the same thing that frustrated the colonists. Taxation without representation, lack of free political speech, and lack of freedom to worship the Creator in one's own way, are just a few of my frustrations with America.

I love the Daily Show. I would like to see more mainstream news organizations put humor into their shows. The ratings would increase and people would be more informed. Two good things for a democracy.

WHAT DO YOU FEEL AMERICA'S ROLE SHOULD BE IN THE GLOBAL COMMUNITY? I think America will continue to be the leader in the global community. We are the only country in the world to consistently check and balance itself. We have high ideals for our national creed. Other countries long to be us. Citizens of the world long to be Americans and risk their lives trying to get here. We must live up to those high ideals that we have set for ourselves and that we project to the world. Americans must remain a strong and compassionate people. When I am president, we will lead the world into the future by example, and not by force, except as a last resort.

WHY SHOULD PEOPLE FOLLOW YOU AND YOUR CAMPAIGN? People will hear new ideas that are well thought out and articulated. The American people are not used to politicians being clear and direct, so the distinction will be dramatic. The people will see that I have a passion, a vision, and the organization and leadership skills that are needed to run the country.

**"How wonderful it is that nobody need wait a single moment before starting to improve the world."
—Anne Frank**

FRIENDS & FAVORITES

TELL US ABOUT YOUR TWO BEST FRIENDS. My two best friends are Esai Morales and Jono Kohan. Esai is a witty, confident man who challenges my political beliefs, or tries to anyway. He is a liberal who supported Kucinich in the primaries. He is funny and fun to be with. He is the godfather of my daughter Olivia.

Jono, also a Democrat, is a friend from Beverly Hills High School. His twin brother and another friend from high school are the creators of "Will and Grace," the television show. Jono is great friend. He loves food and women, like all men. He is extremely supportive of my adventures and loves my children. Jono is the godfather of my son, Christopher. I am blessed to have such great friends in my life.

HOW WOULD YOU DESCRIBE YOUR ROLE IN YOUR CIRCLE OF FRIENDS? I am the storyteller for my group of friends. The other night, Esai called me from his house as he was having a debate with his friends; politics and history were the subjects. They needed a historical outlook, so they called me. At the time, they were arguing about what year women in America were allowed to vote.

I try to put the world's events into perspective and create a big picture for my friends. I was a history major in school and still love reading about public policy and history. When my friends come to my house, we talk politics and history. They are my favorite conversations. Most of my friends are single, so when they need to feel the love of a family, they come over and I feed them and they hang out with my children.

WHAT BOTHERS YOU MOST ABOUT OTHER PEOPLE? I used to get bothered all of the time by other people because I had certain expectations. Now, I don't expect anything from people, not even family. There are as many good people as bad in the world, and I do my best to associate with the good ones who don't bother me and avoid the bad ones who do.

NEWSPAPER: The *Los Angeles Times* is my favorite newspaper, not that I read it much, but it burns well on camping trips. I don't like reading newspapers because they are so dirty (I end up with ink on my hands). Also, paper uses up so many trees to print. I prefer to read the news online, so I can read a variety of sources on one subject. I like hearing different points of view on the same topic.

TV SHOW: "The O'Reilly Factor" is my favorite television show. I mostly watch the 24-hour news shows, and occasionally I'll enjoy a *Nature* show. I love and hate O'Reilly at the same time. I love him because I agree with most of what he says. However, he is against marijuana, and I would love to debate him on the issue because that is one area where we disagree. I hate him because he is so arrogant and it rubs me the wrong way sometimes, but that is part of his appeal. He has strong beliefs and articulates them well. As I said, "Most of the time, I think he is right."

I think it ironic that one of his employees got paid off because he told some off color jokes that were meant to be sexually stimulating and were not, coming from him at least, but it is sad for America that he would feel it easier and cheaper to pay her off rather than fight her on the bogus charge of sexual harassment.

RADIO SHOW: In the afternoon, "John and Ken" on the commercial station KFI 640 a.m. in Los Angeles. These guys are crusaders, using the airwaves the way I imagine they should be used. Their show is all about keeping politicians honest and consumers protected, and most of all, it is entertaining. I love listening to them bust local politicians for being liars and wasting public money. They are driving me nuts recently because I disagree with their stance on immigration reform. I would love to debate these big mouths because I think they are wrong.

My favorite morning show is "Jamie and Danny," but I recently became a fan of "Howard Stern." Now that the FCC is all over him, I decided to listen. I agree with him that the government is going to kick him off the air by fining him out of existence. The police tried to do the same thing to me at 2000 B.C. when I stood up for my right to free speech by calling water pipes "bongs." The First Amendment of the Bill of Rights needs to be protected, and if I am elected, I'll ask Howard Stern to run the FCC. I don't like childish bathroom humor myself, but I will fight to the death for his right to be on the public airwaves.

The "Jamie and Danny" show is more to my taste. I think they rule Southern California's airwaves. What both shows have in common is that the hosts are brutally honest, and I mean brutal. Honesty is so lacking in our society that people take it brutal if that is the only way to get it. Howard's show seems somewhat chauvinistic to me, but truthful even so. I like the female lead aspect of the "Jamie and Danny" show, too. Jamie's name comes first; she is spunky, where on Howard's show, it is Howard's show and Robin is his sidekick. That is why Jamie and Danny are on my radio in the morning. Radio and the Internet have remained bastions of freedom, and when I am president, they will remain that way. At night I listen to Coast to Coast AM. I am more of a radio person than television.

BAND/OR TYPE OF MUSIC: I like all sorts of music, **mostly rock**. Some younger friends of mine turned me on to Marshall Mathers (Eminem) and Christina Aguilera. I love the tracks of them bagging on each other. I think hip-hop is funny. My favorite musician is someone I knew in high school, Lenny Kravitz. I remember when someone's mother in high school said, "What is that nigger doing in my house?" He was very hurt and was shocked that people still thought that way, but not that many years had passed since Dr. King was killed, but to us kids it seemed as if it was a lifetime ago. I think Lenny's music rocks.

MOVIE, MAGAZINE, AND BOOK: My favorite movie is *Gandhi* and my favorite magazine is *High Times*. I read the *Economist* and other heady magazines online, but love the simple freedom of *High Times* best. Don't get me wrong. I am huge critic of theirs, and think I could manage the magazine better than the current administration, but I have my sights on higher goals. I love the fact that they are one of the few magazines promoting hemp. My favorite book is the Bible, the children's version; I read it to my children every night.

FOOD AND WEB SITE: My favorite foods are things made with love—okay, mostly Mexican and Italian. And my favorite Web site is CraigX.com.

"You must be the change you wish to see in the world."
—Mahatma Gandhi

EXPERIENCE

WHAT OTHER CITIES AND/OR COUNTRIES HAVE YOU LIVED IN APART FROM YOUR CURRENT PLACE OF RESIDENCE? I lived 18 months in Mexico. I lived in Merida, the capital city of the state of Yucatan and traveled throughout the country. For six months, I lived in the state of Colorado, nine years in Northern California, and three years in a small town in rural Arizona called Snowflake.

I have visited the Havasupai Indian Reservation over 100 times and probably have spent collectively more than 52 weeks there. The rest of my time has been spent in Southern California. I speak Spanish and English. I am somewhat familiar with Mayan, Havasupai, Italian, French, and Japanese.

HOW DO YOU DEFINE YOUR RELIGION/SPIRITUALITY? I believe in God and read the Bible to my children every night when I put them to bed. I don't go to church or temple because I don't need others to confirm my relationship with the Creator. As far as I am concerned, there is only one true, loving God. The God of Abraham, Isaac, and Jacob who led Joseph and his family into Egypt and helped Moses lead a nation out of servitude. Even though I am Jewish, I think that Jesus understood the law and broke it down into the two most important elements: love God with all your heart and love each other with same passion.

I have a sweat lodge at my ranch in Northern Arizona and I sweat often with the Havasupai (a Native American tribe) of the Grand Canyon. I am close to members of the tribe and have been going there since I was six years old. I don't speak their language, but understand many words. I was married on the reservation in Supai in front of the waterfall, Havasu Falls, during the autumnal equinox in a tribal ceremony, not a Jewish wedding. The wedding ceremony was covered in *High Times* magazine.

I take the First Amendment seriously. It is first for a reason. The reason is that the government should stay out of people's religious practices as long as those practices don't harm others. I don't think religious institutions should receive tax-exempt status, and they won't when I am president. That may not be a popular stand, but I take separation of church and state seriously, even though I am a very religious person. I think people should have the right to change their religion daily that is the true meaning of "freedom of religion."

WHAT IS THE BIGGEST SECRET YOU'VE EVER KEPT FROM YOUR PARENTS, FRIENDS, OR IMMEDIATE

FAMILY? That I kissed a guy once. It is gross, but I did it. Actually, it wasn't that bad, that was the worst part, but I have only told two people in the whole world until now, but one was Nicole Morgan, the undercover LAPD officer I sold weed to, so I am sure it is known on my permanent government record. Other than that, I have never done anything that my friends and family don't know about. I am not great at keeping secrets.

WHO IN YOUR LIFE DO YOU MOST WANT TO BE PROUD OF YOU? My father. I don't know how to describe the feeling of my own conscience. I know what is right and wrong because of my father, who read me the Bible as a child. I want to do the right thing and serve others by being president.

WHAT ARE YOUR THREE BEST QUALITIES? My three best qualities are my calmness under pressure, my ability to communicate complex ideas into easy-to-understand concepts ("the big picture"), and lastly, my ability to inspire people towards positive action.

WHAT ARE YOUR THREE WORST QUALITIES? My three worst qualities are that I sometimes don't know when to stop talking, I don't dress that well (according to my friends), and my family and I use foul language too much. However, I am aware of, and working on, these faults.

WHAT DO YOU DO FOR FUN? DO YOU HAVE ANY HOBBIES? For fun, I spend time with friends and family. We enjoy talking and singing. It is hard to have hobbies when you are the single parent of three small children, but I would have to say that my hobby is writing, studying history, the Bible, and following world events.

DESCRIBE THE BEST DAY OF YOUR LIFE THUS FAR: The best three days were when my three children were born.

DESCRIBE THE WORST DAY OF YOUR LIFE THUS FAR: The worst day of my life was when I was trying to work things out with my wife and she told me that she never really loved me. That still hurts to this day. It is not an easy thing to hear when you have three children with someone and you give them your heart.

WHAT IS THE CRAZIEST THING YOU'VE EVER DONE?
The craziest thing I have ever done is the John Muir trail. It was a 30-day, 240-mile hike along the Eastern Sierras. It was amazing, and I learned many secrets of life along the journey.

WHAT IS THE BIGGEST SCAM YOU'VE EVER PULLED?
The biggest scam I have ever pulled is selling weed to an undercover police officer over a period of several months and never being charged with a crime. I don't know the exact reason that I was never busted, but the undercover officer's name is Nicole Morgan. From what I know, she has now left the department and works as a fraud investigator for an insurance company. An LAPD Intelligence Officer and an investigative journalist confirmed this information for me.

WHAT WAS YOUR MOST HUMBLING MOMENT? It is difficult to find one moment in my life that I was humbled the most. The beauty of God's creation every day humbles me. From the smile on my children's face to standing at the foot of Havasu Falls at the bottom of the Grand Canyon, I am awed by the world daily.

WHAT ACTIONS OR ACCOMPLISHMENTS IN YOUR LIFE ARE YOU MOST PROUD OF? Starting the Free Speech Movement when I was a student at UCLA was an amazingly gratifying experience. My next most satisfying accomplishment was starting a store on Melrose, "2000 B.C. *The Stoned Age Hemp Shop*." I loved making commercials for the shop. The store, being in Hollywood, was a celebrity Mecca. Growing my own food on difficult land in Northern Arizona deepened my respect for farmers and love of the earth. And finally, surviving divorce, raising my children, writing a book, and now running for president are all things that I am proud of.

275

WHAT IS YOUR GREATEST REGRET? Getting my girlfriend pregnant when we were both young is my biggest regret. I think if I had been more of a man at the time, she would have considered having our child, but I was immature at the time, not yet a man.

DESCRIBE AN INTERNATIONAL EVENT THAT AFFECTED YOU:
I was a student at UCLA when the students in China were killed in June, 1989 for protesting. They wanted rights that we take for granted here in America and were willing to die for those rights. That historical event radicalized me as a student. I thought to myself, "What am I doing to make my society a better place?" and "What rights would I die for?"

WHAT IS THE MOST IMPORTANT ISSUE OR PROBLEM FACING YOU TODAY? The biggest issue, or at least the most important one, in my life right now is how to raise my children to be healthy, contributing adults. In my opinion, the world doesn't have too many people. We have too many of the wrong people. Who are the wrong people? They are our friends and neighbors who worship financial profit over each other. I am a capitalist, but we need to teach a generation of thoughtful business leaders to put the health of people and our planet over short-term profits. If we had more people willing to contribute positively, the world would not seem so overpopulated.

WHAT IS THE BIGGEST OBSTACLE YOU HAVE HAD TO OVERCOME IN YOUR LIFE? I am the biggest obstacle I have had to overcome. I have been blessed with a great family, friends, and children. I cause all of the problems in my life and this is difficult to accept, but is not an insurmountable challenge.

DO YOU SMOKE CIGARETTES? I do not smoke cigarettes, but I do smoke pot.

DO YOU DRINK ALCOHOL? I drink beer and wine, but usually less than once a month.

HAVE YOU BEEN TREATED FOR ANY SERIOUS PHYSICAL ILLNESS WITHIN THE LAST THREE YEARS? I recently had skin cancer removed from my shoulder and back.

HAVE YOU BEEN TREATED FOR ANY SERIOUS MENTAL ILLNESS WITHIN THE LAST THREE YEARS? I have not been treated for mental illness ever. I saw a psychologist when I was in high school after my parents divorced. The experience taught me some valuable communication skills that I use to this day.

Henry Ford hitting his hemp car with an iron crowbar. This was to show that it was ten times stronger than steel. The car also ran on hemp fuel.

"It's easy to make a buck. It's a lot tougher to make a difference."
—Tom Brokaw

WORK AND FAMILY HISTORY

PLEASE LIST AND INCLUDE ALL AFFILIATIONS OR ORGANIZATIONS SUCH AS FRATERNAL

277

ORGANIZATIONS, NON-PROFITS, VOLUNTEER, RELIGIOUS, OR POLITICAL ORGANIZATIONS TO WHICH YOU BELONG.

I don't belong to groups. I say that I am Jewish because I was raised Jewish, but I don't belong to a temple. I think Jesus was the Messiah, but I am not Christian and don't belong to a church. I have faith that God keeps His word, and I act accordingly.

I organized a group of students to practice the First Amendment at UCLA when I was a student there, but only because I had to in order to check out the microphone. It was a Free Speech Club that mostly promoted *cannabis*, but we allowed pro and con views on every subject and always encouraged debate. My friend Mike and I were known around Westwood and on campus as "The Free Speech Guys." It was a title I didn't mind having.

When I had a store on Melrose, I organized large groups to visit the Havasupai Indian Reservation, and we would clear fields and chop wood for the elderly. It was my way of thanking them for opening their part of the canyon to me for so many years. I dream often of the Southwest, which I have traveled in extensively, and the Grand Canyon in life, as in my dream, is my favorite destination. Also, I take my children to visit the elderly sometimes.

I don't belong to any group or organization that I can think of. I am a registered Republican, but I don't give them money, and the last time I voted Republican for president was for the first Bush the first time. I voted for Ross Perot when the elder Bush ran the second time. Now, I just voted for his son's reelection.

I believe in the Republican ideals of entrepreneurship, growth in small business, and not depending on government handouts but on your good word and hard work. I love our country and the ideals for which it stands, including that all men are created equal. I know the last sentence sounds like an "American Ideal," but it was the Republican Abraham Lincoln who took the stand against slavery by signing the Emancipation Proclamation. I think the

278

government under my leadership will succeed by taxing less and downsizing.

I did work with various groups to help pass the medical marijuana bill, Proposition 215, in California, but never joined any groups to do so.

HAVE YOU EVER SERVED IN THE MILITARY? No, I have not served in the Armed Forces of the United States. But I have been a warrior on the frontlines of the Drug War here at home, and I did register for the draft upon turning 18 years old.

WHAT IS YOUR CURRENT OCCUPATION? My current occupation is full-time father of three and I just completed this book, which was quite time-consuming. *9021GROW: The Story of Hollywood's Wizard of Weed* is a true and humorous look at America's number one cash crop from a Beverly Hills perspective.

DESCRIPTION OF WORK HISTORY: Before being an author (2003-), I was a farmer (2000-2003). Before that, I was a shop owner on Melrose (1994-2000). Before that, I was the primary caretaker of my elderly grandmother. Before that, I was a full-time student at UCLA/Santa Monica Junior College (1989-1993). Before that, I held various odd jobs, from real estate to stand-up comedy (1984-1993). Before that, I worked in the mailroom of Korn/Ferry International (1982-1984), one of the world's largest executive consulting firms at the time.

IF YOU COULD HOLD ANY JOB OTHER THAN YOUR CURRENT POSITION, WHAT WOULD IT BE? I would be a television producer if I were not a writer.

WHAT WERE YOUR FAMILY'S ECONOMIC CIRCUMSTANCES WHEN YOU WERE GROWING UP? I grew up with everything I ever needed, but not everything I ever wanted. All my needs were taken care of, but because my father had grown up without money, he encouraged a strong work ethic. My first job was a paper route at the age of six, and I worked all

279

through high school. We were wealthy enough to live in Beverly Hills, but we were far from the richest people in town. In fact, my friends were so financially well off that I thought we were actually poor until I got to college and realized how wealthy my father actually was.

DESCRIBE YOUR CHILDHOOD: I grew up in a Republican home. My father and I had contracts as to what type of grades I was going to receive. It was a fairly happy childhood; all of my material needs were met. It ended when my parents divorced, but I fit into the community of alienated youth at "Beverly," my high school, better after their divorce. I was 15 at the time, so I felt like an adult already. I am thankful for my somewhat blissful childhood prior to that. I was involved in acting and in sports.

Section IV

Stony Dictionary: a.k.a. the "420" Glossary

"420" Glossary

This language is regional, extremely fluid, and constantly changing as a result of the prohibition of *cannabis*. This "9021Grow" version of "420 slang" resembles the constantly changing use of words by teenagers who are concealing things from authority figures, such as parents. This section is intended to be both insightful and funny.

This is not a complete authoritative guide to *marijuana speak*, but it helps to point out two things. First, that the 420 Tribe is the world's first unique global sub-culture with regional dialects. Second, what I noticed as I did research for this section is that law enforcement is single-mindedly trying to link marijuana use with hard drug use.

On a Web site designed to give parents advice on raising teenagers, they list slang terms for marijuana. For instance, they list "chronic" as marijuana mixed with crack. I know that terms can vary even within the same small town or city, but I also know that people trying to "educate teenagers" are ignorant. It was like the LAPD narcotics officer telling me that people were smoking crack out of bongs. Please, don't take my word about anything. Do the research.

Afterburner—(verb) The act of burping in which your gaseous release contains marijuana smoke long after you've taken the hit.

Apple Pipe—(noun) A MacGyvered pipe made by carving an apple into a smoking device.

Aromatherapy—(many uses) The use of selected fragrant substances in lotions and inhalants in an effort to affect mood-or hide the smell of weed.

Bio—(adjective) Marijuana grown in soil versus "hydroponically."

Black Finger—(noun) The index finger of your dominant hand that is used to pack the burning bowl of the bong.

Bogart—(noun) A person who doesn't share his or her weed. And when you are sharing your weed with them, they seem to smoke more than you wanted them to.

Bong—(noun) Water pipe, binger, "B," the weapon, the tool, Fred, Bob, the spiritual centerpiece, and "The B-Love'd One." This is a smoking apparatus that filters smoke through water—(verb) to be bonging, B-loading, snapping a "B," and/or "pulling tubes, dude."

Bongitis—(illness) A common form of bronchitis that bong smokers usually come down with once a year.

Buffalo Fart—(noun) The smoke left in a bong after a hit, a.k.a. trash, smog, waste, dirt, haze.

Bunk Weed or **Bud-Light**—(adjective) Marijuana that looks good, but has no medicinal effect. Could be called, "no high."

Coughing up a Lung—(verb) A spastic cough after taking a large hit. Also, called spoofing, gagging, gacking, and chicken boofing.

Chilled Binger—(noun) An iced, chilled bong.

Chillum—(noun) A hippie pipe. It is designed so that you hold the end of the pipe in your hands and don't put it to your lips. This allows you to smoke with strangers without sharing germs.

Chronic—(adjective) This describes the type of marijuana grade. It came from the hip-hop culture of the 1990s, as "high grade" strains became available 12 months a year; it is considered a high grade.

Desperate Loser—(adjective) People who come over to your house only when they run out of weed. I have, unfortunately, been one of these people before, and when it happens to me, I try to be gracious and thankful.

Flake—(noun) This a pot dealer who never shows up even when you have agreed to meet because he or she knows that you'll call back; you want pot.

Fluff Bud—(adjective) Bud with too much green leaf. It is very airy and not at all dense. Not well manicured and has a weak taste.

Ganja—(noun) Yet one more word that means "marijuana," but this word has special meaning around the world. In Jamaica, the island country marijuana is called "ganja," and this island was the birthplace of Bob Marley, a stoner legend.

Gram—(adjective) Describes a quantity. It is a metric measurement for weight, 1/28 of an ounce, a.k.a. a "20 bag" or "dub sack." Pot smokers are the only people in America who are familiar with the metric system.

Gravity Bong—(noun) A homemade smoking device. Typically made from a cylindrical apparatus, such as a two-liter soda bottle, submerged in water, with the bottom of the bottle cut off. The bowl is fixed to the top of the bottle, the mouthpiece, and remains out of the water. The flame is placed above the bowl while the bottle is underwater. Simultaneously ignite the bowl and raise the bottle slowly out of the water. The suction caused by the falling water will fill the chamber with smoke. Then remove the bowl, place your mouth on the hole, and press the cylinder back into the water. (Don't try this unless you have consulted your doctor).

Halfin' the Bag—(verb) The subtle art of splitting a bag of weed without using a scale. Typically, the guy who splits the weed lets the other guys pick the half of the bag they want. This method allows both people to feel happy that the split was fair.

Hydro—(adjective) This is marijuana grown in water instead of soil.

Indoe—(noun) Marijuana grown indoors.

Jack Herer—(noun) This is the man who has dedicated his life to legalizing hemp. He is currently a stroke victim, but recovering quickly with massive marijuana use. He has said of my book, "He's got a hit." Jack has sold nearly 1,000,000 copies of his book, a certified bestseller. He has spent every penny he made on pot, junk food, and legalizing marijuana. He spends up to 200 days a year living on the road. We spent a few hours speaking in July, 2004 and he let me know that he's been reading the Bible for years, having slept in hotels the majority of his adult life, and that was the available reading material. Jack believes that he has "cracked" the Bible code and Magic Mushrooms are the key.

Jah—(noun) As in Jehovah or Jah-ovah, according to the Rastafarian religion.

Joint—(noun) The common vernacular term used to describe a marijuana cigarette, a.k.a. hooter, doobie, "fat man in a white jacket," blunt, torpedo, bomber, fat one, and stick. There are several variations to distinguish the size of the joint, as well. A "pinner" or "toothpick" would be an extremely thin marijuana cigarette, while a "Marley," after the legendary Rasta artist, would be a giant hand-rolled cigarette.

KGB—(adjective) An acronym for Killer Green Buds, this is a description for any high quality pot. Usually "A" grade or better.

Kiefer Sutherland—(noun) The code word for kief, a fine grade of *cannabis* made by isolating the tri-combs of the plant. It is the fine crystalline matter that falls from the bud.

Lid—(noun) Anyone over 50 years old remembers scoring "lids," and they love to tell you how they bought four finger bags for "ten dollars, man." Yeah, but it was mostly seeds and stems and they didn't know the difference.

286

Manicure—(verb) When a plant is harvested, it needs to be manicured (have the excess leaves trimmed off) to have nicely formed buds. A manicure is the act of clipping or trimming evenly or closely to the cola or nug. Well-cured bud is not wet.

Marijuana—(noun) Boo, weed, grass, herb, smoke, hooch, dope, green, purple, the kind, the bomb, you got love, medicine, da kine, ganja, and hemp. Comes in several grades. Here are a few: high grade, "A" bud, chronic, d'kind, kush, Northern Lights, Jack Herer, purple bud, the kills, KGB (Killer Green Bud). Low grade: commercial ("*comersh*") schwagg, Mexican, "beasters" (low-grade bud from Vancouver, B.C.), the seedy shit.

Mr. Potato Head Vision—(verb) This condition is ubiquitous in early stages of initial marijuana use. The state of seeing your friends appear like plastic, with way-too-large heads for their too-small bodies. The uncontrollable shits and giggles usually accompany this symptom.

Munchies—(verb or noun) An uncontrollable craving for snack foods or the snack foods themselves are sometimes called "munchies." This is one of the reasons that marijuana has medicinal value. These strong urges of hunger result in odd, tasty, and inventive concoctions being created.

Nug—(Noun) 1) A hot chick, or 2) One bud, a nug, for smoking.
"O"—(adjective) The letter describes a quantity. Sometimes referred to as an "O.Z." or Oscar, Oscar De la Hoya, or simply as One (1/16 of a pound and 28 grams).

One Hitter Quitter—(adjective) A description of pot that is so powerful that you only need one hit. This is something heard from a lot of older people who are not used to "Hero-Juana" (Pronounced: Hair-O-Wanna. From the words heroin and marijuana combined)—the high THC strains of pot that have been developed since prohibition that are so good that they are hard to stop smoking.

Pot Slobber—(verb) This action typically occurs after giant bong hits and all the toker can do is cough and slobber all over for several minutes while others stare in disbelief and concern.

Puffing Tuff—(verb) The act of smoking bowl after bowl from dawn until dusk, or from dusk until dawn, or the act of chain pot smoking.

Q.P.—(adjective) An abbreviation for "quarter pound."

Roach—(noun) The part of a marijuana cigarette that is left after you smoke half of it or more.

Roach Clip—(noun) A device used to smoke a roach down to the tip, a.k.a. crutch, roach holder, burning fingers.

Schwagg—(adjective) A slang term for low-grade pot that does get you high but is loaded with seeds, so it takes an hour of cleaning your pot before you can smoke it.

Spleef-N-Ator—(noun) The device used to eliminate the smell of marijuana smoke. Typically, a cylindrical tube of toilet paper or paper towel roll stuffed with numerous sheets of fabric softener (unused, of course) to filter "glory smoke" from such unsparing places as dorms, jails, bedrooms, and in unsuspecting parents' homes.

Stoned—(adjective) As in tweaked, faded, lit, toast, burnt, wasted, high, comatose, zooted, loopy, irie, "got Chinese eyes," red eyes, washed up, and tore-up and gone.

Stoner Moment—(noun) This is when you're smoking a lot of pot and you're with a lot of friends, and all of the sudden you find yourself and all the others looking off into the distance and zoning out, and then after the stoner moment is over, every stoned dude there is, "like whoa man!"

Sweet Seat—(noun, the middle seat) The person in the middle of a lazy group of stoners when joint is going by in both directions. Explanation, since the joint has to pass through you in each direction (often seen on ski lifts), the person in the "sweet seat" is able to hit it twice as often (see Bogart).

Spark it!—(interrogative) When visiting Supai, Arizona Natives working on the trail often ask visitors if they have marijuana with these two simple words. To a visitor's ear, it sounds like a statement, but really they are asking a question. "Hey, will you please smoke us out to some good pot?"

Thai Stick—(noun) Pot from Thailand (that I haven't seen since the 70s) wrapped around a bamboo stick and held together with string.

Time Warp—(adjective) An elapsed amount of time spent high on marijuana thinking about complex and elaborate philosophies that may actually work if ever applied when all of sudden, you realize no one is around and you've been "out" for three hours.

Toxic Sludge—(noun) The scraped resin from a pipe or bong. This is usually the last resort of a desperate stoner, an improvised bowl when a dry spell hits your dealer and none of your friends are home. Can cause severe headaches and create a weird, sleepy high. Better than nothing, or is it?

Vaporizer—(noun) Any non-completely-combusted hydrocarbon material is carcinogenic, so a vaporizer allows the user to assimilate THC without any smoking pot.

Wake and Bake—(verb) A person who wakes up and smokes marijuana before brushing their teeth.

Weed-ache—(noun) When someone has smoked so much pot that his or her head hurts. This is usually followed by a prolonged, deep sleep.

Yak—(verb) After a humongous bong hit, the horrifying experience of puking, but not a complete puke, just enough that you remember your last meal.

Zoinks—(exclamation) Popularized by Shaggy of Scooby Doo.

"Z"—(noun) An expression for one ounce. As in, "I am so happy because I just got a 'Z' and I was completely out."